S0-EXA-040

GOD'S SPIES

GOD'S SPIES

Michelangelo, Shakespeare and Other Poets of Vision

Paul Murray O.P.

t&tclark
LONDON • NEW YORK • OXFORD • NEW DELHI • SYDNEY

T&T CLARK
Bloomsbury Publishing Plc
50 Bedford Square, London, WC1B 3DP, UK
1385 Broadway, New York, NY 10018, USA

BLOOMSBURY, T&T CLARK and the T&T Clark logo are trademarks of Bloomsbury Publishing Plc

First published in Great Britain 2019

Copyright © Paul Murray O.P. 2019

Paul Murray O.P. has asserted his right under the Copyright, Designs and Patents Act, 1988, to be identified as Author of this work.

For legal purposes the Acknowledgements on p. viii constitute an extension of this copyright page.

Cover image: The Dream of Human Life (detail), after Michelangelo
© Art Collection 3 / Alamy Stock Photo

All rights reserved. No part of this publication may be reproduced or transmitted in any form or by any means, electronic or mechanical, including photocopying, recording, or any information storage or retrieval system, without prior permission in writing from the publishers.

Bloomsbury Publishing Plc does not have any control over, or responsibility for, any third-party websites referred to or in this book. All internet addresses given in this book were correct at the time of going to press. The author and publisher regret any inconvenience caused if addresses have changed or sites have ceased to exist, but can accept no responsibility for any such changes.

A catalogue record for this book is available from the British Library.

A catalog record for this book is available from the Library of Congress.

ISBN:	HB:	978-0-5676-8580-3
	ePDF:	978-0-5676-8581-0
	ePUB:	978-0-5676-8582-7

Typeset by Integra Software Services Pvt. Ltd.
Printed and bound in Great Britain

To find out more about our authors and books visit www.bloomsbury.com and sign up for our newsletters.

*So we'll live
And pray, and sing, and tell old tales, and laugh
… And take upon us the mystery of things
As if we were God's spies.*

Shakespeare: *King Lear*

To Monk-Scholar and Great Friend
Abbot Jeremy Driscoll O.S.B.

CONTENTS

Acknowledgements   viii

INTRODUCTION   1

CHAPTER 1
PARADISE ON EARTH: EARLY IRISH NATURE POETRY
AND THE *CANTICLE* OF FRANCIS OF ASSISI   7

CHAPTER 2
'I AM MYSELF ALONE': SHAKESPEARE AND
THE HUMAN CASUALTY   45

CHAPTER 3
A MAN TALKING: THE PRAYER AND POETRY OF
CHARLES PÉGUY   63

CHAPTER 4
'BEAUTY, MY ENEMY': PASSION AND PIETY AT WAR IN
THE POETRY OF MICHELANGELO   81

CHAPTER 5
APOCALYPTIC VISIONS: THE POETRY OF NATURE
AND THE CROSS   113

CHAPTER 6
GOD'S SPY: SHAKESPEARE AND RELIGIOUS VISION   129

CHAPTER 7
AT THE THRESHOLD OF WONDER: POETRY AND
RELIGION: FRIENDS OR FOES?   147

FINALLY COMES THE POET:
AN AFTERWORD   169

Index   174

ACKNOWLEDGEMENTS

I am greatly indebted to a number of people who have helped shape the present work. To two friends in particular: Denis O'Brien for his sharp and reasoned criticism and Robert Ombres OP for bright and insightful comments on the manuscript at various stages. To Ben McGuire I am grateful for the scrupulous care with which he read the chapters as they were produced. Also, for unflagging support shown throughout the long period of research and writing, I am grateful to Dr Fernando Cervantes, Philip McShane OP, Susan Portieri, Luke Buckles OP, Katherine Wolff NDS, Shine Raju, Colin Howell and Lisa Simpson. I want also to thank Colmán Ó Clabaigh OSB for wise and illumined advice given at a particular moment. Finally, to my friend, Roderick Strange, I am indebted for helping me to decide on the title *God's Spies*.

Every effort has been made to contact copyright holders of material reproduced in these volumes. If any copyright holders have not been properly acknowledged, please contact the publisher, who will be happy to rectify the omission in future editions.

Translations in *God's Spies*, when not otherwise indicated, are by the author.

Chapter 3 of the present work, 'A Man Talking: The Prayer and Poetry of Charles Péguy', appeared first in *Logos: A Journal of Catholic Thought and Culture* (Fall 2006).

Chapter 6 of the present work, 'God's Spy: Shakespeare and Religious Vision', appeared first in *Communio: International Catholic Review* (Winter 2000)

Extracts from *A Celtic Miscellany*, Kenneth Hurlstone Jackson © 1971 Routledge and Paul, reproduced by permission of Routledge, Taylor & Francis Books, UK

'The Hermit's Song' from *Kings, Lords, Commons: An Anthology From The Irish*, translated by Frank O'Connor © 1970, reproduced by permission of Peters Fraser and Dunlop

Extracts from *Medieval Irish Lyrics*, James Carney © 1985, reproduced by permission of Colin Smythe Limited

Extracts from *Francis of Assisi: Early Documents*, edited by Regis J. Armstrong, Wayne Hellmann and William J. Short © 1999, reproduced by permission of New City Press, https://newcitypress.com/francis-of-assisi-early-documents-set.html

Extracts of Charles Péguy's poetry from *The Portal of the Mystery of Hope*, translated by Daniel L. Schindler ©1996, reproduced by permission of Wm B. Eerdmans Publishing

Extracts from *The Mystery of the Holy Innocents and Other Poems*, by Charles Péguy, translated by Pansy Pakenham ©1956, used by permission of Wipf and Stock Publishers, www.wipfandstock.com

Extracts from *The Poetry of Michelangelo: An Annotated Translation*, by James M. Saslow ©1993, reproduced by permission of Yale Representation Limited

St. Ephrem, Hymn 31 of 'The Cycle on Faith' from *The Luminous Eye: The Spiritual World Vision of Saint Ephrem*, Sebastian P. Brock ©1992, reproduced by permission of Cistercian Publications c/o Liturgical Press

'Zeus is Dead' from *Exhortation to the Heathen*, Book 2, translated by T. Merton in *The Collected Poems of Thomas Merton* ©1980, reproduced by permission of New Directions Publishing

Extract from *The Divine Comedy* by Dante Alighieri, translated by John Ciardi © 1954, 1957, 1959, 1960, 1961, 1965, 1967, 1970 by the Ciardi Family Publishing Trust, used by permission of W. W. Norton & Company, Inc.

Extract from Haicéad's poem 'On Hearing it has been Ordered in the Chapterhouses of Ireland that the Friars make no more Songs or Verses', translated by Thomas Kinsella, used by permission of Thomas Kinsella

INTRODUCTION

The poets of vision represented in the following pages include writers who are among the most celebrated of all time and others whose work, although of no small interest and importance, is much less known. Authors such as the following: Dante Alighieri, Charles Péguy, St Francis of Assisi, Michelangelo, St John of the Cross, the anonymous Irish author or authors of *The Frenzy of Sweeney* (*Buile Shuibhne*) and Shakespeare. A diverse group, it's clear, by any standards. But the choice of these particular writers (and the choice of others represented in *God's Spies*) is not as arbitrary as it might at first appear. For, in spite of the many differences between them, they possess one great and surprising quality in common: audacity.

*

It would not, I think, be difficult to defend the claim that, in all of world literature, no more remarkable poem was ever composed than the *Divina Commedia*. But just as defensible would be the claim that no poem anywhere in any language exists that is even half as audacious as Dante's great work. One brief example will serve to make the point. At the centre of the *Commedia*, and playing nothing less than a *salvific* role, is the young woman, Beatrice, whom Dante had met and loved as a young man in Florence. Years later, in the *Vita Nuova*, he made a bold prophecy that he would, in time, 'write of her that which has never been written of any other woman'.[1] It was a prophecy that would, with the passage of years, be wondrously *and* outrageously fulfilled to the letter in the third part of his *Commedia*, the *Paradiso*.

The elevation of Beatrice to a quasi-divine status within the poem is evidence of Dante's great imaginative daring. But nothing in the *Paradiso* is able to match for boldness of conception the poem's final visionary stanzas. Dante, in a moment of intense rapture, is permitted a direct vision of God. Later, when the moment has passed, he struggles to find words to describe the miracle:

> As one who sees in dreams and wakes to find
> the feelings wrought by it remain
> but nothing of the rest returns to mind,

---

1. *Dante's Vita Nuova: A Translation and an Essay* by Max Musa, XLII (Bloomington, 1973), p. 86.

> Just so am I. With almost all
> the vision gone, still in my heart I feel
> the sweetness born from it distil and fall.[2]

Dante is well aware that words alone will never be able adequately to describe the divine vision once it passes. Nevertheless, in the *Paradiso*, the poet-pilgrim, against all expectation, does find words and images – halting yet illumined – to make tangible and real what is intangible. By any standards of visionary writing, it is a prodigious achievement.

*

St John of the Cross, a Carmelite friar of the sixteenth century, is, by common consent, the greatest mystical poet in the Catholic tradition. One might expect, therefore, from his pen, given the depth and strength of his piety, devotional poems in the style of Henry Vaughan or Richard Crashaw. But the work in which his genius is most in evidence, *La Noche Oscura*, when read for the first time, is startling. Although for centuries revered as one of the most illumined descriptions of the journey towards intimacy with God, the poem itself contains not one single reference to God or to religion. What's more, the voice we hear in the poem is not that of an austere sixteenth-century friar but the voice of a young girl, manifestly in love, recalling with breathless wonder how, on one occasion, feeling overwhelmed by desire for the man she loved, she was able, in spite of all the risks involved, to go out alone into the night to meet with him and, in a lonely place, 'where no one else might appear', fall into his arms with utter and complete abandon.

The use, by St John of the Cross, of not only romantic but also erotic language and imagery to describe the soul's intimate communion with God has not won universal approval. More than a few readers find it objectionable and even scandalous. T.S. Eliot, for example, writing in 1926, had no hesitation in describing the Carmelite saint as *a voluptuary of religion*.[3] In his opinion, works by the Spanish mystic such as *La Noche Oscura* could all too easily be read as displaced or repressed forms of human sexuality and, as a result, be subject to what he called 'the indignities of Freudian analysis'.[4] But John's poem, for all its daring, is not compromised in the least way by such modern concerns and puritan scruples. Being at once more human and more divine in its conception than most if not all current art forms and popular ways of

---

2. Dante Alighieri, *Paradiso*, XXXIII. Parts of this translation have been influenced by a John Ciardi version: *The Paradiso* (New York, 1970), p. 362.

3. The term 'voluptuaries of religion' was used by Eliot to describe both St John of the Cross and St Teresa of Avila. See Eliot, 'On the Metaphysical Poetry of the Seventeenth Century', The Clark Lectures, V, in *T.S. Eliot: The Varieties of Metaphysical Poetry*, ed. R. Schuchard (London, 1993), p. 158.

4. T.S. Eliot, 'Thinking in Verse', *The Listener* III, no. 61 (12 March 1930): p. 443.

thinking, its scandalous purity, like a revealing mirror – if we dare to attend to it – renders us, as moderns, subject in *our* turn to a deep and searching scrutiny.

*

'Audacity' is a word often used by critics when attempting to describe the life and work of the French Catholic poet, Charles Péguy (1873–1914). A man of immense Gallic pride and of quite remarkable integrity, Péguy came to be regarded, during his life, as a prophet as much as a poet. With unfailing energy, and with enormous courage, he dared to speak out on all kinds of controversial issues, not least the Dreyfus Affair. But the flame of his prophetic charism was not restricted to prose broadsides; it burned with no less ardour in two of Péguy's most celebrated works of verse, *The Portal of the Mystery of Hope* and *The Mystery of the Holy Innocents*.

We don't expect a writer in the modern era, in this case a poet of the twentieth century, to compose a work of literature which contains a revelation of the innermost mind and heart of God. Much less do we expect to hear, in page after page of verse, words directly attributed to God by the poet-prophet. But that's exactly what Péguy has had the presumption to achieve. And the words which we hear spoken throughout the two *Mystères* are words of clear Gospel compassion. Henri Bremond, after reading *The Portal of the Mystery of Hope* for the first time, wrote to Péguy, expressing his gratitude, not only on his own behalf but also 'for the masses of people whom no one evangelizes anymore and to whom you have brought the good news'.[5]

A poem by the fourth-century Doctor of the Church St Gregory Nazianzen is cited in the final chapter of *God's Spies*. It repeats again and again, like an incantation, the idea that God's divine mystery cannot be named. Gregory's emphasis is all on *not* knowing God – on the *via negativa* – an emphasis which would seem directly to contradict the clear, *knowing* affirmations in the poetry of Charles Péguy. Péguy's confident placing and naming of emotions such as tenderness and wild pity within the heart of God the Father might well be considered audacious. But, if that's the case, there is an answering audacity, I would suggest, in the way St Gregory piles negation upon negation in his insistence that the true and living God *cannot* be named.

Both of these different emphases, when they assert themselves within the tradition, are declaring something of fundamental importance, as John Henry Newman explains. But both need to experience the challenge and even the opposition of the other. 'By this *method of antagonism*', Newman remarks with his customary brilliance, 'we steady our minds … saying and unsaying to a positive result'.[6]

*

---

5. Henri Bremond, Letter to Péguy, 7 November 1911, cited in *The Portal of the Mystery of Hope*, trans. D.L. Schlinder (Grand Rapids, 1996), p. xvii.
6. *The Theological Papers of John Henry Newman*, Vol. 1, ed. J.D. Holmes (Oxford, 1976), p. 102.

Michelangelo, throughout his life as painter and sculptor, was denied the freedom of being able to choose the subjects of his art. Like most artists of his day, he was almost wholly dependent on the whim of rich patrons. And what these patrons asked him to produce was, with few exceptions, work of a religious character. With a genius second to none, he responded to the challenge by creating in stone and coloured fresco one impressive masterpiece after another. His artistic commitment to the task could hardly have been greater. But what do we know of Michelangelo's own inner conviction as a man? How much of personal faith was invested in the making of this religious art? I doubt if there exists a greater or more effective answer to the question than the radiant, spiritual authority of the work itself. For, how could a man, an artist, be capable of first conceiving and then of bringing to birth a work such as the *Pietà*, if he were not already, at least to some degree in his spirit, quickened by the flame of living faith?

There are, as it happens, innumerable details in the biography of Michelangelo which alert us to the strength of his religious character. Perhaps the most striking detail of all is the fact that more than a quarter of the verses he composed during his life are fired by an urgent longing to attain union with God. This transcendent focus remains strong and undeflected even in the love poems dedicated to two of his greatest friends, Tommaso de' Cavalieri and Vittoria Colonna. The drama enacted in the poems – the struggle between the passion he feels for those he loves on earth and his passion for God – has no equal anywhere in the literature of the period. Its bold, unguarded honesty forges a language of emotional and spiritual courage almost unparalleled in any age.

*

In early Irish poetry, we find two very different visions of nature represented. On the one hand, lyrics composed by a number of inspired hermit-poets celebrate nature as an almost unfallen world. These men, in their solitude, dared to live and write as if the natural world which surrounded them was a veritable paradise (Chapter 1). In contrast, in a text such as *The Frenzy of Sweeney*, a medieval epic composed sometime between 1200 and 1500, nature appears in all its starkness and challenge (Chapter 7). *Frenzy* tells the story of a seventh-century king from the north of Ireland who goes mad on the field of battle after being cursed by a priest. Compelled to assume the shape of a bird, Sweeney finds himself condemned to wander in a wild panic over the glens and mountains of Ireland, a mad outcast, 'a derelict doomed to loneliness'. In time, however, out of the pain and sorrow of exile, out of his unspeakable anguish, he creates a number of astonishing lyrics, astonishing songs – haunting, lonely, beautiful poems.

The author behind Sweeney, the anonymous poet of *The Frenzy*, is revealed throughout the work as a unique celebrant and visionary of the natural world, a bold contemplative of some of nature's most stark and extreme conditions. But Sweeney's anonymous author is also contemplative of a wide range of different states of soul and psyche. For that reason, the author – or, more likely, *authors* of the work – can be numbered among those poets described by T.S. Eliot as being capable of perceiving and distinguishing more clearly than others 'the colours or sounds within the range of ordinary vision or hearing'[7] and capable also of perceiving realities which lie outside that range, allowing us, as a result, to perceive much more of the world than we could ever see without the poet's vision.[8]

*

The poets represented in *God's Spies* belong not only to individual countries of Europe (France, Italy, Spain, Greece, England and Ireland) but also to different periods of European history, from the early Christian period to modern times. A few of these authors are poets of religious vision in the strict meaning of the term 'religious'. Their work, in other words, expresses a devout turning away from the things of this world in order to give wholehearted attention to God. Other authors, in contrast, far from turning away from the world of 'things', are writers whose work is distinguished by a remarkable visionary focus on the many small and great dramas of life, attending with bright, imaginative genius to what Shakespeare calls, at the close of *King Lear*, 'the mystery of things'.

Two entire chapters are devoted to Shakespeare. In Chapter 6, the apparent absence of religion in the plays is explored. In Chapter 2, the focus of attention is on one character in particular, the crookback Richard, Duke of Gloucester (later, King Richard III). Not only is Richard the first major character created by Shakespeare as a young playwright (in the drama *Henry VI, Part 3*), he is also widely regarded as the most truly evil character in all of Shakespeare's work. The majority of critics have no hesitation in joining chorus with the protagonists in the play, denouncing the Crookback as a veritable monster.

Shakespeare, as playwright, does not for a moment ignore the true horror of the evil perpetrated by Richard. But, by making effective use of the dramatic monologue, he allows us to hear, or overhear, Richard talking to himself. And what we hear is a revelation. We are given access, visionary access, to the very soul of an evil character, an access denied to all the other protagonists in the play. And this unique perspective on evil, this privileged knowledge, challenges us to think with perhaps more seriousness than before about the origin and mystery of evil. Following the drama of the play, scene by scene, we find we are watching the crookback Richard, not only from outside, as it were, but also from within, listening and watching 'as if we were God's spies'.

---

7. T.S. Eliot, 'What Dante Means to Me' (1950), in *To Criticize the Critic and Other Writings* (London, 1965), p. 134.
8. Ibid.

Chapter 1

PARADISE ON EARTH: EARLY IRISH NATURE POETRY AND THE *CANTICLE* OF FRANCIS OF ASSISI

A radiant clarity and a wonderful freshness of perception are the two most immediately striking characteristics of the verse and vision of the monk-poets of Ireland in the early Middle Ages. The world in which they were living day to day was, they believed, a world that had been redeemed and restored by Christ. Accordingly, their monastic vocation, whether lived out in community or in solitude, represented not merely an aspiration, an ideal, but a strong and lively conviction of being able to rediscover and re-experience something of the freshness and vigour of the first creation.

The worlds of beauty they saw around them – the rivers and the woods, the plants and the birds, the mountains and the lakes – were to them nothing less than a beginning glimpse of the lost Garden of Eden. Like the first Christian monks and hermits before them – the Desert Fathers – these bold pioneers and adventurers of the spirit, while living lives of great solitude out in the wild, found themselves able to experience the joy of a new sense of harmony with all living creatures, a new fellowship with animals wild and tame, and to experience also the sheer unimaginable joy of 'recapturing in the present moment a taste of the innocence and intimacy with God which Adam knew in paradise'.[1]

This faith-understanding, this bright perspective on the world of nature, goes some way to explain the unique quality of the lyrics composed by these early Irish monks. Commenting on that quality and that achievement, Seamus Heaney says of this startling poetry that it 'makes a springwater music out of certain feelings in a way unmatched in any other European language'.[2] And he notes further: 'We are nearer the first world in that first poetry, nearer to the innocent eye and tongue of Adam as he named the creatures.'[3]

---

1. A phrase describing the faith experience of the Desert Fathers. See Burton-Christie, *The Word in the Desert: Scripture and the Quest for Holiness in Early Christian Monasticism* (Oxford, 1993), pp. 231–2. See also *The Desert Fathers: Sayings of the Early Christian Monks*, ed. Benedicta Ward (London, 2003), p. xii.

2. Seamus Heaney, 'The God in the Tree: Early Irish Nature Poetry', in *Preoccupations: Selected Prose 1968–1978* (London, 1980), p. 182.

3. Ibid., p. 185. Heaney suggests that the early nature poetry of Ireland is sustained both by a conscious awareness of 'the Christian deity, the giver of life, sustainer of nature' and 'by

Something of that unique vision survives in a number of lyrics composed centuries later in Ireland. Thus, as late as the fifteenth century, we find the poet Tadg Óg Ó hÚigínn acknowledging Christ as the origin of all the fruitfulness and beauty he sees around him in the natural world:

> It is you who make the sun bright
> together with the ice;
> you who create the rivers and the salmon
> all along the river.[4]

The few details of nature listed here were originally, in the understanding of the poet, part of the un-fallen realm of Eden, the original paradise of Adam and Eve. That paradise, however, in its fullness and fruitfulness, was lost by the Fall. Ó hÚigínn acknowledges this fact but then he goes on at once to speak of the mystery of the new blessing won for humanity by the saving death of Christ on the Cross:

> Although, as children of Eve, we ill deserve
> the bird-flocks and the salmon,
> it was the Immortal One on the Cross
> who made both salmon and birds.
>
> It is He who makes the flower of the sloes
> grow through the surface
> of the blackthorn, and the nut-flower
> on the other trees.[5]

It's clear from these stanzas that humanity, in spite of its ancient failure, has *not* been robbed of the wonders and riches of the natural world. And it is the Cross, the poet is happy to acknowledge, which stands at the heart of these wonders. Whereas the first creation was ushered in by a seemingly effortless, divine imperative – 'Let there be light, and there was light' – the new creation and the imperishable joy that it brings have not been achieved without the unique sacrifice made by Christ on behalf of humanity and on behalf of the entire cosmos. 'Through Him', as was stated in Colossians, 'are reconciled all things, whether on earth or in heaven, making peace by the blood of his Cross' (Col. 1.20).

Concerning those poets in the Christian tradition who speak or sing of this new creation, two things are especially worthy of note: first, the manifest affection they have for the sharp and clear details of creation, and, second, the fact that the bond existing

---

a deep unconscious affiliation to the old mysteries of the grove' – to the hovering powers of 'the Celtic underworld' (p. 186).

4. Tadg Óg Ó hÚigínn, 'Christ's Bounties', in *A Celtic Miscellany*, trans. K.H. Jackson (London, 1971), p. 300. Ó hÚigínn was not a monk but a married layman.

5. Ibid.

between them and nature is one of fraternal intimacy and joy. Francis of Assisi, more than any other individual in the Christian tradition, is celebrated for his enormous reverence and regard for creatures, and for the way in which even the fiercest of animals, according to reports, became docile and tame when he approached them. Comparable legends and stories – works of hagiography – have survived in Ireland regarding the lives of the early monks and hermits. To take one example from among many, we read in the *Vitae Sanctorum Hiberniae* of the great concern shown by the fifth-century saint Ciarán of Saigir for the protection and well-being of wild beasts: how he intervenes 'to save a hunted animal from its pursuers', how he 'renders fierce animals tame' and how he 'feeds starving wolves out of the herds which he tends'.[6]

On one occasion, according to the legend, while he was living out in the wild surrounded by 'a waste and tangled wood', Ciarán encountered a savage boar. This 'ferocious' creature, instead of attacking and harming the saint, was somehow miraculously tamed and became Ciarán's 'first disciple', serving him 'like a monk in that place'.[7] What follows then – the delightful but truly bizarre account of a monastery consisting not of monks but of wild animals – is one of the most charming tales ever to come out of Ireland.

> Eventually other animals came from their dens in the wilds to St Ciarán, a fox, a badger, a wolf, and a stag. And they behaved with the greatest meekness in his presence, obedient in everything to the holy man's orders as if they were monks. But one day the fox, who was more cunning and more deceitful than all other animals, stole the shoes of the Abbot, St Ciarán – and, abandoning his vow, carried them off to his old den in the waste, intending to chew them there. Discovering this, the saintly Father Ciarán sent another monk or disciple, namely the badger, to bring his brother back to his obedience. The badger, being knowledgeable about woods, at once set out in obedience to his Elder, making his way directly to the den of Brother Fox (*fratris vulpis*'). There, finding him just about to eat his master's shoes, the badger bit the ears and tail of the fox, and cropped his fur, and compelled him to return with him to the monastery, there to do penance for his theft. Yielding to force, the fox came back with the badger to his own cell at the ninth hour carrying the shoes still uneaten, and went to St Ciarán. The holy man said to the fox, 'Brother, why have you done this evil deed which no monk ought to do? (*Quare hoc malum fecisti, Frater, quod non decet monachos agere?*). Behold our water is sweet and common to all, and food here is for us all alike to share. And if you should have a longing to eat flesh, as is your nature, the omnipotent God would make it for you from the bark of these trees if we prayed.' Then the fox, pleading to be forgiven, undertook to do penance by fasting, and would not eat until the holy man commanded him. And from that time on he lived as devout and companionable [*familiaris*] as all the other animals.[8]

---

6. Carolus Plummer, 'Introduction', in *Vitae Sanctorum Hiberniae*, Vol. 1 (Oxford, 1910), p. cxli.
7. '*Vita Sancti Ciarani de Saigir*', V, in *Vitae Sanctorum Hiberniae*, Vol. 1, p. 219.
8. '*Vita Sancti Ciarani de Saigir*', V–VI, in *Vitae Sanctorum Hiberniae*, Vol. 1, pp. 219–20.

This story, though vivid and compelling, is an entirely fanciful tale, legend, not history. Nevertheless, the vision which it expresses of manifest ease and harmony between Ciarán and the world of nature brings at once to mind the figure of Francis of Assisi. What's more, it is even possible that this humble Irish legend marks the first time in the history of Christian literature (prior to the time of St Francis) that a wild creature – a fox in this case – is openly and reverently addressed by a human being as *brother*.

Readers and scholars over the years have often been struck by the similarities existing between the spirit of Francis and that of the early Irish monks. Francis, like them, was 'fond of retiring from time to time into solitude, underneath a cliff or in the heart of a wood'.[9] And, like them, he had a great 'love of nature'[10] and a love also for 'poetry and music'.[11] 'The Irish', writes Anselmo M. Tommasini, 'made poetry and music almost an integral part of religion, and almost all the great Irish saints have left us hymns or poems.'[12] Clearly struck by many of these same links and similarities, the celebrated English scholar Robin Flower remarks:

> I think it may be claimed that the Irish were naturally Franciscan, Franciscan before St Francis. For, when we read the records of the early [Irish] Church, the legends, the poems, the rules, we cannot escape the feeling that we are here in the presence of a rehearsal of the Franciscan drama, centuries before it was first staged at Assisi. For where they are most characteristic and least dulled by later unimaginative repetition, these records have that very air of morning freshness which surrounds the early Franciscan traditions.[13]

Of all these 'records' – the legends, poems and rules – the most impressive by far, I would say, are the nature lyrics composed by monk-poets in the ninth and tenth centuries. A reflection on three of them will constitute the first part of the present chapter. The second part of the chapter will explore the meaning and significance of *The Canticle of the Creatures* by St Francis of Assisi. Probably no work of literature concerned with nature – certainly no poem – is more famous within the Christian tradition.

---

9. Anselmo M. Tommasini, *Irish Saints in Italy*, trans. G. Cleary (London, 1937), p. 475.
10. Edward A. Armstrong, *Saint Francis, Nature Mystic: The Derivation and Significance of the Nature Stories in the Franciscan Legend* (London, 1973), p. 34.
11. Tommasini, *Irish Saints in Italy*, p. 484.
12. Ibid., p. 482.
13. Robin Flower, *The Irish Tradition* (Dublin, 2012), p. 125. When finally, in the fourteenth century, the Franciscans arrived in Ireland, they enjoyed immediate success. According to Colmán Ó Clabaigh, in an illuminating paper on the subject, 'by the 1530s Ireland was host to over one hundred Franciscan communities'. See 'The Other Christ: The Cult of St Francis of Assisi in Late Medieval Ireland', in *Art and Devotion in Medieval Ireland*, eds. C. Ó Clabaigh and S. Ryan (Dublin, 2006), p. 142. On page 147, Ó Clabaigh cites a cheerful, brief salute to St Francis from a fourteenth-century manuscript: 'Hail, Saint Francis, with your many birds – kites and crows, ravens and owls, twenty-four wild geese and a peacock! Many a stout beggar follows your company'.

PART ONE
THREE IRISH LYRICS
MONKS AT HOME WITH NATURE

1
A Hermit Song

The first of the poems under consideration is voiced for Marbán, a poet of the seventh century. It is a truly radiant work. In it we hear the monk describe in detail his beloved hermitage, his demonstrably poor yet happy dwelling place at the heart of nature. (The lyric itself, it is believed, was composed in the tenth century.)

>A hiding tuft, a green-backed yew-tree
>   Is my roof,
>While nearby a great oak keeps me
>   Tempest-proof.

… … … … … … … … … … … … … … … … … …

>Pigs and goats, the friendliest neighbours,
>   Nestle near,
>Wild swine come, or broods of badgers,
>   Grazing deer.

>All the gentry of the country
>   Come to call!
>And the foxes come behind them,
>   Best of all.

… … … … … … … … … … … … … … … … … ….

>All that one could ask for comfort
>   Round me grows,
>There are hips and haws and strawberries,
>   Nuts and sloes.

>And when summer spreads its mantle
>   What a sight!
>Marjoram and leeks and pignuts,
>   Juicy, bright.

>Dainty redbreasts briskly forage
>   Every bush,
>Round and round my hut there flutter
>   Swallow, thrush.

>Bees and beetles, music-makers,
>   Croon and strum;

> Geese pass over, duck in autumn,
> Dark streams hum.[14]

These stanzas represent one side of a conversation or debate which, it was believed, took place between King Guaire of Connaught and Marbán, his half-brother. Marbán had chosen to renounce the life of a prince at court for life as a humble solitary. The king, astonished by this decision, asks his brother why, instead of sleeping in his own bed, he prefers sleeping out in the wilderness on 'a pitch-pine floor'. Marbán's reply – his stout defence of his vocation – takes the form of a bright series of stanzas, some of which are those above. Although Marbán does appear, it's true, to be bereft of all ordinary comforts, he declares that he doesn't feel any less rich than his brother, the king: 'I am richer far through Christ, my Lord, / than ever you were.'[15]

> Though you enjoy all you consume
> and wealth exceeding,
> I am grateful for the riches
> my dear Christ brings me.
>
> No hour of trouble like you endure,
> no din of combat:
> I thank the Prince for all the good
> he grants me in my hut.[16]

So impressed is the king by these words, he declares at once that he would willingly give up his entire kingdom, indeed surrender all claims to wealth and power if only, with his brother Marbán, he could live in joyous solitude the hermit vocation.[17]

2

Another Hermit Song

A comparable lyric, again on the hermit theme, has survived from the ninth century. This time, however, the author, Manchán of Liath, is not writing as an established solitary – an ascetic monk living far from society in a remote hermitage – but rather as someone aspiring to be a hermit, a man, a poet of manifest literary talent, longing for the life of solitude. Here once again, the vision of nature is of

---

14. Marbán, an extract from 'The Hermit's Song', in *Kings, Lords, Commons: An Anthology from the Irish*, trans. Frank O'Connor (London, 1970), pp. 7–8.

15. Only part of 'The Hermit's Song' is translated by O'Connor. The sentence cited here is from a translation by James Carney, *Medieval Irish Lyrics* (Oakland, CA, 1967), p. 73.

16. Ibid. In the last two lines, I have presumed to make changes to the Carney translation, replacing, for example, the word 'bothy' with the word 'hut'.

17. Ibid.

a world entirely beautiful, entirely benign. Not only does the poet speak with manifest warmth and reverence of the great world of nature surrounding his longed-for hermitage, he imagines nature in the form of 'a clear pool' possessing, under divine inspiration, the power to heal and cleanse his soul.

> I wish, O Son of the living God, O ancient,
>   eternal King,
> for a hidden little hut in the wilderness
>   that it may be my dwelling.
>
> An all-grey lithe little lark to be by its side,
>   a clear pool
> to wash away my sins through the grace
>   of the Holy Spirit.
>
> Quite near, a beautiful wood around it
>   on every side
> to nurse many-voiced birds, hiding it
>   with its shelter.
>
> A southern aspect for warmth, a little brook
>   across its floor,
> a choice land with many gracious gifts such as
>   be good for every plant.
> … … … … … … … … … … … … … … … …
>
> This is the husbandry I would take,
>   I would choose,
> and will not hide it, fragrant leek, hens,
>   salmon, trout, bees.
>
> Raiment and food enough for me from the King
>   of fair fame.
> and I to be sitting for a while praying to God
>   in every place.[18]

Alongside the manifest affection for God and nature, a kind of primitive radiance pervades these early Christian poems, a boldness of perception that almost startles. No reader, I imagine, coming upon them for the first time, could fail to be impressed by how memorably, in poem after poem, the tiniest details of place and weather are described: the ice-cold hermitage invaded by Spring, the new winds, the stark beauty of ocean rock and remote woodland. Kuno Meyer, in one of his many reflections on the distinctive character of early Irish verse,

---

18. Manchán of Liath, 'The Hermit's Son', in *Ancient Irish Poetry*, trans. Kuno Meyer (London, 1994), pp. 30–1.

remarks: 'These poems occupy a unique position in the literature of the world. To seek out and watch and love Nature in its tiniest phenomena as in its grandest, was given to no people so early and so fully as to the Celt.'[19]

But what was it that made possible this achievement, and what explains the compelling directness and force of these early lyrics? In the attempt to answer this question, reference has often been made to the likely survival of a robust 'pagan' or pre-Christian spirit. That, I have no doubt, is a telling part of the explanation. But of at least equal importance and significance is the direct influence on these early monastic poems of the decidedly fresh vision and understanding of creation which came with Christianity. To this vision, to this understanding, the lives of the monks and hermits had given bold and vivid expression for three or four centuries. Convinced that by the simple practice of daily work and prayer they could, in a sense, begin to rediscover 'the original garden' of Adam and Eve, the hermits in particular found themselves looking with sheer delight and wonder at the natural world around them, looking at everything as if for the first time.

What they saw – like a revelation to their senses – they found good. Accordingly, each of them would no doubt have recognized as their own the joyous vision of the natural world as we find it expressed, for example, by St Augustine of Hippo. Writing in the fourth century, the great poet-theologian remarked:

> In all the things in creation I find that the sky is good, the sun is good, the moon is good, the stars are good; that the earth is good and that whatever germinates and roots itself in the earth is good; that whatever walks and moves is good; that whatever flies in the air and swims in the water is good. I say too that man is good: for a good man, out of the treasure of his heart, brings forth good.[20]

Augustine's vision of nature, like that of the early monks, is grounded in an understanding of God as the author of all that is good, all that is beautiful. He writes in the same commentary on Psalm 134: 'God made all things very good; not only good but very good. He made the sky and earth and all things which are in them good, and He made them very good.'[21]

3
'The Monk and the Cat'

Birds and badgers, foxes and deer, wolves and horses – animals of all kinds crowd the lines of these monastic poems. But absent, it would seem, are references to what one imagines were the monks' or the hermits' most familiar and most favoured

---

19. Kuno Meyer, *Ancient Irish Poetry* (London, 1994), p. xii.
20. St Augustine of Hippo, *Enarratio in Psalmum* CXXXIV, no. 4, *Enarrationes in Psalmos S. Augustini*, P.L. 37, 1740.
21. Ibid., no. 3, 1740.

domestic animals, those uniquely loyal and devoted ambassadors of nature: dogs and cats. One splendid lyric, however, has come down to us in a medieval manuscript which happily names and celebrates the bond existing between a particular Irish monk of the ninth century and his white cat, Pangur Bán.[22] So truly charming and so unusually intimate is the relationship between man and cat; this ancient poem is unquestionably a candidate for inclusion in what might be called the poetry of Eden. That said, however, the mouse in the poem, living under immanent threat of being devoured by the great Pangur, has absolutely no illusion that this particular monastic cell is paradise restored!

*

Pangur Bán was composed in Carinthia (modern-day Austria) and was written down in Old Irish on one page of a four-page manuscript containing, apart from the actual lyric, study notes on the Greek language. The manuscript of the poem is now preserved in the Reichenau Primer at St Paul's Abbey in the Lavanttal, Austria.

> I and Pangur Bán, my cat,
> 'Tis a like task we are at:
> Hunting mice is his delight,
> Hunting words I sit all night.
>
> Better far than praise of men
> 'Tis to sit with book and pen;
> Pangur bears me no ill will,
> He too plies his simple skill.
>
> 'Tis a merry thing to see
> At our tasks how glad are we,
> When at home we sit and find
> Entertainment to our mind.
>
> Oftentimes a mouse will stray
> In the hero Pangur's way;
> Oftentimes my keen thought set
> Takes a meaning in its net.
>
> 'Gainst the wall he sets his eye,
> Full and fierce and sharp and sly;
> 'Gainst the wall of knowledge I
> All my little wisdom try.

---

22. I have spoken of 'The Monk and the Cat' as if it belonged to the category of hermit poetry, but that is something of a presumption. At this distance in time it's impossible to know if the author lived in community or was a solitary.

> When a mouse darts from its den,
> O how glad is Pangur then!
> O what gladness do I prove
> When I solve the doubts I love!
>
> So in peace our tasks we ply,
> Pangur Bán, my cat, and I;
> In our arts we find our bliss,
> I have mine and he has his.
>
> Practice every day has made
> Pangur perfect in his trade;
> I get wisdom day and night
> Turning darkness into light.[23]

An unmistakable joy – the 'bliss' of Eden – is present in all three of these monastic verses. And something of that same joy, that same feeling of lost innocence restored, and of an almost magical sense of intimacy with nature, is present also three or four centuries later and, in a unique and radiant form, in the great hymn of creation composed by St Francis.

---

23. 'The Monk and His Cat', trans. Robin Flower in *Poems and Translations* (Dublin, 2012). A critical edition of the poem was published by W. Stokes and J. Strachan in *Thesaurus Palaeohibernicus*, Vol. 2, ed. W. Stokes (Cambridge, 1903), p. 293.

PART TWO
FRANCIS OF ASSISI: THE *NEW* CANTICLE

Be praised, my Lord, with all your creatures,
especially Sir Brother Sun
who is the day
and through whom you give us light,
and he is beautiful and radiant with great splendour
and bears a likeness of you, Most High.

No one reading these lines from *The Canticle of the Creatures* can fail to be impressed by the quality and freshness of their language and vision.[24] But what information do we have of the saint and poet behind the work? The knowledge handed down to us over the centuries, is it knowledge of Francis the man or of Francis the myth? According to contemporary scholarship, it is no small challenge to find or recover a clear and accurate image of the historical Francis behind the countless legends and stories, many of them composed years after the death of the saint and by authors who had never known him when he was alive. Scholars and historians such as André Vauchez,[25] Raoul Manselli,[26] Michael Robson[27] and Augustine Thompson[28] have worked hard to separate the more trustworthy sources from those less genuine. Legends celebrated for centuries, for example, such as the story of Francis and the taming of the wolf at Gubbio, are now regarded as just that – mere legends.[29] But on one point, at least both the earliest witnesses and the later chroniclers of Francis's life happily agree, and that is on the startling freshness, the *newness* of the relationship established by Francis with all living creatures.

Nowhere, I would say, is the spirit of that relationship more in evidence than in the *Canticle* itself. But what is it exactly that constitutes the newness of St Francis's vision? If the awareness of God and of nature evoked so memorably in the poem can be thought of as a form of mysticism, how does it differ from the traditional Christian forms of mysticism, medieval and ancient?

---

24. The *Canticle*, even in modest translation, impresses. But, inevitably, much of the poetry is lost – and in particular the play of assonance and alliteration which we find in the original. The phrase, for example, 'and he is radiant and beautiful with great splendour', reads in the Italian: 'et ellu è bellu e radiante con grande splendore.'

25. André Vauchez, *Francis of Assisi: The Life and Afterlife of a Medieval Saint*, trans. M.F. Cusato (London, 2012). According to Vauchez (p. 20), 'each of the lives written in the century that followed the death of Francis reflects an interpretation, a partisan "reading," of the Franciscan phenomenon'.

26. Raoul Manselli, *St Francis of Assisi*, trans. P. Duggan (Chicago, 1988).

27. Michael Robson, *St Francis of Assisi: The Legend and the Life* (London, 1997).

28. Augustine Thompson, *Francis of Assisi: A New Biography* (London, 2012).

29. Ibid., p. viii.

1
Francis: Poet of Affirmation

There are, it could be said, two distinct forms under which Christian poets have been accustomed, over the centuries, to conceive divine reality. The first of these – what one might call the doctrine or the poetry of immanence – invites the poet to look confidently outward towards the material universe and to perceive, in the great power and beauty of nature, the immanent presence of God. All five senses are involved in this act of contemplation. Gerard Manley Hopkins, for example, impressed at the close of one summer by how 'barbarous in beauty' and 'lovely' in 'behaviour' were the elements of nature, felt himself drawn by the sense of the 'wind-walks' above him, by the sudden rising up of the stooks and by the wondrous movement of the 'silk-sack clouds', to search within them, and through them, for a glimpse of the immanent yet unseen presence of divine beauty.

> I walk, I lift up, I lift up heart, eyes,
>   Down all that glory in the heavens to glean our Saviour …
> And the azurous hung hills are his world-wielding shoulder
>   Majestic[30]

The second way of perceiving divine reality in the Christian spiritual tradition is what might be called a doctrine or poetry of transcendence. When most radically expressed, this second mode of vision insists on an almost total separation of the temporal and the eternal worlds. God, or the Supreme Being, is viewed as being separated from our world of multiplicity and variety by an immeasurable distance. Thus, the path of the contemplative in search of perfection, or in search of God, must literally be a *transcendence*, a surpassing: a path of painful self-negation, a closing fast of the door of the senses, a journey inward and upward through a long series of trials and temptations. Poets and mystics associated with this particular way include names such as Richard of St Victor, St Augustine of Hippo, Pseudo-Dionysius and St John of the Cross.

That Francis of Assisi belongs among the poets of immanence and affirmation cannot be doubted if the testimonies of his closest disciples, the earliest witnesses, are to be believed. His first biographer, and one of his contemporaries, Thomas of Celano, writes:

> Who could ever express the deep affection he bore for all things that belong to God? Or who would be able to tell of the sweet tenderness he enjoyed while contemplating in creatures the wisdom, power, and goodness of the Creator? From this reflection he often overflowed with amazing, unspeakable joy as he looked at the sun, gazed at the moon, or observed the stars in the sky.[31]

---

30. Gerard Manley Hopkins, 'Hurrahing in Harvest', in *A Hopkins Reader*, ed. J. Pick (New York, 1966), p. 51.

31. Thomas of Celano, *The Life of Saint Francis*, 'The First Book' Chapter XXIX, 80, in *Francis of Assisi: Early Documents*, Vol. 1: *The Saint*, eds. R.J. Armstrong et al. (New York, 1999), p. 250. Hereafter 'The First Book'.

Francis was clearly enraptured by the natural beauty of the world around him, but his vision of the world cannot be described merely in terms of immanence and affirmation. As with the work of all the great Christian mystics and poets, the contemplative vision of Francis combines elements of both immanence *and* transcendence. Although happily absorbed in the enchantment of immediate, palpable beauty, never for a moment would he have allowed himself to forget the bright source and origin of all beauty. Contemplating the loveliness of this or that aspect of creation, his instinct was always to turn with joy to the thought of 'the wisdom, power, and goodness of the Creator'.[32]

Francis was a man who had discovered for himself the true nature of God. As a result, even when attempting to speak in prose of that divine nature and say something of the God whom he described once as 'the fullness of good, all good, every good, the true and supreme good',[33] the words which Francis uses seem almost to possess the quality and pattern of a prose-poem. He writes:

> Wherever we are,
> in every place, at every hour,
> at every time of the day, every day, and continually,
> let all of us truly and humbly believe,
> hold in our heart and love,
> honour, adore, serve,
> praise and bless, glorify and exalt,
> magnify and give thanks
> to the Most High and Supreme Eternal God,
> Trinity and Unity,
> Father, Son and Holy Spirit,
> Creator of all,
> Saviour of all who believe
> and hope in Him,
> and love Him,
> Who, without beginning and end,
> is unchangeable, invisible,
> indescribable, ineffable,
> incomprehensible, unfathomable,
> blessed, praiseworthy,
> glorious, exalted, sublime, most high,
> gentle, lovable, delightful,
> and totally desirable above all else
> for ever.
> Amen.[34]

32. Ibid.

33. Francis of Assisi, 'The Earlier Rule', Chapter XXIII, 9, in *Francis of Assisi: The Saint*, p. 85.

34. Ibid., Chapter XXIII, 11, pp. 85–6.

That St Francis felt drawn to use so many words when attempting to describe the nature of God is no accident. He was a man fascinated by the power of words. It was almost as if, by themselves, words gave him direct access to reality. By simply pronouncing the name God on occasion he would, we are told, be 'so wholly taken up in joy', so filled with sheer delight that he appeared to his companions like 'a new person', like someone who had come from 'another age'.[35] The sound of words – even it would seem the very *existence* of words – was to Francis a cause of the greatest wonder.

> For this reason he used to gather up any piece of writing, whether divine or human, wherever he found it: on the road, in the house, on the floor. He would reverently pick it up and put it in a sacred or decent place because the name of the Lord, or something pertaining to it, might be written there. Once a brother asked why he so carefully gathered bits of writing, even writing of pagans where the name of the Lord does not appear. He replied: 'Son, I do this because they have the letters which make the glorious name of the Lord God. And the good that is found there does not belong to the pagans nor to any human being, but to God alone "to whom belongs every good thing".'[36]

2
Francis: The Path towards Freedom

One of the paradoxes in the life of Francis is that the act of discovering God or discovering the traces of God in the beauty of the natural world – that capacity to be enchanted by beauty – was in no way hindered but rather helped, it would appear, by an unconstrained commitment to self-denial and by a capacity for fierce detachment. Such bold asceticism did not, however, represent any kind of disdain for the wonders and charms of creation. On the contrary, it represented simply a determination on the part of Francis to keep alive his most hidden, most profound desire. Thomas of Celano explains: 'More than anything else he desired *to be set free and to be with Christ*. Thus his chief object of concern was to live free from all things that are in the world, so that his inner serenity would not be disturbed even for a moment by contact with any of its dust.'[37]

Here Celano could almost be describing the traditional spiritual path of a poet or mystic of transcendence. His statement makes abundantly clear that the Francis who looks out with confidence at the natural world through all his senses as manifesting divine beauty is also the Francis who acknowledges the need, in life and in spiritual life, for some form of radical discipline and radical detachment. Celano writes: 'Francis made himself insensible to all outside noise, gathering his external senses into his inner being and checking the impetus of his spirit,

---

35. Thomas of Celano, 'The First Book' Chapter XXIX, 82, p. 251.
36. Ibid., pp. 251–2.
37. Ibid., Chapter XXVII, 71, p. 243.

he emptied himself for God alone.'[38] Any notion that Celano, with this particular reflection, may have been projecting his own austere spirituality onto the nature-loving man of Assisi is negated as soon as we take time to read the actual writings of Francis himself.

As a young man, according to Celano, Francis had lived a life of disordered passion and self-indulgence.[39] In his *Testament*, Francis himself refers bluntly to a time in his life when he had been living 'in sin'.[40] Once converted, however, with the passion of a convert, he surrendered to a life of prayer and penance, clearly determined to pursue a path that was both rigorist and demanding. Typically, in one of his *Admonitions* to a number of his first disciples (addressing them as 'Brothers and Sisters of Penance'), Francis writes: 'We must deny ourselves and place our bodies under the yoke of servitude and holy obedience.'[41] And again, in another place: 'Let us chastise our body, crucifying it with its vices, concupiscence and sins, because by living according to the flesh, the devil wishes to take away from us the love of Jesus Christ and eternal life.'[42]

Francis, by the grace of prayer and penance, became a free man, his senses and imagination and indeed his very soul liberated from all unnecessary distraction.

> There was in him such harmony of flesh with spirit and such obedience that, as the spirit strove to reach all holiness, the flesh did not resist but even tried to run on ahead, according to the saying: *For you my soul has thirsted; and my flesh in so many ways!* Repeated submission became spontaneous, as the flesh, yielding each day, reached a place of great virtue, for habit often becomes virtue.[43]

'Spontaneous' – the adjective chosen here by Celano – is a key word for understanding the unique spiritual genius of Francis of Assisi. But that spontaneity – the piercing joy he felt, for example, in surrendering to the power and beauty of nature and to the beauty of God – was made possible, firstly, by a naked vulnerability both in sense and thought to all that he perceived and, secondly, by an interior freedom of spirit, a quality of detachment that was by any standards

---

38. Ibid.

39. It's not clear if Celano was exaggerating when he says of Francis that 'beyond all of his peers in vanities, he proved himself a more excessive inciter of evil and a zealous imitator of foolishness'. See Celano, 'The First Book' Chapter I, 2, p. 183.

40. Francis of Assisi, 'The Testament (1226)' 1, in *Francis of Assisi: The Saint*, p. 124.

41. Francis of Assisi, 'Later Admonition and Exhortation to the Brothers and Sisters of Penance', 40 (second version of the 'Letter to the Faithful') in *Francis of Assisi: The Saint*, p. 48. In the same document, Francis goes even further. He writes: 'Let us hold our bodies in scorn and contempt because, through our own fault, we are all wretched and corrupt.' See 'Later Admonition' 46, p. 48.

42. 'Fragments (1209–1223)' 3, in *Francis of Assisi: The Saint*, p. 87.

43. Thomas of Celano, *The Life of St Francis*, 'The Second Book' Chapter IV, 97, *Francis of Assisi: The Saint*, p. 266. Hereafter 'The Second Book'.

remarkable. Umberto Eco, reflecting on the seeming contradiction between the manifest power which beauty has to enthral and the practice of radical asceticism, writes:

> Ascetics, in all ages, are not unaware of the seductiveness of worldly pleasures; if anything, they feel it more keenly than most. The drama of the ascetic discipline lies precisely in a tension between the call of earthbound pleasure and a striving after the supernatural. But when the discipline proves victorious, and brings the peace which accompanies control of the senses, then it becomes possible to gaze serenely upon the things of this earth.[44]

3

Approaches to Nature: Two Paths, Two Visions

Francis of Assisi and Augustine of Hippo were both converted sinners and both writers of genius. In the Christian literary tradition, almost no one before Francis speaks or sings of the beauty of the natural world with more eloquence and conviction than Augustine. And yet these two authors and saints are often seen in opposition one to the other: Francis the affirmative nature mystic and Augustine the austere rigorist, the man who, even years after conversion, still remained (according to some) suspicious of nature, his wariness almost Manichean.[45]

That Francis was far more at home in the world of nature than Augustine, I have no doubt. There is a wonderfully relaxed quality in the *Canticle* that is unique to the saint of Assisi. But Augustine, although he certainly deserves his place among the poets and mystics of transcendence, has a striking capacity all the same to be stirred by the beauty of the natural world. At times, in fact, Augustine writes of the immense variety of nature with an almost Franciscan sense of wonder and delight:

> How could any description do justice to all these blessings? The manifest diversity of beauty in sky and earth and sea; the abundance of light, and its miraculous loveliness, in sun and moon and stars; the dark shades of woods, the colour and fragrance of flowers, the multitudinous varieties of birds, with their songs and their bright plumage; the countless different species of living creatures of all shapes and sizes, amongst whom it is the smallest in bulk that moves our greatest wonder – for we are more astonished at the activities of the tiny ants and

---

44. Umberto Eco, *Art and Beauty in the Middle Ages*, trans. H. Bredin (London, 1986), p. 6.
45. Roger D. Sorrell speaks of 'an unease with the beauty of the created world characteristic of the "the converted Manichee Augustine"'. Sorrell is prepared to acknowledge, however, that some of Augustine's ideas 'could easily be the basis for a Christian nature mysticism'. See Sorrell, *St Francis of Assisi and Nature* (New York, 1988), p. 86.

bees than at the immense bulk of whales. Then there is the mighty spectacle of the sea itself, putting on its changing colours like different garments, now green, with all the many varied shades, now purple, now blue.[46]

In similar vein, elsewhere Augustine puts this question to his readers: 'Ask the loveliness of the earth, ask the loveliness of the sea, ask the loveliness of the broad, airy spaces ... ask the serried ranks of the stars, ask the sun making the day glorious with its beams ... ask all these things, and they will answer you, "Here we are, look. We are indeed beautiful."'[47] Then Augustine adds: 'Their beauty is their confession. Who made these beautiful yet changeable things if not One who is both beautiful and unchangeable?'[48] Here, the contemplation of natural beauty serves as a catalyst for a beginning awareness of divine beauty. And something of that movement, from the contemplation, that is, of the beauty of creatures to the recognition and praise of the source of all beauty – from nature to the author of nature – takes place also in the *Canticle* of St Francis. That said, however, what is achieved in the *Canticle* is something so new that even this statement of Augustine, though apparently informed and comprehensive, doesn't begin to describe the world of vision opened for us with such genius and simplicity by the saint and poet of Assisi.

4

A Song of Fellowship and Praise

Composed in the spring of 1225, *The Canticle of the Creatures* is the most beloved and celebrated of all the writings of Francis of Assisi.[49] It divides into three separate parts corresponding to the three stages in which it was composed. The first part begins with the poet lifting up in joyous song to God the praise of all creation – sun, moon, stars and the four elements, earth, air, water and fire. Part two, in contrast, is concerned with forgiveness and reconciliation. It

---

46. St Augustine of Hippo, *Concerning the City of God against the Pagans*, Book 22, Chapter 24, trans. H. Bettenson (Harmondsworth, 1967), p. 1075.

47. St Augustine, Sermon 241, *In diebus Paschalibus: De resurrectione corporum, contra Gentiles, Sermones ad populum*, Chapter 2, no. 2, P.L. 38, 1134.

48. Ibid.

49. Many books and articles have been written concerning the *Canticle* over the years. See for example: Eloi Leclerc, *Le Cantique des créatures ou Les symboles de l'union* (Paris, 1970); Carlo Paolazzi, *Il Cantico di Frate Sole* (Genova, 1992); Timothy J. Johnson, 'Francis and Creation', in *The Cambridge Companion to Francis of Assisi*, ed. M.J.P. Robson (Cambridge, 2012), pp. 142–58; Edward A. Armstrong, *Saint Francis, Nature Mystic: The Derivation and Significance of the Nature Stories in the Franciscan Legend* (London, 1973); Roger D. Sorrell, *St Francis of Assisi and Nature* (New York, 1988); Ewert H. Cousins, 'Francis of Assisi: Christian Mysticism at the Crossroads', in *Mysticism and Religious Traditions*, ed. S.T. Katz (Oxford, 1983), pp. 163–90; Brian Moloney, *Francis of Assisi and His 'Canticle of Brother Sun' Reassessed* (New York, 2013).

was occasioned by a quarrel in Assisi which had broken out between civil and religious authorities. Francis, in an attempt to restore peace between the warring sides, added two verses to the *Canticle*, praising those who, out of love for God, bear with tribulation and suffering and who learn to forgive their enemies. The third part, in which we find the stunning reference to Sister Death, was composed by Francis when he himself was dying. It has been suggested that the final verse *Praise and bless my Lord and give him thanks and serve him with great humility* may possibly have been 'a refrain used after each verse of the entire Canticle'.[50]

But – enough commentary for the moment. It is time to read in its entirety, albeit in modest English translation, the Little Poor Man's song:

The Canticle of the Creatures

Most high, all-powerful, good Lord,
yours are the praises,
the glory, the honour, and all blessing.
To you alone, Most High,
do they belong, and no human being
is worthy
to speak your name.

Be praised, my Lord, with all your creatures,
especially Sir Brother Sun
who is the day
and through whom you give us light,
and he is beautiful and radiant with great splendour
and bears a likeness of you, Most High.

Be praised, my Lord, for Sister Moon
and the stars.
In heaven you have formed them bright
and precious and beautiful.

Be praised, my Lord, for
Brother Wind,
and for the air, cloudy and serene,
and for all weather
through which you give sustenance
to your creatures.

Be praised, my Lord, for
Sister Water

---

50. See the editorial introduction to 'The Canticle of the Creatures', in *Francis of Assisi: The Saint*, p. 113.

who is most useful and humble and
precious and chaste.

Be praised, my Lord, for
Brother Fire
through whom you illumine the night,
and he is beautiful
and playful and robust and strong.

Be praised, my Lord, for our Sister
Mother Earth,
who sustains and governs us,
and produces diverse fruits with coloured flowers
and herbs.

Be praised, my Lord,
for those who forgive out of love for you,
and bear infirmity and tribulation.

Blessed are they
who endure in peace for, by you,
Most High,
they shall be crowned.

Be praised, my Lord, for our
Sister Bodily Death
from whom no living man can escape.

Woe to those who die in mortal sin.
Blessed are those
whom death will find in your most holy will,
for the second death shall do them
no harm.

Praise and bless my
Lord,
and give him thanks
and serve him with great humility.[51]

At the time when Francis began writing the *Canticle*, he was suffering intolerably. For days on end, owing to an eye disease, he was 'unable to bear the

---

51. Translation by the author. For the original text of the *Canticle*, see Carolus Paolazzi, ed., *Francisci Assisiensis: Scripta* (Rome, 2009), pp. 121–3. See also Vittore Branca, 'Il Cantico di Frate Sole, Studio sulle fonti e testo critico', in *Archivum Franciscanum Historicum* 41 (1948): pp. 3–87.

light of the sun or the light of a fire at night.'[52] He was almost certainly suffering from a form of trachoma. But Francis had other ailments as well: among them, pain from the wounds of the stigmata he had received on Mount La Verna, severe malnutrition and something like malaria. 'One night', we are told by an early source, 'as blessed Francis was reflecting on all the troubles he was enduring, he was moved by pity for himself. "Lord," he said, "make haste to help me in my illnesses, so that I may be able to bear them patiently"'.[53] Help came to him at once. In his inmost spirit, Francis heard the Lord say to him: 'Be glad and rejoice in your illnesses and troubles, because as of now you are as secure as if you were already in my kingdom.'[54]

No words could have pleased Francis more. As soon as he got up the next day, he shared the news of what had happened with his companions, and he shared something else as well. He had come to a decision overnight, a decision which was in time to prove momentous not only for his own spiritual life and mission but also for his work as a poet. To the companions who were with him he declared:

> I must rejoice greatly in my illnesses and troubles, and be consoled in the Lord ... In his mercy he has given me, his unworthy little servant still living in the flesh, the promise of his kingdom. Therefore, for his praise, for our consolation and for the edification of our neighbour, I want to write a new *Praise of the Lord* for his creatures.[55]

5

God's Troubadour and Preacher

Francis not only wrote the words of *The Canticle of the Creatures*, he also composed the melody (now lost) to accompany it. After revealing to his brethren his intention 'to write a new *Praise of the Lord*', he withdrew into himself and meditated for a while. Then, with the opening words of the *Canticle* already on his lips, 'He composed', we are told, 'a melody for these words and taught it to his companions so that they could repeat it.'[56] This event was by no means out of the ordinary for Francis – the experience, that is, of finding himself so ecstatically moved that he was unable to suppress the need, the desire, to break into song. Quickened by what his inner ear perceived in secret of the 'divine whisper', he would sometimes experience 'a sweet melody of the spirit' bubbling up within him and then bursting forth from him as 'a song of joy'.[57] This, apparently, would often happen when he

---

52. *The Assisi Compilation (1244–1260)*, 83, in *Francis of Assisi: Early Documents*, Vol. 2, *The Founder*, eds. R.J. Armstrong et al. (New York, 2000), p. 185. *The Assisi Compilation* contains anecdotes which could only have come from people close to Francis.
53. Ibid.
54. Ibid.
55. *The Assisi Compilation*, 83, in *Francis of Assisi: The Founder*, pp. 185–6.
56. Ibid., p. 186.
57. Celano, *The Remembrance of the Desire of a Soul*, 'The Second Book' Chapter XC, 127, in *Francis of Assisi: The Founder*, p. 331.

was walking out in the open with his companions wholly absorbed in the task of prayer and praise.[58]

Few images of the saint are more appealing than this open-air picture of the *poverello* singing in a 'rapture of spirit' at the heart of nature. But the experience, the rapture, was not always singing for its own sake. Francis, the festive troubadour, was an apostle as well as a genius. Often with strong insistence, 'especially to the Lesser Brothers who had been given to the people for their salvation, he would say "What are the servants of God if not His minstrels, who must move people's hearts and lift them up to spiritual joy?"'[59]

Francis, being both genius and apostle, subverts the strict either/or approach of the Danish philosopher Søren Kierkegaard. In his celebrated essay 'Of the Difference between a Genius and an Apostle' (1847), Kierkegaard declared:

> The lyrical author is only concerned with his production, enjoys the pleasure of producing ... but he has nothing to do with others, he does not write *in order that*: in order to enlighten men or in order to help them along the *right* road ... No genius has an *in order that*, but the Apostle has, absolutely and paradoxically, an *in order that*.[60]

Behind *The Canticle of the Creatures*, there does exist an undeniable *in order that*, a clear and generous concern for the good of others. But not for a moment does this concern negate the genius of the work. Here it is not a matter of either/or, either genius *or* apostle, but rather of both/and – both genius *and* apostle.

One of the friars of St Francis, before joining the Order, had been known in the secular world as 'the King of Verses' and 'a very courtly master of singers'.[61] His name was Brother Pacifico. As soon as Francis had finished working on the *Canticle*, his spirit was filled, we are told, with 'such sweetness and consolation' he decided at once to send for Pacifico so that this singing friar together with 'a few good and spiritual brothers' might go throughout the world 'preaching and praising God'.[62]

> He said that he wanted one of them who knew how to preach, first to preach to the people. After the sermon they were to sing the *Praises of the Lord* as minstrels of the Lord. After the praises, he wanted the preacher to tell the people: 'We are minstrels of the Lord, and this is what we want as payment: that you live in true penance.'[63]

---

58. Celano, 'The Second Book' Chapter IX, 115, p. 284.
59. *The Assisi Compilation*, 83, in *Francis of Assisi: The Founder*, p. 186.
60. Søren Kierkegaard, 'Of the Difference between a Genius and an Apostle', in *The Present Age*, trans. A. Dru (London, 1962), pp. 107–10; cited by Robert Kiely in *The Fountain Light: Studies in Romanticism and Religion*, ed. J.R. Barth (New York, 2002), p. 34.
61. *The Assisi Compilation*, 83, p. 186.
62. Ibid.
63. Ibid.

6
Brother to All Creation

When for the first time Francis read or sang to his brethren the words of his *Canticle*, those present would have been reminded at once of *The Song of the Three Young Men*. This particular song or canticle, taken originally from the Book of Daniel, is one which the friars would often have sung together at the Office of Lauds. It contains a series of brief exhortations encouraging all living things, both on earth and in heaven, to give God praise. Here are some extracts from the prayer:

> All things the Lord has made, bless the Lord:
> give glory and eternal praise to him ...
> Sun and moon, bless the Lord ...
> Stars of heaven, bless the Lord ...
> Winds, all bless the Lord ...
> Fire and heat, bless the Lord ...
> Everything that grows on the earth, bless the Lord ...
> Springs of water, bless the Lord ...
> Sea beasts and everything that lives in the water,
> bless the Lord ...
> Birds of heaven, all bless the Lord ...
> Animals wild and tame, all bless the Lord:
> give glory and eternal praise to him.[64]

Several years before the mark of this great canticle was apparent in St Francis's own poetry, it was evident in his life. According to Thomas Celano, just as 'the three young men ... invited all the elements to praise and glorify the Creator of all things, so this man, full of the spirit of God never stopped glorifying, praising, and blessing the Creator and Ruler of all things in all the elements and creatures'.[65] The image Celano gives us here and elsewhere of Francis the joyous celebrant of both nature *and* of nature's author is unforgettable: 'Fields and vineyards, rocks and woods, and all the beauties of the field, flowing springs and blooming gardens, earth and fire, air and wind: all these he urged to love of God.'[66]

Being a man of the Gospel, Francis all his life expressed unique warmth and affection for human beings. But he also, and in innumerable ways, showed particular regard for 'mute, brute animals: reptiles, birds, and all other creatures whether sensate or not'.[67] And these creatures, in turn, would show respect for him. Even animals wild and dangerous to others would, we are told, become tame in his

---

64. The Book of Daniel, 3: 57–81.
65. See Celano, 'The First Book' Chapter XXIX, 80, pp. 250–1.
66. Ibid., Chapter XXIX, 81, p. 251.
67. Ibid., Chapter XXVIII, 77, p. 248.

presence.[68] Some of these creatures Francis came to regard as particular favourites. According to Celano, 'He used to embrace more warmly and to observe more gladly anything in which he found an allegorical likeness to the Son of God.'[69] As a result, 'among all the different kinds of creatures, he loved lambs with a special fondness and spontaneous affection, since in Sacred Scripture the humility of our Lord Jesus Christ is frequently and rightly compared to the lamb'.[70] What's more, 'Whenever he had to walk over rocks, he would walk with fear and reverence out of love for Him who is called "The Rock".'[71]

Francis not only showed unusual affection and regard for the small and great things of creation, he also spoke to them, and he sang to them. Behaving with the exuberant freedom and joy of a holy fool, he would, we are told, diligently exhort 'all birds, all animals, all reptiles, and also insensible creatures, to praise and love the Creator'.[72] In effect, with regard to the natural world, Francis was repeating some of the great prayers of exhortation from the biblical *Canticle of the Three Young Men*.

But the man of Assisi was doing something else as well, something unheard of up to that time. The birds of heaven, the animals wild and tame, the stars, the winds, the plants, the living springs were not addressed by Francis simply as creatures of the one God. They were addressed by him as nothing less than brothers and sisters. Francis did not have the least hesitation, therefore, in addressing doves, crows and jackdaws as 'my brother birds',[73] and a tiny chirping cricket as 'my sister',[74] and the great element of fire (a thing in his opinion not only 'useful' but 'noble') as 'my brother fire'.[75] This way of viewing the natural world has, over succeeding centuries, become so familiar it is by now almost a commonplace in art and literature. At the time of St Francis, however, it was a vision startlingly new.

An observation made by Gerard Manley Hopkins comes to mind at this point. It occurs in a letter he wrote to a friend in which he raised the question of Wordsworth's 'spiritual insight into nature'.[76] In Hopkins's opinion, the quality of insight which Wordsworth enjoyed was so remarkable that it was, he declared, a gift, a *'charisma'*, granted 'to very few men since time was – to Plato and who else?'[77] Two months later, in a letter to the same friend, he returned once again to the question:

68. *The Assisi Compilation*, 110, p. 218.
69. Celano, 'The First Book' Chapter XXVIII, 77, p. 248.
70. Ibid.
71. *The Assisi Compilation*, 88, p. 192.
72. Celano, 'The First Book' Chapter XXI, 58, p. 234.
73. Ibid.
74. *The Assisi Compilation*, 110, p. 217.
75. Ibid., 86, p. 190.
76. Letter XXXV, Hopkins to Dixen, 7 August 1886, *The Correspondence of Gerard Manley Hopkins to Richard Watson Dixen*, ed. C.C. Abbott (London, 1935), p. 141.
77. Ibid.

> There have been in all history a few, a very few men, whom common repute ... has treated as having had something happen to them that does not happen to other men, as having *seen something*, whatever that really was. Plato is the most famous of these ... human nature in these men saw something, got a shock ... [and] is in a tremble ever since.[78]

What Hopkins has particularly in mind at this point is Wordsworth's immortality ode. Once this work became known, 'human nature', Hopkins believes, 'got another of those shocks, and the tremble from it is spreading'.[79] The claim Hopkins makes here regarding Wordsworthian vision can be made – and with perhaps more justice – regarding the new and original vision of Francis of Assisi. I say this because through the eyes of the humble *poverello*, human nature saw something which it had never seen before. And this new understanding of the natural world must have greatly surprised the contemporaries of St Francis. What's more, that first visionary knowledge, the immediacy of beholding the world of nature afresh, did not end then and there – 'the tremble from it', we can say, is still spreading.

Thomas Celano in his *Life of St Francis*, when attempting to describe this 'spreading', this newness, employs the image of a great and powerful river flowing out of Eden. He writes: 'In these last times, a new Evangelist, like one of the rivers of Paradise, has poured out the streams of the gospel in a holy flood over the whole world ... In him and through him an unexpected joy and a holy newness has come into the world.'[80] There are of course other impressive rivers and streams of Gospel spirituality in the Middle Ages. But in the view of the Cambridge historian Dom David Knowles, there is nothing in the work of even the most celebrated authors to compare with 'the limpid freshness of Francis'.[81] Knowles is not for a moment questioning the sincerity and depth of texts such as the letters and dialogues of Bernard of Clairvaux and Aelred of Rievaulx. But, set them alongside the work of Francis and, in his opinion, they appear 'artificial and rhetorical'. He writes: 'They are of a school and of a date', whereas 'the most characteristic utterances of Francis have something of the dateless purity of the Gospels.'[82]

7
Praising the Divine Lord

'Be praised, my Lord, with all your creatures.' This brief statement by Francis is nothing if not inclusive. And yet, in the *Canticle*, no names of living creatures are actually mentioned: no birds or reptiles, no plants or whales, no flowers or fish.

---

78. Letter XXXVIII, Hopkins to Dixen, 23 October 1886, pp. 147–8.
79. Ibid., p. 148.
80. Celano, 'The Second Book' Chapter 1, 89, pp. 259–60.
81. David Knowles, 'Francis of Assisi', in *Francis of Assisi: Essays in Commemoration*, ed. M.W. Sheehan (New York, 1982), p. 7.
82. Ibid.

Instead, what we find named as brothers and sisters are the celestial bodies (sun, moon and stars) and the four elements (earth, air, fire and water). All of these had, of course, already been named in the great *Canticle of the Three Young Men*. But what Francis achieves in his *Canticle* is something unexpected. He does not simply name the sun and the moon and the four elements. Instead, like a new Adam, looking at them afresh and referring to them in turn, he describes each one in a way no one had ever done before, naming without hesitation their strong, distinctive and beautiful attributes as if they were indeed living creatures. At one point in the *Canticle*, for example, evoking the elements of water and fire, he exclaims:

> Be praised, my Lord, for
> Sister Water
> who is most useful and humble and
> precious and chaste.
>
> Be praised, my Lord, for
> Brother Fire
> through whom you illumine the night,
> and he is beautiful
> and playful and robust and strong.

The authority and charm of Francis's *Canticle* depends in no small part on the remarkable balance achieved by naming the terrestrial and celestial elements as either masculine or feminine. What emerges as a result is a pattern which is truly magical. In clear and harmonious balance with Brother Sun, for example, we have Sister Moon, and with Brother Wind, Sister Water, and with Brother Fire, Sister Mother Earth.

*

An unmistakable delight in the natural world is something manifest throughout the *Canticle*. It is not, however, the beauty of nature to which the words of praise are addressed but rather to the *author* of nature, a point underlined in the very first sentence of the work:

> Most high, all-powerful, good Lord,
> yours are the praises,
> the glory, the honour, and all blessing.

The adjectives 'most high', 'all-powerful' and 'good' might appear at first hearing to be the only words in the *Canticle* descriptive of the author of creation. But that is not actually the case. Later, when we find the sun and the moon, the wind and the stars and so on, being described by Francis with such vividness, something also of the power and beauty of the Creator is being revealed. This is particularly the case with Sir Brother Sun 'through whom', Francis declares, addressing the Creator, 'you give us light, / and he is beautiful and radiant with great splendour / and bears a likeness of you, Most High'.

The 'Most High' – the Divine Lord addressed in the *Canticle* – is for Francis the Creator of all living things. Owing to the way, over the last few hundred years, creation has been depicted in art and literature, Christian believers in the West have become accustomed to thinking of the Divine Father, the Ancient of Days, as the sole Creator – not the Son, therefore, and not the Spirit. In the Middle Ages, however, there was a greater, more profound awareness of the roles played at creation by all three Persons of the Trinity. Accordingly, it was not unusual in certain works of art to find the *Logos*, the Second Person of the Trinity, depicted as the one Creator.[83] Francis himself, in his writings, refers more than once to all three Persons of the Trinity together as 'the Creator of all'.[84]

So the question arises: to whom exactly is the *Canticle* of St Francis being addressed? The Dominican Augustine Thompson and along with him I suspect many other readers today are of the opinion that the one addressed at the beginning as the 'subject of all praise' is 'God the Father'.[85] I am not so sure. For years, I took for granted that Francis was addressing God *simpliciter* and that no individual person of the Trinity was the subject of all the praises. That still seems to me a valid way of reading the *Canticle*. More recently, however, I have been stuck by another way of understanding the work. It occurs to me now that if indeed one particular person of the Trinity is being addressed throughout, it is most likely not God the Father but rather the *Incarnate* Lord, Christ Jesus.

Of probable significance in this context is the following brief passage from Celano concerning the focus of Francis's words of praise with regard to the 'elements', earth, air, fire and water. Neither the word 'God' nor the word 'Father' is mentioned; it is instead the name 'Jesus' which we find highlighted. 'Often as he walked along a road, thinking and singing of Jesus', he would become so absorbed in the task of praise he would forget where he was going and would instead 'start inviting all the elements to praise Jesus'.[86]

In the *Canticle* three adjectives are used to describe the subject of praise – 'Most High', 'all-powerful' and 'good' (*Altissimo, onnipotente* and *buono*).[87] All three of them are words which could indeed be used to describe the Father. But they are also words, in the view of St Francis, descriptive of the Divine Son. The saint, in his *Letter to the Entire Order*, has no hesitation in speaking of Christ Jesus as 'Most High' (*Altissimo*),[88] and in his *Later Admonition and Exhortation*, actively inviting all creation to praise Christ the Saviour, Francis refers to him as

---

83. See, for example, the fourteenth-century bas-relief of the creation of Eve on the facade of Orvieto Cathedral in Italy.

84. 'Fragments (1209–1223)', 59, in *Francis of Assisi: The Saint*, p. 91.

85. Thompson, *Francis of Assisi: A New Biography*, p. 123.

86. Celano, 'The Second Book' Chapter IX, 115, p. 284.

87. The opening address in the original Umbrian script of St Francis reads as follows: '*Altissimu, onnipotente bon Signore.*'

88. Francis of Assisi, 'A Letter to the Entire Order (1225–1226)', 14, in *Francis of Assisi: The Saint*, p. 117.

not only 'wonderful' and 'glorious' but also '*buono*' (good) and '*onnipotente*' (all-powerful).[89]

The opening words of the *Canticle*, therefore, could well be words addressed most particularly by Francis to the Incarnate Lord. And, likewise, the strong declaration in the sentence which follows: 'No human being is worthy to speak your name.' It's almost impossible to imagine a reverence greater than that which St Francis felt for the name of Christ Jesus. In *A Letter to the Entire Order* he declared: 'When you hear his name, the name of our Lord Jesus Christ, who is blessed forever, adore his name with fear and reverence, prostrate on the ground!'[90] By all accounts, the name of Jesus was never far from his thoughts or from his lips. According to Celano, 'He was always with Jesus: Jesus in his heart, Jesus in his mouth, Jesus in his ears, Jesus in his eyes, Jesus in his hands, he bore Jesus always in his whole body.'[91] And again, in another place, Celano notes: 'So thoroughly did the humility of the Incarnation and the charity of the Passion occupy his memory that he scarcely wanted to think of anything else.'[92]

The contemporaries of Francis were clearly astonished at the way in both prayer and in conversation that Francis kept alive the memory of 'Christ Jesus and him crucified'.[93] In time, this mystery would not merely be impressed on his mind and heart but on his very flesh. I am referring, of course, to what happened to him on the Mountain of La Verna. One morning in the autumn of 1224, two years before his death, Francis had a vision of a brilliant, fiery seraph hovering in the air before him. The seraph's beauty, we are told by Celano, 'was beyond comprehension'.[94] To the saint's astonishment, however, between the wings of the seraph there appeared the figure of a man crucified. Francis was so deeply moved he felt at once both intense sorrow and intense joy. Then something extraordinary

---

89. Francis of Assisi, 'Later Admonition and Exhortation to the Brothers and Sisters of Penance', 60, in *Francis of Assisi: The Saint*, p. 49.

90. Francis of Assisi, 'A Letter to the Entire Order', 2, p. 116. In another place, with reference again to Christ Jesus, Francis remarked: 'Whenever I find our Lord's most holy names and written words in unbecoming places I want to gather them up and I beg that they be gathered up and placed in a becoming place. And we must honour all theologians and those who minister the most holy divine words and respect them as those who minister to us spirit and life.' 'The Testament', 12, in *Francis of Assisi: The Saint*, p. 125.

91. Celano, 'The Second Book' Chapter IX, 115, p. 283. To anyone who has knowledge of early Irish literature, these lines will sound familiar. In *St Patrick's Breastplate*, for example, we read: 'Christ with me, Christ before me, Christ above me … Christ in every eye that sees me, / Christ in every ear that hears me.' The name of Christ, we are told by Frank O'Connor, is the name which 'rings out again and again in the poetry'. He quotes these lines: 'Christ, Christ hear me! / Christ, Christ of Thy meekness! / Christ, Christ love me! / Sever me not from Thy sweetness!' See O'Connor, *Kings, Lords and Commons: An Anthology from the Irish* (London, 1959), p. 17.

92. Celano, 'The First Book' Chapter XXX, 84, p. 254.

93. Celano, 'The Second Book' Chapter IX, 115, p. 284.

94. Ibid., Chapter III, 94, p. 264. The vision of St Francis immediately brings to mind the vision of Isaiah in the Old Testament, Isaiah 6: 1–13.

happened. In the words of St Bonaventure, 'As the vision disappeared, it left in his heart a marvellous ardour and imprinted on his body markings that were no less marvellous. Immediately the marks of nails began to appear in his hands and feet just as he had seen a little before in the figure of the man crucified.'[95] Francis, as Celano puts it so memorably, had been 'stamped with Christ's brilliant seal'.[96] It was shortly after this event that Francis was inspired to start writing *The Canticle of the Creatures*.

If there is one detail which more than any other has encouraged me to think that the focus of Francis throughout the *Canticle* is on the Lord Incarnate, it is the short phrase which occurs in the third sentence of the work and is then repeated several times: 'Laudato sie, mi' Signore': 'Be praised, my Lord.'[97] To my knowledge Francis never uses the phrase '*mi' Signore*' when referring to God the Father. He does, however, use this particular form of address when referring to Christ Jesus.

One example can be found in his *Later Admonition and Exhortation to the Brothers and Sisters of Penance*. Rendered incapable due to illness of visiting in person many of his brothers and sisters, Francis chose instead to send a message to 'all Christian religious people: clergy and laity, men and women, and to all who live in the whole world'.[98] At one point in the *Admonition*, we find Francis referring explicitly to Christ. He writes: 'Because I am the servant of all, I am obliged to serve all and to administer the fragrant words of my Lord to them.'[99] On another occasion, not long after his conversion, Francis was noticed by a stranger walking along the road 'crying loudly and wailing'. The man thought Francis might be 'suffering some painful illness' but Francis replied: 'I should go through the whole world this way, crying and bewailing the Passion of my Lord.'[100]

So entirely focused was Francis on poverty as a religious ideal – 'conforming himself to the poor in all things'[101] – it might seem that the attainment of a stark asceticism was his one great obsession. Such a view, however, obscures

---

95. St Bonaventure, *Legenda maior S. Francisci*, XIII, 3; cited in Ewert Cousins, *Bonaventure: The Soul's Journey into God* (New York, 1978), pp. 305–6.

96. Celano, 'The Second Book' Chapter IX, p. 284.

97. *Laudato si'* is the form of 'Be praised' which occurs throughout the rest of the *Canticle*. Only once does the spelling '*sie*' appear.

98. Francis of Assisi, 'Later Admonition and Exhortation to the Brothers and Sisters of Penance', 1, p. 45.

99. Ibid., 2, p. 45. In another place Francis speaks of being 'closely united and joined with my Lord'. The 'Lord' here is Christ 'through whose mercy [*per sua misericordia*]' Francis says he is able to 'rejoice' in God the Father, that is 'in the Most High Himself [*posso ben esultare nell'Altissimo*]'. See *The Assisi Compilation*, 99, p. 203.

100. *The Assisi Compilation*, 78, pp. 180–1. In Celano's *Remembrance of the Desire of a Soul*, Chapter VI, 11, in *Francis of Assisi: The Founder*, p. 250, we read that after receiving the stigmata at La Verna Francis 'could not hold back his tears, even weeping loudly over the Passion of Christ, as if it were constantly before his eyes. He filled the roads with his sobbing, and, as he remembered the wounds of Christ, he would take no comfort'.

101. Celano, 'The First Book' Chapter XXVIII, 78, p. 247.

what is at the heart of the Little Poor Man's vision. The greatest poverty for Francis, the focus of all his thoughts and thus his one abiding obsession, was not the achievement of some entirely new and radical practice of self-negation. It was rather the stark self-emptying of God in the Incarnation, a poverty almost impossible to imagine, a *kenosis* deliberately chosen by 'that most exalted King, who though He was Lord of all, willed for our sake to become the servant of all and, although he was rich and glorious in majesty, came as one poor and despised in our humanity'.[102]

That humility of God was for Francis particularly manifest in the presence of Christ in the humble Eucharistic bread on the altar during the celebration of the Eucharist. That, more than anything else, I would say, is what captured his imagination as a man and compelled his sense of wonder and awe. He writes:

> Let everyone be struck with fear, let the whole earth tremble, and let the heavens exult when Christ, the Son of the living God, is present on the altar in the hands of the priest! O wonderful loftiness and stupendous dignity! O sublime humility! O humble sublimity! The Lord of the universe, God the Son of God, so humbles Himself that for our salvation He hides himself under an ordinary piece of bread! Brothers, look at the humility of God.[103]

The Lord of heaven and earth to whom the praises of the *Canticle* are sung has, by virtue of the Incarnation, become a Brother to all humanity and a Brother also in a sense to all created nature. St Francis, in one of his late writings, exclaims: 'O how holy and how loving, gratifying, humbling, peace-giving, sweet, worthy of love, and above all things desirable it is to have such a Brother and such a Son: our Lord Jesus Christ.'[104]

When the praises of the *Canticle* are read in light of this understanding, the work acquires a new freshness and a new depth of meaning. The 'likeness', for example, which Brother Sun bears to the divine Lord, we now perceive as something of much greater force and importance than we had earlier realized. I say this because no image in Christian tradition is more associated with Christ the risen Lord than that of the sun. It is therefore possible to say that throughout the *Canticle* the joy and meaning of Incarnation is present in every image and in every line: Christ the Son of God revealed in sun and fire, in moon and stars, in earth and wind – Christ the Incarnate Lord 'beautiful and radiant with great splendour'.

---

102. Francis of Assisi, *The Assisi Compilation*, 97, p. 201.
103. Francis of Assisi, 'A Letter to the Entire Order (1225–1226)', 26–8, in *Francis of Assisi: The Saint*, p. 118.
104. Francis of Assisi, 'Later Admonition and Exhortation to the Brothers and Sisters of Penance', 54, p. 49.

8
Redemptive Music: *The* Canticle *and the Cross*

When Francis wrote the *Canticle*, he was almost completely blind. And yet his vision – his *inner* vision – was never more open, never more joyous. With regard to most of the verses of the work, this is undeniably the case, but can the same be said with confidence of the entire *Canticle*? If the vision of Francis is indeed as open and joyous as suggested, how are we to explain the difference between the first part of the *Canticle* (on which our attention has been focused almost exclusively up to now) and the final two brief segments at the end? In these second and third parts of the work, we see St Francis confronting head-on the realities of human conflict and woundedness, illness and sin, final judgement and death. In contrast, in the first part of the *Canticle*, there is not the least hint of shadow. Each radiant line, each brief prayer to the Creator, breathes an air of manifest ease and freedom.

What then is the relationship between the different parts of the *Canticle*? Is the opening section with its calm, illumined stanzas in any way related to the concern of St Francis for the weak and wounded condition of humanity, or is it something entirely separate? To answer this question, it will be necessary to look back to the moment Francis decided to compose his new *Canticle*. And here, worth remembering, are the motives he gave for composing the new work, namely 'for [God's] praise, for our consolation, and for the edification of our neighbour'.[105] Of these three motives the second – consolation – is the only one to which we have not so far given attention.

Francis speaks of 'our', not *my*, consolation, but it's clear that he was not shy at times to speak about his own need for consolation, especially when he was enduring almost unbearable affliction. On one occasion, knowing that music, if played on a lute, would bring balm to his spirit he said to one of his companions:

> I would like you to obtain secretly from some upright person a lute on which you could play for me a decent song and, with it, we will say the words and praises of the Lord, especially because my body is tormented with disease and pain. So I wish by this means to change that pain of my body to joy and consolation of spirit.[106]

For Francis, a key part of the consolation was always the opportunity to praise and thank God for the marvels of creation. According to an early witness,

> He did this and continued to do this gladly, whether he was healthy or sick. And he encouraged others to praise the Lord. Indeed, when his illness grew more serious, he himself began to say the *Praises of the Lord* [the *Canticle of the Creatures*], and afterwards had his companions sing it, so that in reflecting on

---

105. *The Assisi Compilation*, 83, p. 186.
106. Ibid., 66, p. 169.

the praise of the Lord, he could forget the sharpness of his pains and illnesses. He did this until the day of his death.[107]

As soon as Francis had finished work on the *Canticle*, he found himself experiencing great 'sweetness and consolation'[108] and at once wanted others who were low in spirit like himself to experience something of the same blessing. Francis entertained the idea, the hope, that if those in distress could hear the *Canticle* sung by a group of his friars, their hearts would be lifted up to 'spiritual joy'.[109] For Francis few things were more important in following the path of Christ than 'spiritual joy' or what he would sometimes call 'holy cheerfulness'.[110] According to Celano, he used to say: 'When the spirit is teary-eyed, feeling abandoned and sad, it will easily be swallowed up in sorrow, or else be carried away toward empty enjoyment.'[111] For Francis, especially at times of trial, music was one of the great ways of keeping the heart joyful and of keeping fresh within oneself and in others 'the anointing of the spirit and the oil of gladness'.[112] This helps explain why the great hymn of joy which constitutes the first part of the *Canticle*, although offered first and last as praise and worship of God, is offered also by St Francis as *consolation*, as healing balm for those who find themselves in any kind of sorrow or affliction.

The second part of the *Canticle* derives its inspiration directly from the words of Jesus in the Gospel and, in particular, from the teaching of the Beatitudes.

> Be praised, my Lord,
> for those who forgive out of love for you,
> and bear infirmity and tribulation.
>
> Blessed are they
> who endure in peace for, by you,
> Most High,
> they shall be crowned.

No matter how challenging or radical the Gospel message, Francis's 'foremost desire', Celano tells us, was 'to follow the teaching of our Lord Jesus Christ and to retrace his footsteps completely'.[113] Time and time again, he would encourage his brethren 'to love those who persecute, rebuke and find fault with us, because the Lord says ... *Blessed are those who suffer persecution for the sake of justice, for theirs*

---

107. Ibid., 83, pp. 186–7.
108. Ibid., p. 186.
109. Ibid.
110. Celano, *Remembrance of the Desire of a Soul*, Chapter LXXXVIII, 'The Second Book' 125, p. 329.
111. Ibid.
112. Ibid.
113. Celano, *The Life of Saint Francis*, 'The First Book' Chapter XXX, 84, p. 254.

is the kingdom of heaven'.[114] In his *Earlier Rule* Francis wrote: 'We must rejoice when we fall into various trials, and in this world, suffer every kind of anguish or distress of soul or body for the sake of eternal life.'[115] Once accepted and lived out in practice, the teaching of Christ, in the view of St Francis, bestowed unique blessings. The actual words of Jesus he came to regard as 'words through which we have been made and redeemed from death to life'.[116] Accordingly, trials and crosses which almost everyone else would instinctively avoid as 'bitter and painful' Francis endured gladly. According to Celano, 'Worn out with suffering on all sides, it was amazing that his strength could bear it. But, in fact, he did not call these tribulations by the name of "pains," but rather "Sisters".[117] And again: 'Even death itself, terrible and hateful to everyone, he exhorted to praise, and going to meet her joyfully, invited her to be his guest, saying: "Welcome, my Sister Death!"'[118]

9
The Groaning of Creation

I have spoken of three motives behind the composition of the *Canticle*. But there was in fact a fourth motive. After listing the first three, Francis remarked:

> I want to write a new *Praise of the Lord* for his creatures, which we use every day, and without which we cannot live. Through them the human race greatly offends the Creator, and every day we are ungrateful for such great graces, because we do not praise as we should our Creator and the Giver of all good.[119]

Here Francis has in mind, we may presume, animate and inanimate creatures such as plants, birds, trees, cows, rabbits, flowers and lambs. What distresses him most is not merely the tendency we have as human beings to take these things for granted but also the way these 'graces' can often be used and abused.

One early witness remarks that Francis had so much sympathy and regard for creatures that when he witnessed any of them being ill-treated or handled without proper respect, he found it impossible to bear.[120] One day when he was walking along the road, he encountered a man carrying two lambs hung over his shoulder.

---

114. Francis of Assisi, 'The Later Rule (1223)' Chapter X, 11–12, in *Francis of Assisi: The Saint*, p. 105.
115. Francis of Assisi, 'The Earlier Rule' Chapter XVII, 8, in *Francis of Assisi: The Saint*, p. 75.
116. Francis of Assisi, 'Exhortation to the Clergy, Later Edition (1220)', 3, in *Francis of Assisi: The Saint*, p. 54.
117. *The Legend of Three Companions*, Chapter CLXI, 212, in *Francis of Assisi: The Founder*, p. 384.
118. Ibid., Chapter CLXII, 217, p. 388.
119. *The Assisi Compilation*, 83, p. 186.
120. Ibid., 86, p. 191.

The small creatures were crying out so piteously Francis said to the man, 'Why are you torturing my brother lambs, binding and hanging them in that way?'[121] After a brief conversation in which it emerged that the lambs were about to be sold because the man needed the money, Francis, in order to rescue them from their fate, at once offered his cloak to the man in exchange for the two frightened animals.

On another occasion Francis released a live rabbit,[122] and in time other animals would also find themselves liberated – among them a fish,[123] a water-bird[124] and a pheasant.[125] It seemed there was no limit to Francis's devoted concern for these 'lesser creatures': 'Even for worms,' Celano tells us, 'he had a warm love, since he had read the text about the Saviour: *I am a worm and not a man*. That is why he used to pick them up from the road and put them in a safe place so that they would not be crushed by the footsteps of passersby.'[126] And that was not all. 'In the winter', according to Celano, 'he had honey or the best wine put out for the bees so that they would not perish from the cold'.[127] What's more, he would speak to these small creatures – to rabbits and lambs, to crickets and birds, to flowers and fish, as if each one of them had been 'endowed with reason'.[128]

Animals great and small and even the elements themselves responded to Francis in ways which, to his contemporaries, seemed truly miraculous. But no matter how surprised they were at times at the manner in which Francis received 'the obedience of creatures',[129] what must have completely astonished them was the saint's willingness to be submissive to the things of nature as if they had actual authority over him. This marked a complete reversal of ordinary Christian thinking or, at the very least, a radical transformation of it. In his *Salutation to the Virtues*, Francis declares that obedience, when it is lived properly as a virtue, is 'subject and submissive to everyone in the world, not only to people but to every beast and wild animal as well, that they may do whatever they want with it insofar as it has been given to them from above by the Lord'.[130]

The most striking example of how St Francis put this vision into practice is the way he reacted when, on one occasion, some of his clothes, his 'linen pants', went on fire. The companion who was with him at the time rushed to put out the flame, but Francis said: 'No, dearest Brother, do not hurt Brother Fire.' Only when

---

121. Celano, *The Life of Saint Francis*, 'The First Book' Chapter XXVIII, 79, p. 249.
122. Ibid., Chapter XXI, 60, p. 235.
123. Ibid., 61, pp. 235–6.
124. St Bonaventure, *The Major Legend of St Francis*, Chapter Eight, 8, in *Francis of Assisi: The Founder*, p. 592.
125. Celano, *Remembrance of the Desire of a Soul*, 'The Second Book' Chapter CXXIX, 170, pp. 356–7.
126. Celano, 'The First Book' Chapter XXIX, 80, p. 250.
127. Ibid.
128. Ibid., 81, p. 251.
129. Ibid., Chapter XXI, 61, p. 236.
130. Francis of Assisi, 'A Salutation of the Virtues', 14, in *Francis of Assisi: The Saint*, p. 165.

another companion, a more senior friar, intervened was the flame extinguished. If this story is to be believed, why would Francis behave in such a manner? Why would he insist on his own determined vision of things to the point of seeming idiocy?

Absolutely nothing of what Francis says or does regarding nature makes sense unless we take into consideration the degradation of nature which he would have witnessed during his lifetime – not merely the shameful lack of reverence shown to created things but also the arrogant behaviour of individual men and women using and abusing the gifts of nature as their selfish desires dictated. Francis knew instinctively that it would never be enough simply to express his vision in rational terms. What was needed was a bold, prophetic witness. G.K. Chesterton says of Francis:

> Many of his acts will seem grotesque and puzzling to a rationalistic taste. But they were always acts and not explanations … From the moment when he rent his robes and flung them at his father's feet to the moment when he stretched himself in death on the bare earth in the pattern of the cross, his life was made up of these unconscious attitudes and unhesitating gestures.[131]

*

The word which brings *The Canticle of the Creatures* to a close is 'humility', a word which derives from the Latin word *humus* meaning earth. Francis was a man, a poet, who strove all his life to remain humble, to keep close to the earth. And it is humility, I would say, more than any of the other virtues, which shines most clearly in and through his words and deeds. In the *Canticle*, when referring to the sun, Francis does something more than merely speak in a charming, fraternal manner – he expresses himself with a marked reverence. Not simply Brother Sun, therefore, but *Sir* Brother Sun. Likewise, when referring to 'our Sister Mother Earth', he praises God not only for the way the earth 'sustains' us but also for the way she 'governs' us. This, I would say, betrays on the part of St Francis an instinctive desire to challenge, by means of his *Canticle*, certain proud and arrogant ways of thinking about the earth, a desire in effect to radically change the minds and hearts of those among his readers or listeners who thought they had a God-given right to rule with impunity the world of nature.

This same desire, this bold determination, is evident also in the 2015 Encyclical Letter composed by Pope Francis entitled *Laudato Si'*. 'We have forgotten', the Pope declares, 'that we ourselves are dust of the earth (cf. Gen. 2.7); our very bodies are made of her element, we breathe her air and we receive life and refreshment from her waters.'[132] The Pope then goes on to quote these lines from the *Canticle*: 'Praise be to you, my Lord, through our Sister, Mother Earth, who sustains and

---

131. G.K. Chesterton, *St Francis of Assisi* (London, 1943), p. 106.
132. Pope Francis, *Laudato Si': On Care for Our Common Home*, 2 (New York, 2015), p. 6.

governs us, and who produces various fruit with coloured flowers and herbs.'[133] One has the impression, reading *Laudato Si'*, that the calm, simple radiance of this image serves to intensify the sadness Pope Francis feels at the thought of the damage done out of greed and selfishness to the beauty and fruitfulness of 'our Sister, Mother Earth'. He writes in the very next line:

> This Sister now cries out to us because of the harm we have inflicted on her by our irresponsible use and abuse of the goods with which God has endowed her. We have come to see ourselves as her lords and masters, entitled to plunder her at will. The violence present in our hearts, wounded by sin, is also reflected in the symptoms of sickness evident in the soil, in the water, in the air and in all forms of life. This is why the earth herself, burdened and laid waste, is among the most abandoned and maltreated of our poor; she 'groans in travail' (*Rom* 8:22).[134]

10
The Return to Paradise

In the year 1837, while on holiday in Italy, William Wordsworth together with a friend, Henry Crabb Robinson, visited a number of the most famous sites and places of pilgrimage associated with St Francis. First, he visited Assisi itself and then a few days later travelled to La Verna. That Wordsworth, the celebrated poet of nature, should find himself drawn to the figure of St Francis will come as no surprise, even though he had never shown any particular affection for the Catholic religion and his own view of nature was decidedly different from that of Francis. By the time the English poet reached Assisi, the weeks of sightseeing had taken a great toll. He had begun to lose all enthusiasm for the task. But when he reached La Verna, something happened. Wordsworth at this stage in his journey was already familiar with *The Canticle of the Creatures* and familiar also with a number of the principal places of Franciscan pilgrimage. But, visiting the site at La Verna, he was enabled and in a new way to shape and crystallize his thoughts concerning the saint and poet of Assisi. Before he left Italy he had already composed a poem prompted by the experience.

In 'The Cuckoo at Laverna, May 25, 1837', Wordsworth notes that a strong ascetic impulse lay behind the decision of St Francis to spend time 'among these sterile heights of Apennine'.[135] There was, however, a marked difference between

---

133. Ibid., 1, p. 6. The phrase cited by Pope Francis, 'Praise be to you, my Lord, through our Sister, Mother Earth', is a translation of the original '*Laudato si', mi Signore, per sora nostra matre terra*'. Pope Francis takes the word '*per*' to mean 'through'. But '*per*' in this context can also mean 'for': 'Praise be to you, my Lord, *for* our Sister, Mother Earth.'

134. Ibid., 2, p. 6.

135. William Wordsworth, 'The Cuckoo at Laverna, May 25, 1837', *Memorials of a Tour in Italy. 1837*, XIV, in *The Poetical Works of Wordsworth*, ed. T. Hutchinson (London, 1959), p. 286.

the asceticism of Francis and that of some of the friars who came after him. Because of his 'milder genius', the stringent discipline he practised daily did not dull for a moment his love for the natural world. On the contrary, although rapt quite out of his senses on occasion when at prayer, Francis remained wonderfully alive to the beauty of created things both great and small:

> Rapt though He were above the power of sense,
> Familiarly, yet out of the cleansed heart
> Of that once sinful Being overflowed
> On sun, moon, stars, the nether elements,
> And every shape of creature they sustain,
> Divine affections.[136]

What further impressed Wordsworth was how both 'beast and bird' were drawn to the saint, enchanted, it would appear, by the words he spoke to them and by his manifest innocence of life – creatures of the air and of the earth happily abandoning for a time 'their own pursuits in field or grove'.[137] The open, joyous character of Francis's engagement with 'beast and bird' Wordsworth describes as follows:

> He wont to hold companionship so free,
> So pure, so fraught with knowledge and delight,
> As to be likened in his Followers' minds
> To that which our first Parents, ere the fall
> From their high state darkened the Earth with fear,
> Held with all Kinds in Eden's blissful bowers.[138]

Here what is being highlighted is the rare knowledge and great happiness which Francis enjoyed as a result of his communion with the world of nature, a state of freedom and joy so great that the followers of the saint compared it to the happiness which was experienced by Adam and Eve, 'our first parents', when they walked in the original garden – in the 'bowers' of Eden – before the Fall. Wordsworth is touching here on a theme – the recovery of paradise – which perhaps more than any other opens a door into the mystery of the Little Poor Man's unique relationship with nature.

Wordsworth was not mistaken when he suggested that the 'followers' of Francis regarded his easeful, radiant way of being with the things of nature as in some way comparable to the state of innocent joy experienced by 'our first parents'. St Bonaventure, for example, probably the best known of all the saint's followers, suggested that the wonderful ease which creatures experienced in the presence of Francis was a sign not only of a life wholly converted but of a life 'in some way'

---

136. Ibid.
137. Ibid.
138. Ibid.

actually restored to the state of innocent goodness which had been lost with the Fall. Bonaventure writes:

> To the degree that an individual is reformed and returned to the state of innocence that person will discover that animals are at ease in his presence, and he will be moved by piety towards them. It is written of the Blessed Francis that he experienced this kind of tender piety towards creatures because in a certain way he had recovered [the state] of innocence. And a sign of this recovery was that irrational creatures obeyed him.[139]

A number of years before Bonaventure wrote these lines, Thomas Celano noted in the first biography of Francis, 'It was certainly a marvel that even irrational creatures recognized his feeling of tenderness toward them, and sensed the sweetness of his love.'[140] Those friars who were close to Francis from the beginning are unanimous in their reports: 'We who were with him saw him always in such joy, inwardly and outwardly, over all creatures, touching and looking at them as if his spirit was no longer on earth but in heaven.'[141] That St Francis felt free to bestow on creatures, wild and tame, the names of 'brother' and 'sister' was already remarkable, but his closest companions observed something else as well which they found even more striking: 'In a wonderful way, unknown to others', Celano writes, 'he could discern the secrets of the heart of creatures like someone who had already passed into the freedom of the children of God.'[142]

This gift of discernment manifest in the day-to-day life of Francis also found expression in his wonderfully insightful and imaginative reading and naming of the celestial bodies in the *Canticle* and his naming also of the beauty and usefulness of the four elements, earth, air, fire and water. These fine illumined stanzas helped restore to the world of nature a dignity which all too often had been obscured by human selfishness and greed. Creation itself, St Paul explains in Romans Chapter 8, has been 'waiting in eager expectation for the revelation of the sons of God' in order to be 'set free from its bondage' (Rom. 8.19-21). Francis, as visionary poet of the new creation, clearly deserves to be numbered among these 'sons', and not least because of his concern to liberate with words as well as with deeds whatever is in travail in the world of nature.

---

139. St Bonaventure, *Commentarius in Dist.* XXVIII, q. 1, *Commentaria in Quatuor Libros Sententiarum Magistri Petri Lombardi, Opera Omnia* (Quaracchi, 1887), p. 622. Timothy J. Johnson in 'Francis and Creation' compares the approach taken by Bonaventure regarding the question of loving irrational animals with that of Thomas Aquinas. Whereas Aquinas 'spent precious little time on this issue and emphasized why these creatures are not to be loved, Bonaventure appealed to the experience of Francis in nature as the entry point into consideration of love and the nature of human interaction with animals'. See *The Cambridge Companion to Francis of Assisi*, ed. Michael J.P. Robson (Cambridge, 2012), p. 150.

140. Celano, 'The First Book' Chapter XXI, 59, p. 235.
141. *The Assisi Compilation*, 88, p. 192.
142. Celano, 'The First Book' Chapter XXIX, 81, p. 251.

Francis's 'new' *Canticle* invites us to live in the radiance of a world that is still coming into being – invites us, in other words, 'to understand our destiny in the created world as a very simple one, that of walking in paradise'.[143] In the opinion of the contemporary Franciscan Friar Murray Bodo, 'Francis lived out of an essential vision of paradise, a vision of what is God's original design for creation and what will be again when Creator and creation are reconciled.'[144] 'This', Bodo concludes, 'is what Celano meant when he said that Francis "had already escaped into the freedom of the glory of the children of God"'.[145]

That 'escape' into freedom also characterized the lives of the hermit-poets of Ireland centuries earlier. Both in their lives and in their writings they, like Francis, dared to look at the world afresh, encouraging not only their own contemporaries but all those who came after them to live and to act with something of the same courage, the same freedom. Much of what has been said concerning early monastic poetry in Ireland can also be said here of the visionary work of St Francis. For with the *Canticle* in particular, with the vision it provides, we come as near as it is possible to come – at least within the realm of literature – 'to the innocent eye and tongue of Adam as he named the creatures'.[146]

---

143. Murray Bodo, *The Way of St Francis* (New York, 1984), p. 110.
144. Ibid.
145. Ibid.
146. Seamus Heaney, 'The God in the Tree: Early Irish Nature Poetry', in *Preoccupations: Selected Prose 1968–1978* (London, 1980), p. 185.

Chapter 2

'I AM MYSELF ALONE': SHAKESPEARE AND THE HUMAN CASUALTY

On 4 February 2013 the name of one of the most famous characters in Shakespearian drama – King Richard III – was highlighted on the front pages of newspapers across the world. The name, for days, was repeated in countless television broadcasts and news reports on the World Wide Web. What prompted the excitement was the dramatic unearthing of bones from underneath a parking lot in the city of Leicester, bones belonging to the actual historical figure, Richard III.

A spinal curvature in the spine was one of a number of signs indicating that the skeleton was indeed that of Richard, the infamous hunchback king, the man who is arguably the most reviled royal figure in all of English history. This particular king was the man blamed for the ruthless murder of the young princes in the Tower of London and blamed also for countless other atrocities. In fact, so manifestly deliberate and so hideous were his purported crimes, King Richard came to be regarded, over time, as a true monster of evil. And, as we know well, he is not alone in that category. Other no less appalling figures have appeared in almost every period of human history.[1]

The phenomenon of evil, when manifest in such figures, provokes many different kinds of response, few of them are effective. Politicians respond, of course, as do soldiers on the ground, and there are the very different but no less engaged responses of judges, lawyers, novelists, historians and poets. Shakespeare's response to the phenomenon is, as one would expect, distinctive and compelling. Of the many different characters he creates in his plays, one figure stands out as the most truly demoniacal, and that is Richard, the crookback King of England.

1
'The Devil's Butcher'

Our first glimpse of Richard is his appearance in *3 Henry VI* as the ruthless Duke of Gloucester. Not only is this particular play one of the first composed by

---

1. That the actual Richard III of history was a monster of evil has been challenged by contemporary historians. See, for example, John Ashdown-Hill, *The Mythology of Richard III* (Stroud, 2015).

Shakespeare, it was while engaged in creating its central character – the villainous, outrageous Crookback – that Shakespeare's genius as a playwright first caught fire. The appalling Duke of Gloucester was, we can say, his first major creation.[2] As the drama of the play unfolds, we find Richard being described, by the other protagonists in the play, not only as a truly evil individual but also as someone physically misshapen. In Act V, Scene 6, for example, King Henry, when speaking to Richard directly, does not mince his words, calling him 'an undigested and deformèd lump'. Queen Margaret, in Act II, Scene 2, can barely contain her horror at the sight of him, exclaiming: 'Thou art neither like thy sire or dam, / But like a foul misshapen stigmatic, / Marked by the destinies to be avoided, / As venom toads or lizards' dreadful stings.' Prince Edward, in Act V, Scene 5, dismisses Richard with equal disdain, referring to him as 'scolding crookback' and 'thou misshapen Dick'.

Henry VI, Part 3, is a play awash with blood, its stage littered with heavy armour, and with men and swords dripping with blood, and with dead bodies and severed heads. It is a veritable jungle of revenge and torture, of murder, mockery and mutilation. And there, standing at its centre, as if at home in this world of hate and chaos, is Richard, Duke of Gloucester. In the opening scene of the play, we see him holding out in his hand, with unconscionable glee, the severed head of a man he has just murdered. Addressing the head, as if it were still alive, Richard exclaims: 'Speak thou for me, and tell them what I did.' Then, actually shaking the head, he announces his stark, murderous ambition: 'Thus do I hope to shake King Henry's head.' At a point later in the drama (Act I, Scene 2), with words no less deadly, no less eloquent, he declares:

> I cannot rest
> Until the white rose that I wear be dyed
> Even in the lukewarm blood of Henry's heart.

Hearing or overhearing these alarming statements, what are we to conclude about the character of Richard? The judgement of those most opposed to Richard in the Wars of the Roses – King Henry among them – has already been noted. In the opinion of these witnesses, Richard is almost Satan incarnate, 'the devil's butcher', as one of them puts it. And this judgement, it's worth noting, is shared by almost all the critics who have commented over the years – indeed over the centuries – on Shakespeare's play. 'Richard', writes R.W.S. Mendl, 'is the very embodiment of evil in human form … a kind of Miltonic Satan living on earth as a man'.[3] This opinion echoes that of the eighteenth-century critic Thomas Whately. Whately believed that the misshapen form of Richard's twisted body was intended by Shakespeare

---

2. In Shakespeare's career as a dramatist, only one figure stands out from the rest prior to Richard in *3 Henry VI*, and that is Jack Cade in *2 Henry VI*. On stage, however, Cade never commands the same attention as Richard.

3. R.W.S. Mendl, *Revelation in Shakespeare* (London, 1964), p. 34.

to represent a fundamental monstrosity of spirit, his appalling deeds, therefore, proceeding not from some mere external or accidental circumstance but rather from what Whately called 'a savageness of nature'.[4]

In marked contrast to the demonic figure of the Duke of Gloucester, King Henry is generally regarded by critics of the play not merely as a good man but as a veritable saint. John Dover Wilson, in the Cambridge commentary, has no hesitation in telling us, for example, that 'Henry is the only sketch of a saint in the [Shakespearian] canon.'[5] Quite often commentators view Henry as a kind of pacifist hero, his gentleness of spirit thrown into relief by the fierce clamour of the battles raging around him. We see him, for example, at one point in the drama (Act II, Scene 5), grieving for those whom he calls 'the harmless lambs', the unprotected men and women who are caught up in an interminable spiral of vengeance and hatred not their own.

> O piteous spectacle! O bloody times!
> Whiles lions roar and battle for their dens,
> Poor harmless lambs abide their enmity.

Henry is presented in the play as the near opposite of a roaring lion of war. He is a lamb of piety, a man more at home with whispered prayers than with tumultuous battle cries, his holiness – or what looks like holiness – appearing in complete contrast, therefore, to the evil character of Richard, a man described again and again in the play as a monster in human form.

But is this the way Shakespeare wants us to regard these two individuals – Henry as perfect saint and Richard as devil incarnate? Are these two characters in opposition no more than archetypal figures, fixed 'types' reminiscent of the strict, oppositional structure of medieval drama, one man representing absolute good, and the other absolute evil?

2
Richard and Henry: Devil and Saint?

Towards the end of *3 Henry VI*, we are given an opportunity to see the two men alone together in the Tower. It is, by any standards, a remarkable encounter. John Dover Wilson, in the Cambridge commentary, reflecting on the characters of Richard and Henry, sums up in one brief sentence the most commonly held opinion among critics. 'Devil and saint', he writes, 'are here for the first time brought face to face in private colloquy'.[6] But these stark terms – 'devil and saint' –

---

4. Thomas Whately, *Remarks on Some of the Characters of Shakespeare* (1889), p. 36; cited in The Arden Shakespeare edition of *King Henry VI, Part 3*, eds. J.D. Cox and E. Rasmussen (London, 2001), p. 75.

5. John Dover Wilson, 'Introduction', in *The Third Part of King Henry VI* (Cambridge, 1968), p. xxxiv.

6. Ibid., p. xxxvii.

are they really the most helpful and accurate terms we can find to describe our two protagonists in the Tower?

At first sight, the facts of the case do appear to confirm the Dover Wilson view of a stark opposition between simple goodness and sheer evil. Murder does take place – a brutal murder – and the King, with his last breath, as he lies bleeding on the ground, is heard to utter a brief, manifestly Christian prayer: 'O God, forgive my sins, and pardon thee.' These words, at such a moment, are indeed worthy of a saint, words of impressive forgiveness. But how truly forgiving in reality, how *saintly*, is the way Henry treats Richard at this final meeting? What kind of sanctity, if any, is manifest when the King finds himself confronting face-to-face his most ruthless enemy, the man who has come to slaughter him?

*

When the Tower scene opens, we see King Henry sitting alone in his prison cell reading what is thought to be some kind of prayer book.[7] Then Richard enters. He greets the King: 'Good day, my Lord. What, at your book so hard?' The greeting, though it sounds friendly enough, is, of course, entirely cynical. Henry reacts with a swift mockery of his own, making clear that any attempt to link the word 'good' with Richard, Duke of Gloucester, would be unthinkable:

> Ah, my good Lord. 'My Lord' I should say, rather,
> 'tis sin to flatter; 'good' was little better.
> 'Good Gloucester' and 'good devil' were alike,
> And both preposterous. Therefore, not 'good Lord.'

The wit is convoluted and somewhat forced, but it allows King Henry the opportunity to state exactly what he thinks of his visitor, declaring in so many words that, far from being good, Richard is, if anything, a 'devil'. Later, after some initial conversation between the two men, Richard asks the King: 'Think'st thou I am an executioner?' To this Henry replies in the affirmative and refers back to those 'innocents' Richard has already slaughtered.

> A persecutor I am sure thou art;
> If murdering innocents be executing,
> Why then, thou art an executioner.

What follows is a long speech from Henry in which, at one point, he delivers a calculated dagger blow with words, a sharp thrust straight to the heart. For those who have been attentively following the drama up to this point, this verbal attack is disturbing in a number of ways. It's almost as if the King knows Richard from the inside and knows just where the words will most hurt, mocking not only the man's misshapen body – a cheap and obvious jibe – but actually telling Richard

---

7. The stage direction at 3.1.12 reads: 'Enter King with a prayer book.'

that, from the very moment of his birth, it was clear to all that he was ordained to be misshapen in *spirit* as well as in body, a human monster:

> The owl shrieked at thy birth, an evil sign;
> The night-crow cried, aboding luckless time;
> Dogs howled; and hideous tempests shook down trees;
> The raven rooked her on the chimney's top;
> And chattering pies in dismal discords sung.
> Thy mother felt more than a mother's pain,
> And yet brought forth less than a mother's hope:
> To wit, an undigested and deformèd lump …
> Teeth hadst thou in thy head when thou wast born
> To signify thou cam'st to bite the world.

These words, so venomous and deadly, find at once their mark. Richard, stung to the quick, and determined to prevent Henry reciting any further mockeries, exclaims: 'I'll hear no more! Die, prophet, in thy speech!' Then he stabs the King. But that is not all. This man predestined, in Henry's judgement, to become pure evil, this vilified Crookback, declares at once, and with brilliant sarcasm, 'For this amongst the rest was I ordained.' Then he stabs the King a second time: 'Down, down to hell, and say I sent thee thither!'

The gleeful brutality exhibited here and the sheer theatricality of the character of Richard account in no small measure for the stage appeal of this early play of Shakespeare. Although Richard's appalling wickedness is never disguised, much less downplayed, as soon as he makes an appearance on stage, as here in the Tower scene, there is such an engaging, villainous zest to his every word and gesture, the attention of the audience is inevitably riveted.[8]

He has stabbed the King not once but twice. And now, as if to match with words the shocking nature of the deed, he declares (although, of course, there is no one to hear him) that he has 'neither pity, love nor fear'. The statement is chilling. Richard, it would seem, is content to damn himself with an assassin's gleeful boast. But then something happens. Almost as if asking us to pause in our judgement, Shakespeare opens for us a window into the soul of this man, and we are permitted to hear or overhear Richard talking to himself about his own character and history.

We learn a number of things, and one of them is that Richard has accepted as gospel truth the ferociously negative statements made by the King. And even worse, and more cruel to contemplate, and more unjust, he has been forced to listen to the same kind of statements from the lips of his own mother since he was a boy.

---

8. Telling, in this context, is the observation Coleridge makes about Shakespeare and the villains in his plays: 'It was in characters of complete moral depravity but of first-rate wit and talents that Shakespeare delighted.' Coleridge in conversation with J.P. Collier, *Coleridge's Writings on Shakespeare*, ed. T. Hawkes (New York, 1959), p. 246.

> Indeed 'tis true that Henry told me of,
> For I have often heard my mother say
> I came into the world with my legs forward …
> The midwife wondered and the women cried,
> 'O, Jesus bless us, he is born with teeth!'
> And so I was, which plainly signified
> That I should snarl, and bite and play the dog.

Not only has Richard suffered the indignity of being misshapen from birth, he has been persuaded by those closest to him that the unnatural hump on his back, the twisted nature of his limbs and his ungainly, limping gait are all clear signs that he has an evil, twisted spirit and that he has been ordained to bring nothing but misery to the world. Earlier (Act III, Scene 2) in a no less poignant, no less disturbing soliloquy, he declares:

> Why, Love forswore me in my mother's womb:
> And, for I should not deal in her soft laws,
> She did corrupt frail Nature with some bribe,
> To shrink mine arm up like a wither'd shrub;
> To make an envious mountain on my back,
> Where sits Deformity to mock my body;
> To shape my legs of an unequal size;
> To disproportion me in every part,
> Like to a chaos, or unlick'd bear-whelp
> That carries no impression like the dam.
> And am I then a man to be belov'd?
> O monstrous fault to harbour such a thought!

It goes without saying that few torments are more terrible to endure than the tragedy of being misshapen physically from birth and with having then to bear that suffering all one's life. That said, however, an even greater torment for the individual thus afflicted is the unhappy conviction that this is not accidental but that, from the beginning, you have been predestined in hate by divine providence – an idea as wounding as it is wholly perverse. Hard to imagine, therefore, a more grim autobiographical declaration than Richard's 'Love forswore me in my mother's womb'.

The reputation of the Duke of Gloucester within the play – a reputation well deserved it would appear – is of a man obsessed with power, a cynic of Machiavellian proportion, a ruthless, calculating upstart. It comes, therefore, as something of a surprise that when, on a few occasions, we find Richard alone and are able to overhear him talking to himself, the thought of love – of love denied and love frustrated – is as much an obsession for him as the thought of power. His wondrous dream, his 'heaven', would have been to charm and win the affection of beautiful women like any other man. And, for a few moments, it's precisely that submerged dream of intimacy achieved, that vivid thought of a lover's conquest, which comes to the surface:

> I'll make my heaven in a lady's lap,
> And deck my body in gay ornaments,
> And 'witch sweet ladies with my words and looks.

But the idea is, of course, mocked by his manifestly ugly and misshapen form:

> O miserable thought! and more unlikely
> Than to accomplish twenty golden crowns.

Denied the ordinary expectation of a fulfilled life, Richard decides to repress within himself, once and for all, the impulse to love and be loved. From this point on, his focus will be on power and on power alone. His last, remaining dream – his only 'heaven' – is the throne and crown of England:

> Then, since this earth affords no joy to me
> But to command, to check, to o'erbear such
> As are of better person than myself,
> I'll make my heaven to dream upon the crown;
> And, whiles I live, t'account the world but hell,
> Until my misshap'd trunk that bears this head
> Be round impaled with a glorious crown.

Here what we see being enacted before us is the momentous shift from love to power, from a condition of frustrated desire for human affection to a state of cold and wilful superiority. Richard, because of the perceived wrong done to him by nature, believes he is now entirely justified in doing any wrong he chooses. He has been excluded from the common hopes and dreams of other men; why then should he be subject to their rules and laws? He has, he believes, the right to think of himself as an exception.

3
Richard 'the Exception'

Sigmund Freud, in an essay entitled 'Some Character-types Met with in Psycho-analytic Work', offers a fascinating reflection on the pathology of those among his patients whom he calls 'the exceptions'.[9] The neuroses of these particular men and women are of an unusually striking character. They behave, in day-to-day life, as if they have the right to transcend all the ordinary ethical norms of society. All of them, Freud explains, were casualties of 'some experience of suffering … in their earliest childhood', some wounded by 'the circumstance of a congenital

---

9. Sigmund Freud, 'The Exceptions', in *Some Character-types Met with in Psycho-analytic Work* (1916), *The Standard Edition of the Complete Psychological Works of Sigmund Freud*, Vol. XIV, ed. and trans. J. Strachey (New York, 1957), p. 312.

disadvantage' for which they knew they were not responsible.[10] But any feeling of deficiency which they had endured was turned bizarrely into a stance of utter and complete superiority, their attitude to themselves and to the world confused by the illusion of standing on 'special ground'. Freud writes: 'They say they have renounced enough and suffered enough, and have a claim to be spared any further demands; they will submit no longer to any disagreeable necessity, for they are *exceptions* and, moreover, intend to remain so.'[11]

Freud, in order to illustrate his point, instead of citing the example of one of his patients, points to the figure of none other than Richard III and, in particular, to the impressive monologue with which the play of that name begins. Here is the brief paraphrase Freud offers of Richard's words:

> Nature has done me a grievous wrong in denying me the beauty of form which wins human love. Life owes me reparation for this, and I will see that I get it. I have a right to be an exception, to disregard the scruples by which others let themselves be held back. I may do wrong myself, since wrong has been done to me.[12]

These sentiments, at first hearing, are so manifestly irrational and disturbed we might imagine the last thing an audience will feel, at this point, is sympathy for Richard or any kind of fellow feeling. But that, apparently, is not the case. While the audience – ourselves in this case – are listening to Richard deliver his monologue, we are, according to Freud, likely to register at least some form of sympathy 'even for a villain like him'.[13] And the reason? Because we recognize 'that we ourselves might become like Richard, that on a small scale, indeed, we are already like him'.[14]

This is an extraordinary claim, and it is an observation made about humanity in general. Can it be true? Freud clearly believes that it is the case. Richard's condition, he explains, is nothing less than 'an enormous magnification of something we find in ourselves'.

> We all think we have reason to reproach nature and our destiny for congenital and infantile disadvantages; we all demand reparation for early wounds to our narcissism, our self-love. Why did not Nature give us the golden curls of Balder or the strength of Siegfried or the lofty brow of genius or the noble profile of aristocracy? Why were we born in a middle-class home instead of in a royal palace? We could carry off beauty and distinction quite as well as any of those whom we are now obliged to envy for these qualities.[15]

10. Ibid., p. 314.
11. Ibid., pp. 314–15.
12. Ibid., p. 315.
13. Ibid.
14. Ibid.
15. Ibid.

Two centuries earlier, the English critic Samuel Johnson made a similar observation when discussing the nature of Richard's character and the issue of deformity. He wrote: 'Whoever is stigmatised with deformity has a constant source of envy in his mind, and would counterbalance by some other superiority these advantages which he feels himself to want.'[16] This fact, however, does not set those who are afflicted with some obvious deformity completely apart from the rest of humanity. 'The truth is', Johnson notes, 'that the deformed, *like all other men*, are displeased with inferiority, and endeavour to gain ground by good or bad means, as they are virtuous or corrupt'.[17]

Far from regarding Richard as the personification of evil – a monster in human form – Johnson encourages us to see him, in the portrayal by Shakespeare, as a real human being and not as a mere cypher of hell. As already noted, the opportunity to overhear Richard talking to himself, in a number of the monologues, offers us a perspective on his character and history we would never have had otherwise. And yet the majority of critics persist in seeing him as evil incarnate and as nothing else. No wonder Samuel Taylor Coleridge felt constrained to remark on one occasion: 'Shakespeare's characters, like those in real life, are very commonly misunderstood, and almost always understood by different persons in different ways.'[18] The reason for this 'misunderstanding', he explains, is that 'the characters of the *dramatis personae*, like those in real life, are to be inferred by the reader; – they are not told to him'.[19]

4

An Excursus on George Eliot

Some authors, as it happens, simply cannot hold back from telling us how they think we should react to the characters they have created. A case in point is the strong, authorial voice we hear intervening again and again in the narrative of *Middlemarch* by George Eliot. Eliot deliberately interrupts the flow of her story to share her thoughts, for example, regarding the Reverend Edward Casaubon, one of the least likeable figures in all of English fiction. The way Eliot is able to open a window for the reader into the soul of this wholly unattractive character is worth comparing and contrasting with Shakespeare's way of depicting the character of Richard.

Casaubon is a cold and pedantic individual. It's impossible not to find distasteful, therefore, the way he treats his young wife, Dorothea. Selfishly wrapped up in an arid pursuit of learning, he takes little or no account of her interests and seems,

---

16. Samuel Johnson, *Johnson on Shakespeare*, Vol. 8, *The Yale Edition of the Works of Samuel Johnson*, ed. A Sherbo (New Haven, CT, 1968), p. 605; cited in *King Henry VI, Part 3*, p. 65.
17. Ibid. My italics.
18. Samuel Taylor Coleridge, 'Shakespeare's Distinguishing Characteristics', in *Coleridge: Poems and Prose*, ed. K. Raine (Harmondsworth, 1957), p. 235.
19. Ibid.

in fact, to resent her youth and her enthusiasm. The more we learn about him, as the novel progresses, the more we instinctively recoil from him, and the more we come to sympathize with Dorothea and with her tragic disillusionment. But George Eliot, as author, decides on a number of occasions to interrupt her own narrative and challenges us to think more deeply about Casaubon, giving a halt to our judgements. Here are some of the relevant passages in *Middlemarch*:

> Poor Mr Casaubon felt (and must not we, being impartial, feel for him a little) that no man had juster cause for disgust and suspicion than he.[20]

> Dorothea ... was as blind to his inward troubles as he to hers; she had not yet learned those hidden conflicts in her husband which claim our pity. She had not yet listened to his heart-beats, but only felt that her own was beating violently.[21]

> As Dorothea's eyes were turned anxiously on her husband she was ... more conscious of that new alarm on his behalf which was the first stirring of a pitying tenderness fed by the realities of his lot and not by her own dreams.[22]

> she had felt the waking of a presentiment that there might be a sad consciousness in his life which made as great a need on his side as on her own. We are all of us born in moral stupidity, taking the world as an udder to feed our supreme selves.[23]

> For my part I am very sorry for him. It is an uneasy lot at best, to be what we call highly taught and yet not to enjoy: to be present at this great spectacle of life and never to be liberated from a small hungry shivering self – never to be fully possessed by the glory we behold, never to have our consciousness rapturously transformed into the vividness of a thought, the ardour of a passion, the energy of an action, but always to be scholarly and uninspired, ambitious and timid, scrupulous and dim-sighted.[24]

> Mr Casaubon had an intense consciousness within him, and was spiritually a-hungered like the rest of us.[25]

Such a clarifying, authorial voice breaking into the narrative, and interpreting for us, in an explicit way, the inner state of soul of a particular character, is, of course, unthinkable in Shakespearean drama. As in real life, so also here on

---

20. George Eliot, *Middlemarch* (New York, 1998), p. 350.
21. Ibid., p. 187.
22. Ibid., p. 196.
23. Ibid., p. 197.
24. Ibid., p. 261.
25. Ibid., p. 259.

stage, the characters we see performing their allotted roles within the drama are not restricted by the clear, authoritative voice of an author talking offstage, as it were, but are left open and vulnerable to a plethora of different interpretations by different people within the audience. Shakespeare, unlike George Eliot, does not *tell* us what we should think or how we should feel about one of his characters. No, he does something else, something much more subtle, much more effective. Employing with characteristic genius the art of the dramatic monologue (as we have already noted), he allows a key protagonist such as Richard to reveal aspects of his character and history which would otherwise have remained hidden. And the effect of this disclosure is to make the audience – ourselves in this case – begin to think again about our judgements regarding Richard.

5
Richard: Monster and *Casualty?*

Take the soliloquy which opens *Richard III*. At first hearing, it might seem to confirm the popular conviction that Richard is indeed a truly monstrous individual. Without shame he declares that he is 'false and treacherous', and he admits to having already devised, for his own evil purpose, all kinds of plots and libels, prophecies and dreams. This portrait of Richard corresponds exactly with the portrait we find in the principal historical source on which Shakespeare relied for information about Richard, *The Union of the Two Noble and Illustre Famelies of Lancastre and Yorke* by Edward Hall. Concerning Richard, Hall notes that not only was he 'eivill featured of limnes, croke backed' and with 'a crabbed face', he also possessed an evil character: 'malicious, wrathful and envious … a depe dissimuler … despiteous and cruell'.[26] All this, we know, Shakespeare carried over into his portrayal of Richard. But, if we listen attentively to what is actually said by Richard in the monologues (in both 3 *Henry VI* and *Richard III*), it soon becomes clear that Shakespeare is deliberately adding something new to the Hall portrait. He is offering a perspective on Richard not even hinted at in the sources, alerting his audience to the presence in Richard – at the very quick of his being – of an aching desire to experience, like any other man, the natural joys and pleasures of love.

Here, Shakespeare is not being in any way sentimental. Again and again he makes it clear that Richard is a man lusting for power and willing to do any wrong to achieve his aim. But Shakespeare also allows his theatre audience to see, and from the *inside* as it were, how the fact of deformity has twisted the threads of Richard's life and destiny and how it has effectively cheated him of the possibility of love, helping to precipitate him towards a career of unspeakable sadness and badness. 'Therefore, since I cannot prove a lover', Richard exclaims, 'I am

---

26. Edward Hall, *The Union of the Two Noble and Illustre Famelies of Lancastre and Yorke* (1548), Appendix 1, in The Arden Edition of *The Third Part of King Henry VI, Part 3* (London, 1964), p. 174.

determined to prove a villain.' In the same speech (*Richard III*, Act I, Scene 1), he describes himself as a man,

> scarce half made up,
> And that so lamely and unfashionable
> That dogs bark at me as I halt by them.

In spite of all that we know about Richard, it's impossible not to acknowledge the pain, the desperate anguish contained in these words. Shakespeare does not intervene at this point with the question: 'Must not we, being impartial, feel for him a little?' Nevertheless, by allowing us to come so near to the innermost world of his protagonist, permitting us to hear, as it were, his very heartbeats, Shakespeare leaves us in no doubt whatever that Richard does indeed possess, 'an intense consciousness within him', and that, 'like the rest of us', he desires, at the core of his being, not to be left alone, not to be mocked or laughed at because of his appearance, not to find himself rejected out of hand by those to whom he is most attracted. But that was, of course, the actual fate which befell him. Richard is, therefore, I would suggest, a particularly striking example of what might be called the human casualty.

6
Revelations in the Tower

At this point, let us turn our attention back once again to the scene in the Tower of London and to the meeting between Richard and King Henry, the former regarded as a veritable devil, the latter as a saint. Henry, the prisoner, is intent on reading his holy book. Richard, in marked contrast, when he enters, comes armed with a sword and with the clear intent to kill. Here, at the beginning of the scene, King Henry has all the appearance of a martyr-victim, and at the end of the scene, that appearance is further underlined when, after being brutally stabbed by Richard, we hear him exclaim: 'O God, forgive my sins, and pardon thee.'

These are indeed words which a saint might use. But words are proven by deeds. A saint does not simply ask pardon for his enemy; a saint actually forgives, hating the crime with all his heart – yes – but choosing in the end, and in spite of whatever humiliation or suffering he may endure, *not* to hate but to love the enemy. By that standard King Henry is, I would suggest, anything but a saint. With more concentrated venom than any of the others who mock and attack the Crookback, Henry expresses a truly profound disdain for the man. His words, when they meet in the Tower, certainly cut like a sword. But words, at this point, are his only defence, the sole weapon left to him. By most ordinary standards, therefore, his reaction is not unreasonable. But is it the reaction of a saint?

This question does not emerge out of an arbitrary preoccupation imposed on the text. No – it is a question raised again and again by what might be called the moral action of the play. King Henry has assumed, from the beginning, the role of a man whose mind is 'bent on holiness'. Instead of relishing the trappings of power, for example, he has made clear his desire to be set free from all regal responsibility, even offering on one occasion to hand over his power to two of his supporters, Warwick and Clarence:

> I will make you both Protectors of this land,
> While I myself will lead a private life
> And in devotion spend my latter days,
> To sin's rebuke and my creator's praise.

At one particularly grave moment during the battle of Towton, Henry, being found ineffectual both as a leader and as a soldier, and being dismissed from the fray by his wife, the Queen, seeks out a place for quiet meditation. Sitting himself down on a molehill, he exclaims:

> Would I were dead, if God's good will were so.
> For what is in this world but grief and woe?
> O God! Methinks it were a happy life
> To be no better than a homely swain
> To sit upon a hill, as I do now,
> To carve out dials quaintly, point by point.

A 'swain' is, of course, a shepherd. One critic, wryly commenting on Henry's dream-fantasy of living as a humble shepherd, remarks: 'Had he had his wish to be a shepherd, he would certainly have lost his sheep!'[27]

Henry, as a king, was not always ineffective. In fact, if his own account is to be believed, he was, as a ruler of the country, exceptional in the way he responded to the needs of his people:

> My pity hath been balm to heal their wounds.
> My mildness hath allayed their swelling griefs.
> My mercy dried their water-flowing tears.
> I have not been desirous of their wealth
> Nor much oppressed them with great subsidies,
> Nor forward of revenge, though they much erred.

Pity, mildness, mercy – these are unquestionably great virtues in a king. But such insistently self-referring phrases as 'my pity', 'my mildness', 'my mercy', are they really the kind of phrases we expect to hear on the lips of a saint? Here, one almost has the impression King Henry is holding up a mirror to catch a glimpse of his own quite exceptional pity, mildness and mercy. And that doesn't sound like holiness.

---

27. M.M. Reese, *The Cease of Majesty* (London, 1961), p. 200; cited in the 2001 Arden Shakespeare Commentary on *King Henry VI, Part 3*, p. 74.

One of Shakespeare's greatest gifts is the remarkable inner consistency of the characters he creates. It's something truly uncanny, an achievement unsurpassed in world literature. And that explains why, having once gained more complete knowledge of the complexity of Henry's character, when we turn our attention back to the Tower scene, we are not surprised to find the King capable of uttering, as he dies, the acceptable saintly words and yet incapable of responding with a saint's gift of attentiveness and compassion to Richard, his executioner.

What Richard hears from Henry in the Tower are the dagger words of defamation to which he has had to listen all his life. And the tragedy is that he believes them. He finds confirmed, as never before, the appalling lie that somehow, by providence, he has been ordained to be a scourge of evil and that his twisted body represents a soul rotten at its core. It comes, therefore, as no surprise, in the long soliloquy after the death of Henry, to hear him exclaim: 'Then, since the heavens have shaped my body so, / Let hell make crooked my mind to answer it.' These are truly terrible words, but they are words as least as desperate and despairing as they are blasphemous. And they are followed by a declaration which is, I would say, the most sad and revealing in the entire play:

> I have no brother; I am like no brother.
> And this word 'love,' which greybeards call divine,
> Be resident in men like one another
> And not in me: I am myself alone.

This statement has been interpreted by a number of commentators as Machiavellian Richard, exulting with glee in the thought of being free of all familial ties, all moral constraints. But, behind the bravado, if bravado it is, behind the seeming boast of separateness, there is an unmistakable anguish. And it is the anguish, more than anything else, which comes through most powerfully.

7
Søren Kierkegaard on the Crookback

Of all the authors and critics who have commented on the character of Richard over the last few centuries, by far the most insightful is an author who was himself 'deformed, crooked, hunchbacked and sickly'.[28] That author was the Danish nineteenth-century philosopher, Søren Kierkegaard. In Kierkegaard's opinion, Richard, as a result of being born so horribly misshapen, is thrust into 'the paradox'.[29] He is 'set outside of the universal'. And that fateful event, that casualty of nature, marks 'the beginning of the demoniacal, for which the individual himself however

---

28. See Theodor Haecker, *Kierkegaard the Cripple* (New York, 1950), p. 24. See also Walter Lowrie, *A Short Life of Kierkegaard* (Princeton, 1946), pp. 40–2.

29. Søren Kierkegaard, *Fear and Trembling*, trans. W. Lowrie (Princeton, NJ, 1954), p. 115.

is not to blame'.[30] Speaking of Richard's monologue in the first act of *Richard III*, Kierkegaard says that it is 'worth more than all the moral systems which have no inkling of the terrors of existence or of the explanation of them'.[31] Then, by way of brief illustration, he cites the following lines from that famous soliloquy:

> I that am rudely stamped, and want love's majesty
> To strut before a wanton ambling nymph;
> I, that am curtail'd of this fair proportion,
> Cheated of feature by dissembling nature,
> Deformed, unfinished, sent before my time
> Into this breathing world, scarce half made up,
> And that so lamely and unfashionable
> That dogs bark at me as I halt by them.

It is already a huge misfortune for any human being to find himself 'deformed' and 'unfinished' in this way, but the suffering does not end there. According to Kierkegaard, 'from time out of mind ... every man on seeing a deformed person has at once an inclination to associate this with the notion of moral depravity'.[32] And he adds at once: 'What a monstrous injustice! The situation must rather be inverted, in the sense that existence itself has corrupted them, in the same way that a wicked stepmother makes the children wicked.'[33]

Here Kierkegaard might seem to be suggesting that those who are casualties of nature or of circumstance have no freedom whatever to change the direction of their lives. But that is not, in fact, what he is suggesting. 'Essentially', he writes, 'such natures are in the paradox'. Either they can be 'lost in the demoniacal paradox or saved in the divine'.[34] And the latter, blessed condition was how he understood his own life. *Saved in the divine.*

Writing in his private journal in 1854, he speaks of two different ways in which people can react to the deep hurt of being denied ordinary human joy: one, his own way, and the other, that of Richard III:

> Alas, in an earlier period I felt all too deeply the pain that it was impossible for me to enjoy life, this beautiful human life. The effect on Richard III was that he decided to make life bitter for others. Not so with me. I intended to conceal my suffering and then make life beautiful for others.[35]

---

30. Ibid.
31. Ibid., p. 114.
32. Ibid., p. 115.
33. Ibid.
34. Ibid.
35. Kierkegaard, No. 6882, *Journals and Papers*, Vol. 6, Autobiographical, Part Two (1848–1855), eds. H.V. Hong and E.H. Hong (London, 1978), p. 514. In another place, speaking of his ability to make the paradoxical leap of faith, Kierkegaard writes: 'I am able to make from the springboard the great leap whereby I pass into infinity, my back is like that of a tight-rope walker, having been twisted in my childhood, hence I find this easy'. See *Fear and Trembling*, p. 47.

In another place, he writes: 'It depends upon the individual which way he turns, whether that solitary inner suffering finds its demoniacal expression and satisfaction in hating mankind and cursing God, or else the very opposite. The last was the case with me.'[36]

Richard, in Shakespeare's play, deliberately chose to pursue the demonic route, and for that he must take responsibility. But Richard never asked – Kierkegaard reminds us – to be thrown into 'the paradox', never asked to be 'set outside of the universal', never asked to be born misshapen, or to be mocked by his companions all his life, and treated as a freak. In all these appalling events, whether of nature or of circumstance, he is the victim, he is the unhappy casualty and he is 'not to blame'.

When, in the Tower scene, King Henry finds himself face-to-face with his adversary, if he were indeed a saint – if Shakespeare, that is, had intended to portray him as such – he would surely have manifested at least something of the wide and wise compassion of Kierkegaard. Instead, we find Henry condemning the man outright with every word he speaks, prophesying a future as black as the past and thereby effectively imprisoning Richard, once and for all, in the paradox of the demoniacal.

It might be objected, at this point, that it makes no sense to talk of Richard as a casualty or victim in any sense. The real victims in the story are they not those many hundreds of innocent people, small children among them, for whose murder and torture Richard is directly responsible? As it happens, Shakespeare in the play never for a moment ignores the unspeakable horror which lies behind this question, but neither does he allow us to ignore the other question, the other tragedy, which concerns individuals like Richard, people who are also victims, but victims who in the end choose to behave like monsters.

So is there such a thing as an innocent monster? This question was raised once in a prose-poem by Charles Baudelaire and put directly to God. Here is an extract:

Life is aswarm with innocent monsters. Lord, my God ... have pity, O have pity on mad men and mad women! O Creator! can there exist such things as monsters in the eyes of Him who alone knows why they exist, how they have made themselves what they are, and how they could not have made themselves any different?[37]

---

36. Cited in Theodor Haecker, *Søren Kierkegaard*, trans. A. Dru (Oxford, 1937), p. 3. Haecker, in another work, writes: 'After Kierkegaard had realized that, in spite of his hump, in spite of his psychic-physical exclusion from the "universal" of human existence, he had chosen (by the grace of God) the good rather than the demonic (represented by Richard III) to which he was potentially inclined, he was so enraptured by the experience and the realization that God loved all men and therefore him also, that he perceived the true meaning of human equality.' See *Kierkegaard the Cripple*, trans. C.V.O. Bruyn (New York, 1950), p. 15.

37. Baudelaire's prose-poem 'Mademoiselle Bistouri' is number 47 of a series of poems published posthumously in 1864 under the title *Le Spleen de Paris: petits poèmes en prose*.

That last phrase strikes a note never sounded in the work of Kierkegaard (Baudelaire's exact contemporary), but the passage is remarkable all the same. It betrays, first phrase to last, the fascination we have as moderns with all the contradictions and complexities we find around us and within us. As Browning puts it,

> Our interest's on the dangerous edge of things.
> The honest thief, the tender murderer,
> The superstitious atheist.[38]

When confronted by the phenomenon of evil, the challenge at times can be so great, we may be tempted to deny that evil exists or perhaps tempted to give it another name, allowing it to be psychologized into something less threatening, and start calling everyone victims, becoming in the end sentimental instead of purposeful and alert. But such temptation, it should be noted, is not one to which Shakespeare ever succumbed. 'Keeping at all times in the high road of life', according to Coleridge, 'Shakespeare has no innocent adulteries, no interesting incests, no virtuous vice: – he never renders that amiable which religion and reason alike teach us to detest.'[39]

But neither, I would say, does Shakespeare ever allow the disturbing criminals and adulterers he creates in his work to become caricatures of themselves. He never encourages us to despise them. His 'freaks' and 'monsters', in fact, are not at all unlike those who crowd the short stories of Flannery O'Connor. When O'Connor refers to the characters of her fiction as 'figures of our essential displacement, images of man forced to meet the extremes of his own nature',[40] she could be describing, and with telling accuracy, a number of the most celebrated characters in Shakespearean drama, Richard – 'the devil's butcher', the 'foul misshapen' human casualty – among them.

---

38. Robert Browning, 'Bishop's Blougram's Apology', in *Robert Browning: Selected Poems* (New York, 2010), p. 306.
39. Coleridge, 'Shakespeare's Distinguishing Characteristics', p. 233.
40. Flannery O'Connor, in Betsy Fancher, 'My Flannery O'Connor' (1975), in *Conversations with Flannery O'Connor*, ed. R.M. Magee (London, 1987), p. 112.

Chapter 3

A MAN TALKING: THE PRAYER AND POETRY OF CHARLES PÉGUY

> God, I love ever and always the human voice,
> The voice of leave-taking and the voice of sorrow,
> The voice whose prayer has often seemed vain,
> But which still goes forward down the painful road.[1]
>
> Péguy: Jeanne D'Arc

Two years after Péguy's death in 1916, in a series of University Extension Lectures at Oxford, T.S. Eliot included Péguy in the syllabus for his course.[2] And in the autumn of that same year, in a short review of a book about Péguy, Eliot remarked: 'There may be passages in his verse which are pure poetry; there are certainly passages in his prose which are of the best prose.'[3] And again:

> There have been finer poets, more subtle thinkers, than Péguy. But there was no one who had just what Péguy had. Emphatically, he was not *fumiste*. There is not a trace of affectation about him. And in Paris ... which was surfeited with criticism, Paris given up to radical and reactionary movements which were largely movements for the sake of moving, Péguy represented something which was real and solid. He stood for a real re-creation, a return to the sources.[4]

More than twenty years later, in a 1940 article, Eliot spoke, in passing, of 'the man whom I consider the greatest journalist, in the best sense of the term, of my time: Charles Péguy'.[5] The enthusiasm is clear. But what Eliot would seem to

---

1. « Jeanne D'Arc », in *Charles Péguy: Oeuvres poétiques complètes* (Paris, 1957), p. 48.
2. See a reproduction of the entire syllabus in A.D. Moody, *Thomas Stearns Eliot: Poet* (Cambridge, 1979), pp. 41–9.
3. T.S. Eliot, review of « Charles Péquy, de la Lorraine à la Marne (août-septembre, 1914) » by Victor Boudon, *The New Statesman* (7 October 1916), p. 20.
4. Ibid.
5. T.S. Eliot, 'Views and Reviews: Journalists of Yesterday and Today', *The New English Weekly* (8 February 1940), p. 237. In the same year, on 28 August, writing as guest editor of the *Christian News-Letter*, Eliot remarked: 'We must not forget, either, those great Catholic

be suggesting is that Péguy is primarily important as a kind of 'presence' to his generation, a necessary social and religious journalist, a prose writer of sharp and prophetic insight. With regard, however, to Péguy's status as a poet, Eliot, writing in 1916, is far more circumspect: 'There is not a great deal, certainly,' he notes, 'of the finest verse.'[6] Whether or not Eliot changed his mind later concerning the poetry of Péguy is difficult to say. But it's interesting to note that there are traces of Péguy's work in Eliot's mature verse. In a letter, composed in the autumn of 1956, Eliot openly acknowledged the 'probable' influence of Péguy on one of the most mysterious phrases in *Four Quartets*: 'The line, "Garlic and sapphires in the mud"', he wrote, 'is an echo of a line of a sonnet by Mallarmé (« Tonnerre et rubis aux moyeux ») with probable recollection also of Charles Péguy's description of the Battle of Waterloo (« de la boue jusqu'aux essieux »).'[7]

Perhaps the most immediate difficulty we confront when we begin to read Péguy is in determining just what kind of poetry he was attempting to write. If, in assessing his work, we insist on placing him in the company of modern poets such as Paul Valéry, or Jules Laforgue, or even the young Eliot himself, and judge him exclusively by their distinctive aims and aesthetic standards, then Péguy will certainly appear as a very poor cousin indeed. But what, I think, has to be understood is that Péguy's project as a poet, at least in the context of modern literature, was something altogether unique. It is hardly surprising, therefore, that what the first readers of Péguy discovered, when confronted by his work, still holds true to some extent today. For then, as now, Péguy, the man, the poet, appears somehow to resist precise definition. His work simply refuses to be contained by most of our literary and religious categories. And this fact alone should help explain why Péguy's work has been largely ignored in the English-speaking world. Here, from the contemporary American critic William Logan, is a summary portrait of the man and the work: 'Péguy, a French poet never much regarded in English, is a figure ridiculous in his propriety: a peasant with a pince-nez, a bookshop owner whose unsold books were used by his friends as tables and chairs, a squanderer of his in-laws' money.'[8]

Eventually, however, Péguy's achievement did receive clear and insightful recognition within the English-speaking world and from an unexpected source. In 1984 there appeared in print a long poem by Geoffrey Hill entitled 'The Mystery of the Charity of Charles Péguy'. 'Footslogger of genius', Hill called him, 'skirmisher

---

writers, such as Charles Péguy and Léon Bloy, who have united a fervent devotion to a passion for social justice.' See 'The Diversity of French Opinion', in *The Idea of a Christian Society and Other Writings* (London, 1982), p. 135.

6. Ibid.

7. Letter to Philip Mairet, 31 October 1956. Harry Ransom Humanities Research Center, Austin. See *T.S. Eliot: Inventions of the March Hare: Poems 1909–1917*, ed. C. Ricks (London, 1996), p. xxv. The 'mud up to the axles' passage which Eliot recalled is from Péguy's *À nos amis, à nos abonnés*. See T.S. Eliot, *Collected and Uncollected Poems*, Vol. 1, eds. C. Ricks and J. McCue (London, 2015), p. 914.

8. William Logan, *Reputations of the Tongue: On Poets and Poetry* (Florida, 1999), p. 189.

with grace / and ill-luck'.[9] In an afterword to the poem, Hill spoke of 'the tragicomic battered élan of Péguy's life'.[10] His poem is nothing less than a homage to the triumph of what he calls Péguy's 'defeat'.[11] 'Péguy, stubborn rancours and mishaps and all', Hill declared, 'is one of the great souls, one of the great prophetic intelligences of our century'.[12]

1
Péguy: The Style, the Man

In the matter of style, Péguy hardly seems to belong to the literature of the early twentieth century. He appeared then, and still appears today, as a poet out of his time. And yet there is one factor in his work which immediately connects him with the work of his contemporaries, his use of free verse. To his friend Joseph Lotte, Péguy remarked in 1910: 'All the attempts in free verse of the last twenty years have put into my hands an excellent instrument.'[13] One writer Péguy may have had in mind here is the American poet Walt Whitman. Some years earlier, in 1901, Péguy's great friend Halévy had written an enthusiastic article on Whitman in the *Pages Libres*. And there does appear to be something, in the incantatory quality of Péguy's verse, reminiscent of Whitman. But if the 'Good Gray Poet' is indeed an influence of some kind, it has to do more with style than content. I say this because it's almost impossible to imagine Péguy approving of any aspect of Whitman's American vision. In 1903 he wrote: 'It will never be known how many stupid things the Catholic Church has done in her effort to modernize herself, even to Americanize herself. In this she forgets, she belittles all her power and all her greatness.'[14]

In parenthesis here, it's interesting to note that a contemporary of Péguy, the Jesuit poet Gerard Manley Hopkins, was familiar with some of Whitman's verse. In a letter to Robert Bridges, he spoke of Whitman's 'marked and original manner' and of the striking 'rhythm' of his verse. But then he added: 'I always knew in my heart Walt Whitman's mind to be more like my own than any other man's living. As he is a very great scoundrel this is not a pleasant confession. And this also makes me the more desirous to read him and the more determined that I will not.'[15]

---

9. Geoffrey Hill, *The Mystery of the Charity of Charles Péguy* (London, 1983), p. 10.
10. Ibid., p. 31.
11. Ibid.
12. Ibid. Great praise is also accorded to Péguy in an impressive paper by George Steiner: 'Drumming on the Doors – Péguy', in *No Passion Spent: Essays 1978–1996* (London, 1996), pp. 160–70.
13. Péguy to Lotte, Conversation: 1 April 1910. See *Lettres et entretiens*, ed. M. Péguy (Paris, 1927), p. 138.
14. « Reprise politique parlementaire » (1903), in *Oeuvres en prose de Charles Péguy: 1898–1908* (Paris, 1959), p. 611.
15. Letter to Robert Bridges, 18 October 1882. See *A Hopkins Reader*, ed. J. Pick (New York, 1961), pp. 172–3.

Critics have found it difficult over the years to ascertain, with any certainty, the important influences on Péguy's style as a poet. He never attempted to write poetry as such until 1908, just six years before his death. And so plain and simple is his language, and so close to prose at times, it seems hardly to be a literary style at all. Indeed, if it is to be thought of as a style, it is perhaps one which answers only to a kind of Wordsworthian idea or ideal – a language that is free of all ornament, a discourse of give and take, a style similar to that of an ordinary, easeful conversation: the language of 'a man talking to men'.[16]

But the model Péguy had in mind for his work as a poet – the principal model – was not Wordsworth, nor indeed any other poet or author within the great literary tradition. The model to which he looked, the example from which he drew his greatest and most immediate inspiration, was the language of Christ the Word, the inspired, colloquial language of the Gospel. The genius of Péguy, his gift as a poet, his content, his style – the very words he uses throughout his work – are all, we can say, *under* the Word. It's not an accident, therefore, that when he sets out to describe the manner in which Jesus speaks in the Gospel, Péguy might almost be describing the language of his own verse, the distinctive cadence of his own speech.

> He came to tell us what he had to tell us.
> Didn't he.
> Calmly.
> Simply, honestly.
> Directly. Right from the start.
> Ordinarily.
> Like one honest man speaks to another honest man.
> Man to man …
> He spoke to us without digressions or complications.
> He didn't put on airs, embellish things.
> He spoke uniformly, like a simple man, crudely like
>   a man from town.
> A man from the village.
> Like a man in the street who doesn't search for his
>   words and doesn't make a fuss
> When he chats.[17]

---

16. Although in my opinion the best of Péguy's work is in *vers libre*, a number of his more formal lyrics are also impressive. I am thinking in particular of the justly famous « Présentation de la Beauce à Notre Dame de Chartres. »

17. « Le Porche du mystère de la deuxième vertu » (1912), in *Charles Péguy: Oeuvres poétiques complètes*, pp. 597–8. See *The Portal of the Mystery of Hope*, trans. D.L. Schindler (Grand Rapids, MI, 1996), pp. 68–9.

2
Literature and Truth

'I am no longer capable of reading anything after Péguy. All the rest is just literature.'[18] This comment was made by the writer Romain Rolland in his private journal in 1912. Given the fact that Rolland's views differed greatly from those of his friend Péguy, and that he found 'exasperating faults' even in the poet's best work, the remark is astonishing.[19] But what exactly does the comment mean? When is writing something more than 'just literature'? Péguy, in one of his own poems, actually characterizes « la littérature » – understood in its decadent form – as something under the thrall of evil: « Les armes de Satan c'est la literature »![20] Here, with a shocking and deliberate wilfulness, Péguy is laying down a stumbling block at the entrance to his work, determined to scandalize that part of us, or that part of modern sensibility, which would insist that all art and poetry – *la poèsie pure* – be kept separate from the contamination of moral, social and religious considerations. But if that is indeed Péguy's aim, why should we bother to read him?

This question brings to mind one of the most interesting and unexpected testimonies in modern times concerning the relationship between literature and truth. It was an observation made by Katherine Mansfield in the last months of her life. Mansfield herself had been part of a confident, modern movement in literature. But, towards the end, she remarked to her friend, A.R. Orage, 'There is something wanting in literary art even at its highest. Literature is not enough.'[21] And she went on:

> The greatest literature is still only mere literature if it has not a purpose commensurate with its art. Presence or absence of purpose distinguishes literature from mere literature, and the elevation of the purpose distinguishes literature within literature. That is merely literature that has no other object than to please. Minor literature has a didactic object. But the greatest literature of all – the literature that scarcely exists – has not merely an aesthetic object, nor merely a didactic object, but, in addition, a creative object: that of subjecting its readers to a real and at the same time illuminating experience. Major literature, in short, is an initiation into truth.[22]

---

18. See *Une amitié française, correspondence Péguy-R. Rolland*, ed. A. Saffrey (Paris, 1955), p. 155.

19. Writing many years later, Rolland did not hesitate to endorse his original statement. He wrote: 'After Péguy I can read nothing else. All the rest is fine writing. Compared with him how hollow today's great figures seem ... I am not in sympathy with his outlook, but I admire him.' Cited in Margorie Villiers, *Charles Péguy: A Study in Integrity* (London, 1965), p. 281.

20. « La Tapisserie de Sainte Geneviève », in *Charles Péguy: Oeuvres poétiques complètes*, p. 864.

21. 'Talks with Katherine Mansfield', in *Selected and Critical Writings*, ed. A.R. Orage (London, 1935), p. 126.

22. Ibid.

Charles Péguy wrote little or nothing in the nature of an *ars poetica*. But Katherine Mansfield's statement would surely have won his enthusiastic assent. Again and again in his work as a poet, Péguy sought to attain a level of writing far above and beyond what Mansfield calls 'mere literature'. The risk, of course, was of producing verse that was merely didactic. But, happily, that was not the end result. On the contrary, by daring to whistle literary correctness down the wind, Péguy managed to bring a new vigour and freshness to the literature of his time. André Gide, in a review of *Le Mystère de la Charité de Jean d'Arc*, wrote: 'Never has [our language] been less Latin, less concise; never has it been freer or at the same time more disciplined; never has it responded more quickly to the slightest breath of the spirit. Here one finds it as it was in Rabelais – quite young, in process of formation.'[23]

3
Péguy among the Theologians

'It is very important not to rig me out as a Father of the Church. It is already quite a lot to be a son'![24] This comment was made by Péguy more than a hundred years ago. If, today, Péguy could read the enthusiastic responses to his work from certain theologians, his response, I suspect, would be just as sharp. That said, however, it's hard to fault the theologians for their enthusiasm. No poet in modern times has written at such length, and with such deep understanding, of the mysteries of the faith. In poem after poem, Péguy appears not only able to speak out of the core of the mystery he is describing but also able (in the view of Hans Urs von Balthasar) 'to penetrate more deeply than any other Christian poet into the secrets of the tenderness of God's heart'.[25] Balthasar even goes so far as to suggest that, as a writer, Péguy was given 'the privilege of uttering words beyond all the fluency of theology to date'.[26]

Again and again in his mature work, Péguy does not simply meditate on some of the great dogmatic truths and mysteries of the faith. Instead, he assumes, as it were, the role of a prophet of the *New* Testament. And, in line after line of plain but rhythmic prose, he allows the Father of Jesus – the living God revealed by the Son – to speak out for Himself.

> I am their father, God says ...
> My Son told them often enough that I am their father ...

---

23. André Gide, 'Review of *Le Mystère de la Charité de Jean d'Arc*', in *La Nouvelle Revue Française*, cited in Villiers, *Charles Péguy*, p. 248.

24. Péguy to Lotte, Letter: 1 May 1912. See *Lettres et entretiens*, ed. M. Péguy (Paris, 1927), p. 87.

25. Hans Urs von Balthasar, 'Péguy', *The Glory of the Lord*, Vol. 3, *Lay Styles* (San Francisco, 2006), p. 415.

26. Ibid.

> *Our Father who art in Heaven*, those three or four words
> ... Happy is the man who goes to sleep under the
> protection of the vanguard of those three or four words.
> Those words which go before every prayer as the hands
> of a supplicant before his face.
> As the two hands of a supplicant advance, joined
> together before his face and the tears on his face.
> Those three or four words which conquer me – me, the
> unconquerable.
> Words which are sent forward in front of their distress,
> like two invincible hands joined together ...
> And every prayer rises towards me concealed behind
> those three or four words ...
> Not, however, as a text only, in so far as the prayer has
> become a text. But, in its very invention, and in its
> source, and its breaking forth.
> When it was itself a birth of prayer, an incarnation, and
> a birth of prayer. A hope. A birth of hope.
> A word coming to birth.
> A branch and a germ and a bud and a leaf and a flower
> and a fruit of speech.
> A seed, a birth of prayer.
> A word among all words.
> That first time it came forth in the flesh, in Time, from
> the human lips of my Son.[27]

Prayer, the practice of prayer, is not so much a theme in Péguy's work as the very lifeblood of his verse. It is significant that on the Contents page of his *Oeuvres poétiques complètes*, we find titles which refer directly to the subject of prayer: « Les cinq prières dans la Cathédral de Chartres » for example and « Présentation de la Beauce à Notre Dame de Chartres ». These titles might, at first, suggest that Péguy's work belongs to what is now considered the faded and dusty world of nineteenth-century piety. But nothing could be further from the truth. The fact is that, by instinct, both as man and poet, Péguy is a fighter. He is a soldier on the march, a *miles Christi*. And his work, both prose and verse, far from inhabiting a dull, sacristy realm, or a narrow mental enclosure, or a physical cloister, always seems to breathe an atmosphere that is fresh, robust and open air.

---

27. « Le Mystère des Saints Innocents », in *Charles Péguy: Oeuvres poétiques complètes*, pp. 693–6. The translation is based in large part on P. Pakenham's translation in *The Mystery of the Holy Innocents and Other Poems* (New York, 1956), pp. 86–9.

4
The Temporal and the Eternal

Péguy's project, his great ambition as a writer, was nothing less than 'a real re-creation, a return to the sources'.[28] And, for Péguy, this meant one thing and one thing only: a return to what he called 'the mystical life, the Christian operation' (« l'opération mystique, l'opération chrétienne »).[29] The phrase « l'opération mystique » or 'the mystical life', in the spiritual literature of the period, generally referred to a special state or stage in the life of prayer, a grace of interior illumination, an ecstasy of thought and vision which, in this life, only a small number of contemplatives could hope to attain. The ideal proposed to 'serious Christians', therefore, was to pursue a path of radical detachment from the things of this world, and even to abandon the world completely, and embrace a life of strict enclosure.

But, for Péguy, this concept of mysticism amounted almost to a heresy. With sharp insistence he noted again and again in his writings that 'the mystical operation, the Christian operation, was one which moved towards the world and not an operation which turned away from it. The world was incontestably its object'.[30] An authentic mystical life, therefore – as, for example, the life manifest in Christ – was the most engaged life imaginable. It was a life which strove not to separate but to link the eternal and the temporal. It was, in Péguy's words, 'an inexhaustible, vivifying spring, nourishing the world, overflowing onto the age, penetrating, inundating the world; a mystical spring temporally in the world, flowing and overflowing towards it'.[31]

What was achieved in the Incarnation was 'an incredible interlocking', an insertion, once and for all, of 'the temporal in the eternal, and of the eternal in the temporal'.[32] But if that 'interlocking' is denied or negated, we will fall inevitably, Péguy reminds us, into all kinds of seductive « mystiques » and 'vague spiritualities' – 'idealisms, immaterialisms, religiosities, pantheisms, philosophisms', etc.[33] Péguy, it should be noted, always seemed to reserve his most trenchant satire for those apparently 'spiritual' people who disdained the temporal, that is the carnal, the natural and the historical, and who sought to identify themselves only with the eternal. He wrote:

> Because they have not the strength and the grace to be one with nature, they think they are one with grace. Because they have not got temporal courage, they

---

28. T.S. Eliot, 'Types of English Verse', p. 20. Unpublished draft lecture in King's College Cambridge. The work was originally intended for a cancelled British Council Tour of Italy, 1939.
29. « Clio: Dialogue de l'histoire et de l'âme païenne », in *Oeuvres en prose de Charles Péguy, 1909-1914* (Paris, 1961), pp. 358-9. See 'Clio I' in *Temporal and Eternal*, trans. A. Dru (New York, 1958), p. 105.
30. Ibid., p. 370, Dru, p. 104.
31. Ibid., p. 384, Dru, p. 113.
32. Ibid., p. 387, Dru, p. 116.
33. Ibid.

believe themselves to have entered upon a penetration of the eternal. Because they lack the courage to be of the world, they believe they are of God. Because they lack the courage to belong to one of the parties of men, they believe themselves to be of the party of God ... Because they love no one, they believe they love God.[34]

In Péguy's eyes, such people are traitors to the true mystical secret of Christianity. They may appear very spiritual, but they are dangerous because they regard the world as a sort of 'blank', as if it was created by God 'not only badly but pointlessly, emptily'.[35] And as a result, Péguy asserts, there is 'a worm of dishonesty at the heart, in the hollow of their prayer'.[36] For what they have renounced, in the name of the eternal, is nothing less than an 'integral part' of the Christianity they would serve, 'not the essential, but an almost more than essential part ... the source of fermentation, the part which is not only the salt of the earth, but the salt of heaven, the yeast, the ferment of the heavenly bread'.[37]

5
Amazement into Song: The Poetry of Incarnation

In 1897, at the age of twenty-four, Péguy published his first literary work, a dramatic trilogy called *Jeanne d'Arc*. Although Péguy was a committed socialist at the time, and not a Catholic, some of the statements made in the play about Christ, and about the imitation of Christ, could well have come from the pen of one of Péguy's religious contemporaries such as Blessed Columba Marmion (1858–1923) or St Thérèse of Lisieux (1873–97). In the play, Péguy made three statements about Christ, and he repeated them, word for word, thirteen years later, in a verse drama called *Le Mystère de la Charité de Jeanne d'Arc*:

Jesus preached; Jesus prayed; Jesus suffered. We must imitate him just as far as our strength allows. Oh, we are unable to preach divinely; we are unable to pray divinely; and we will never have infinite suffering. But we must try with all our human might to speak as best we can the divine word; we must try with all our might to pray as best we can according to the divine word; we must try as best we can ... [to undergo] all we can of human suffering.[38]

Madame Gervaise, to whom this speech is given, explains to Jeanne that if we want to help or save others, not only we must imitate Christ, we must *listen*

---

34. « Note conjointe sur M. Descartes et la philosophie cartésienne », in *Charles Péguy: Oeuvres en Prose 1909–1914* (Paris, 1961), p. 1444.
35. « Clio: Dialogue de l'histoire et de l'âme paienne », pp. 358–9, Dru, p. 97.
36. Ibid.
37. Ibid., pp. 359–60, Dru, p. 98.
38. « Jeanne d'Arc », in *Charles Péguy: Oeuvres poétiques complètes*, p. 38.

to him as well.[39] This is advice Péguy seems to have taken to heart. In the later play, written shortly after his conversion,[40] Péguy expresses an excitement about the mystery of the Word Incarnate. Moved by the thought of Christ's presence among the people of his time, and stunned by the image of the Word walking as an ordinary man down the lanes and along the thoroughfares of Palestine, Péguy writes:

> To think, Lord, to think that you were there, that all that was needed was to come near you, awe-inspiring mystery. Really to think that it happened once. That it was once seen on earth. That everyone could touch you, *visible shepherd*, the womenfolk, the children, the beggars on the highways. And that you spoke like a simple man who speaks.[41]

Here, as in almost all Péguy's work, the quiet repetition of a few simple words, and the dogged, easeful incantation of a few phrases, draw the reader, in calm and purposeful meditation, into the heart of the vision being expressed. Possessed by that vision, Péguy writes with a manifest sense of awe about the Last Supper and, in particular, about the experience of those who were privileged, at that final meal, on that unique day, to be in such direct, physical contact with Jesus:

> Blessed were those who ate, one day, one unique day, one day among all days, blessed with a unique happiness, blessed were those who ate one day, one unique day, that holy Thursday, blessed were those who ate the bread of your body; you yourself consecrated by yourself; in a unique consecration; one day that will never come again; when you yourself said the first Mass; on your own body; when you celebrated the first Mass; when you consecrated yourself; when of that bread ... you made your body; and when of that wine you made your blood.[42]

One day that will never come again – that short telling phrase points to what is, I am convinced, Péguy's deepest concern in the *Mystère*. Yes, Christ has come; yes, his coming marked a moment of grace unparalleled in human history. But what if, in all the years that have passed since that unique moment, we can see no signs on earth of the kingdom that was promised? What if, in practice, even now, people are not being *saved*?

---

39. Ibid.

40. Péguy never accepted the idea that he was a 'convert'. He liked to think his return to Catholicism simply represented a deepening of mind and spirit.

41. « Le Mystère de la Charité de Jeanne d'Arc», in *Charles Péguy: Oeuvres poétiques complètes*, pp. 407–8. See *The Mystery of the Charity of Joan of Arc*, trans. J. Green (New York, 1950), pp. 62–3.

42. « Le Mystère de la Charité de Jeanne d'Arc », in *Oeuvres poétiques complètes*, p. 407. See Green translation, p. 62.

6
A Poet's Hope, a Man's Despair

There are few passages in Péguy's work more poignant than the long prayer that is said by Jeanne d'Arc at the opening of *Mystère*:

> O God, if only the beginning of your kingdom would come. If only the sunrise of your kingdom would come. But there is nothing, nothing to see, ever. You sent us your Son whom you loved so much, your Son came, who suffered so much, and He died, and there is nothing, nothing ever. If only we could see the dawn of your kingdom begin to break ... fourteen centuries of Christendom, alas! since the birth, and the death, and the preaching. And nothing, nothing, nothing ever. And what reigns on the face of the earth is nothing, nothing, nothing but perdition ... God, God, can it be that your Son died in vain? That He came, and it was all for nothing?[43]

There is no simple answer given in the *Mystère* to this sharp question. But, at a certain moment in the play, there occurs an explosion of insight when the nun Madame Gervaise realizes, all of a sudden, the significance – the eternal and *saving* significance – of the cry of Jesus from the cross: a cry, Gervaise explains, 'louder than the two thieves hanging beside him; / And who howled at death like famished dogs'.[44] His cry was different. It was 'as if God himself had sinned like us; / As if God himself had despaired'.[45] The cry that rose from the two thieves was 'a cry of human death' – that only. Christ, 'the Just one' – He alone uttered 'the everlasting cry'.

> Cry still ringing in all humanity;
> Cry that made the Church militant totter;
> In which the suffering Church too recognized its
>   own fear;
> Through which the Church triumphant
> experienced its triumph;
> Cry ringing at the heart of all humanity;
> Cry ringing at the heart of all Christendom;
> O culminating cry.[46]

In *The Portal of the Mystery of Hope*, the second *Mystère* composed by Péguy and arguably his greatest work, the virtue of hope is represented as a small child:

---

43. « Le Mystère de la Charité de Jeanne d'Arc », pp. 368–9. See Daniel Halévy, *Péguy* (London, 1946), p. 99.
44. Ibid., p. 437. See Green translation, p. 101.
45. Ibid.
46. Ibid.

> What surprises me, says God, is hope.
> And I can't get over it.
> This little hope who seems like nothing at all.
> This little girl hope.
> Immortal.[47]

At a first reading, one might imagine that the emphasis on childlike simplicity and trust, and indeed the insistence on this Gospel attitude in the poem, sprang from a distinctly serene and uncomplicated mind and heart. But Péguy's devotional and theological vision – his profound faith-awareness – was, from the beginning, tested and purified in the crucible of certain very painful and unusual circumstances. To his friend Joseph Lotte, Péguy made the following stark confession: 'My second *Mystery* was an anticipation; when I wrote it, I did not believe in hope.'[48]

Much of Péguy's prose, it could be said, emerges out of a struggle with society. But his best verse springs from what Yeats, the Irish poet, would call a struggle with himself. Not far beneath the surface of the poems one can hear the cadence of an intensely personal, questioning voice. In the second *Mystère*, for example, one has the impression that certain key statements voiced for God the Father are statements which, at one level, Péguy is addressing to his own heart and addressing at a time of almost unbearable anguish:

> I tell you: Put off till tomorrow
> Those concerns and those worries that are
>   eating at you today
> And that might devour you today.
> Put off till tomorrow those sobs that choke you
> When you see today's misery.
> Those sobs which rise in you and strangle you.
> Put off till tomorrow those tears that fill your
>   eyes and cover your face.
> That flood you. That fall down your cheeks.[49]

Péguy's vision of hope is childlike but never sentimental. Hope he regards as a grace like no other, a force able to rise up like new blood, or like sap in the month of May, and break through 'the thick skin of our hearts, / Through the skin of anger, through the skin of despair, / Through the thick skin of sin'.[50] In *The Portal* Péguy speaks of 'carnal pride', our human pride, and distinguishes it from the pride of the fallen angels. Their pride, he insists, was 'a poor pride of ideas. / A pale pride,

---

47. « Le Porche de la Deuxième Vertu », in *Oeuvres poétiques complètes*, p. 533. See Schindler translation, *The Portal of the Mystery of Hope*, p. 7.

48. See Daniel Halévy, *Péguy et les Cahiers de la Quinzaine* (Paris, 1941), p. 278.

49. « Le Porche de la Deuxième Vertu », in *Oeuvres poétiques complètes*, p. 657. See Schindler translation, p. 127.

50. Ibid. *Oeuvres poétiques complètes*, p. 583; Schindler, p. 55.

a vain pride all in the head'. Human pride, in contrast, is 'a thick and heavy pride nourished by fat and blood. / Brimming with health. / The skin glowing'.[51]

> Pride of the blood, pride of the flesh.
> Which swells and buzzes throughout the body like a
>   buzzing storm.
> And which throbs at the temples like the beating of a
>   drum.[52]

This 'pride of the flesh' was not redeemed by spirit alone but by Incarnation, by 'the flesh and blood' of Christ. And the parables of Christ form part of the grace of that redemption. They speak directly to the heart of the sinner. And, of all the parables, the parable of greatest hope, in Péguy's view, is the story of the prodigal son. 'This one has awakened the deepest echo. / The most ancient echo … The only one that the sinner has never been able to silence in his heart.'[53] The 'word of hope', then, is the one word that the sinner, even as he turns away from God and 'buries himself in lost countries', and tries to put everything that is sacred out of his mind, will never be able to forget.

> Once this word of hope has bitten into his heart
> Into his believing or unbelieving heart,
> No pleasure will ever more be able to erase
> Its teeth-marks.
> Such is this word. She's a word that stays with you.
> She follows like a dog
> That remains even though you beat it.[54]

The image is as unexpected as the reality it describes. Hope, for Péguy, is a mystery of God's love. It is the signature of God's purpose, the grace and surprise of a loving, relentless pursuit, the one pressure of grace that the sinner will never be able to finally negate or escape, 'because she's a mystery that follows, she's a word that follows / Into the most extreme / Estrangements'.[55]

7

Life and Liturgy

One of the 'extreme estrangements', endured by Péguy as an adult believer, was his lifelong estrangement from the sacraments of the Church and, in particular,

---

51. Ibid. *Oeuvres poétiques complètes*, p. 584; Schindler, p. 56.
52. Ibid.
53. Ibid. *Oeuvres poétiques complètes*, p. 624; Schindler, p. 94.
54. Ibid. *Oeuvres poétiques complètes*, p. 624; Schindler, pp. 94–5.
55. Ibid. *Oeuvres poétiques complètes*, p. 625; Schindler, p. 95.

his estrangement from active reception of the Body of Christ in the Eucharist.[56] In spite, however, of finding himself living at the outer circumference (it seemed) of ecclesial life, Péguy was utterly convinced that his work as a poet sprang from the innermost core of Catholic piety and practice. In an anonymous review of one of his own poems, published towards the end of his life, Péguy went so far as to claim that as a poet he had, *in the matter of faith*, 'descended to the depths where liturgy and theology, that is to say, the spiritual life and the spiritual proposition are as yet undifferentiated'.[57] The reference to 'liturgy' is worth noting. For, paradoxically, it was the very sacramental life of the Church from which, as a man, Péguy had found himself excluded – or had in some way perhaps excluded himself – which, as a poet, he was able so powerfully to evoke and celebrate.

A work written some years later by Péguy's fellow countryman, the Jesuit priest and poet-theologian Pierre Teilhard de Chardin, comes to mind here. Entitled *The Mass on the World*, the work – a long prose-poem in the form of a prayer – was composed by Père de Chardin when, during the course of a scientific expedition, he found himself in a remote part of the Ordos Desert where it was impossible to celebrate Mass in the ordinary way. Accordingly, he attempted to create for himself a kind of alternative Mass, a work or a 'celebration' composed not from ritual signs and actions but instead from a simple pattern of words and images.[58] I draw attention to this work here because it occurs to me that Péguy's own best work as poet is itself a kind of alternative liturgy, a form almost of initiation into the mysteries of the faith, a series of prose-poems and lyrics in which many of the great truths of the Gospel are named and celebrated.

The adjective 'alternative' should not be taken to suggest that the new 'liturgy' of words and images created by Péguy was in any way eccentric or esoteric with regard to faith-tradition. If Péguy was able to descend to the foundations of the Catholic mystery, this was due first and last to his own great dedication to prayer. To his friend Joseph Lotte, he confided: 'Since priests administer the sacraments, they like it to be thought that there is nothing but the Sacraments. They forget to say that there is prayer as well, and that prayer is at least half. Sacraments and prayer are two separate things. The priests control the first, but the second is at our disposal.'[59]

The prayers favoured by Péguy were certain simple prayers repeated over and over again. 'I am one of those Catholics', he remarked, 'who would give the whole of St Thomas Aquinas for the *Stabat*, the *Magnificat*, the *Ave Maria*.'[60] Clearly,

---

56. For a reflection on how Péguy's marriage outside the Church affected his life as a Catholic, see 'Péguy' by Hans Urs von Balthasar, pp. 413–15.

57. « L'Ève de Péguy, » in « Notes et variantes », in *Oeuvres poétiques complètes*, p. 1519.

58. See 'The Mass on the World' (1923), in *Hymn of the Universe* (New York, 1965), pp. 17–37.

59. See Halévy, *Péguy et les Cahiers de la Quizaine*, p. 240.

60. Péguy to Lotte, Conversation: 3 April 1912, *Lettres et entretiens*, pp. 151–2.

much that was potentially wilful or eccentric in Péguy's vision was chastened and purified, over the years, by his incessant, devoted prayer, as well as by his experience of suffering. 'Everything is going along as it should,' he remarked to his friend, 'incredible suffering in the private sphere; immense graces for my production.'[61] And again to Lotte: 'You cannot imagine the abundance of graces. I see very simple things. That flabbergasts priests; the liturgy is full of such things, but they have never seen them. And so they are distrustful. When I am dead they will begin to have confidence in me.'[62]

8
The Poet 'at the Frontier'

At two o'clock in the afternoon of 5 September 1914, Péguy, the leader of a small company of French army soldiers, was killed fighting to defend the city of Paris. It was a brave death and, in fact, the kind of death which Péguy himself had described once in a poem and with such vividness and authority that today the words read almost like a prophecy:

> Happy are they who die for a temporal land,
> When a just war calls, and they obey and go forth,
> Happy are they who die for a handful of earth …
>
> Happy are they who die in their country's defence
> Lying outstretched before God with upturned faces.
> Happy are they who die in those last high places.[63]

Péguy, when he received the mobilization order on Saturday, 1 August 1914, immediately put down his pen, interrupting the work on which he was engaged in mid-sentence. It was a work concerned with what Péguy saw as the very core of the Catholic mystery. And, concerning that core, he wrote in one of the final paragraphs: 'We are entering … an unknown domain, a strange realm, the domain of joy. A hundred times less known, a hundred times more strange than the kingdom of sorrow.'[64]

Deep anguish clearly marked the life of Charles Péguy. But, as soon as we open up his *Collected Poems* and begin to read the work, the realm we enter into is, to our great surprise, not so much a kingdom of sorrow but rather a domain of joy. The sorrow is there, of course, an anguish often evident between the lines and

---

61. Ibid., 27 September 1913, p. 168.
62. Ibid.
63. « Ève », in *Charles Péguy: Oeuvres poétiques complètes*, p. 1026; trans. P. Pakenham, *The Mystery of the Holy Innocents and Other Poems*, p. 58.
64. « Note conjointe sur M. Descartes et la philosophie cartésienne », in *Charles Péguy: Oeuvres en Prose 1909–1914*, p. 1551.

even on occasion in the lines themselves. Nevertheless, far from being maudlin in any way, Péguy's verse is distinguished throughout by a hard flame-like spirit and a virile joy and also by a surprising nonchalance at times in the writing – by a relaxed, colloquial form of discourse like that of an ordinary conversation, one man speaking to another.

The stated aim of the most famous French poet in those years, Stephane Mallarmé, was to purge poetry of all prosaic contamination. And he very nearly succeeded. But Péguy's verse, in contrast, retained much of the vigour and strength of prose. Whereas for years Mallarmé had sought to assimilate poetry to music, Péguy's verse aimed at being a sort of springboard towards active involvement in society, a preparation for even heroic action. It is significant, therefore, that many of the qualities Péguy identifies with 'heroic action' are the very qualities which distinguish his own best work as a poet. In a 1907 essay, he wrote:

> Heroic action is essentially an operation of health, of good humour, of joy, even of gaiety, almost of banter, an act, an operation of ease, of bounty, of readiness, of dexterity, of fecundity; of well-being, of mastery and self-possession; almost of habit, so to speak, and as it were, of usage, of good usage. Of inner fecundity, of strength ... an over-flow of sap and of blood. Without any tension, without any rigidity. Without drudgery. Without sweat.[65]

The seeming nonchalance with which Péguy was capable of making a declaration like 'To set off and to fight at the frontiers is fine'[66] is typical of the man and typical also of Péguy the soldier. '[W]hen a free people is threatened with military invasion', he had written two years earlier, 'the free people needs only to perfectly prepare its national military mobilization [and] ... continue in the greatest peace and ease ... its life of culture and liberty'.[67] An external invasion was obviously a profound threat to a free people. But, for Péguy, there was something 'infinitely more dangerous' than an *external* invasion, and that was what he called, in a significant phrase, 'the invasion which crosses the threshold of *inner* life' (« l'invasion qui entre en dedans, l'invasion de la vie intériere »).[68] The seemingly endless pages of Péguy's prose and verse can be considered as nothing less than a passionate defence of that life and also an articulation of it. And that is the reason why, in almost all his verse, prayer occupies such an important place.

---

65. « De la situation faite au parti intellectuel dans le monde moderne devant les accidents de la gloire temporelle » (1907), in *Oeuvres en prose de Charles Péguy: 1898–1908*, p. 1198. See *Charles Péguy: Men and Saints, Prose and Poetry*, trans. J. Green (New York, 1943), p. 33.
66. Cited in Halévy, *Péguy et les Cahiers de la Quizaine*, p. 211.
67. «Louis de Gonzaque, » (1905), in *Oeuvres en prose de Charles Péguy: 1898–1908*, pp. 944–5. See *Charles Péguy: Men and Saints*, p. 29.
68. Ibid., p. 945; *Charles Péguy: Men and Saints*, pp. 28–9.

Conclusion

In the end, it is impossible to separate Péguy the poet from Péguy the prophet or indeed from Péguy the soldier. What significance he has, as man and author, cannot be perceived within the context of literature alone – within the pages of his *Oeuvres poétiques complètes* – isolated from the witness of his extraordinary life. Looking back on his involvement in the Dreyfus conflict (he was a convinced and passionate Dreyfusard), Péguy remarked – and the statement is one that could be used as an epigraph to introduce his entire biography: 'We achieved an existence full of care and preoccupation, full of mortal anguish and anxiety for the eternal salvation of our race. Deep down within us we were men of eternal salvation, and our adversaries were men of temporal salvation.'[69]

The cost, of course, must have been enormous to Péguy, first of all as a married man and father but also as a writer. It was, however, a price that he was more than willing to pay, regarding the burden as both a privileged and necessary defence of the 'inner life'. He wrote: 'All of us stand in the breach today. We are all stationed at the frontier. The frontier is everywhere.'[70]

According to the philosopher Henri Bergson, Péguy possessed the marvellous gift of somehow penetrating to the very core of a person's mind: 'He knew my most secret thought, such as I had never expressed it.'[71] I think something of that penetrating gaze still survives today in Péguy's prose and poetry. One may well decide, at a certain moment, to take up Péguy's verse, and scrutinize it at some length, as in a chapter such as this. But soon one begins to realize, and even in the act of scrutiny itself, that while we readers are casting a critical eye at the work, and a critical eye at the man, that man, the stubborn celebrant of hope, the defeated, undefeated guardian and prophet of the 'inner life', that man of enormous sorrow and of enormous joy, is scrutinizing us and piercing us with his gaze.

---

69. « Notre jeunesse, » (1910), in *Charles Péguy: Oeuvres en prose complètes*, Vol. III (Paris, 1992), p. 152.

70. « Un nouveau théologien, M. Fernand Laudet, » (1911), in *Charles Péguy: Oeuvres en prose complètes*, p. 464.

71. Cited in Yvonne Servais, *The Pursuit of Salvation* (Cork, 1953), p. 294.

Chapter 4

'BEAUTY, MY ENEMY': PASSION AND PIETY AT WAR IN THE POETRY OF MICHELANGELO

> I want to want, Lord, what I do not want:
> between your divine fire and my own heart
> lies a veil of ice which quenches
> the fire and makes my page a liar.[1]

These lines comprise the first stanza of a work which, in terms of both mood and content, is characteristic of a number of Michelangelo's greatest poems. That the Florentine genius, apart from his work as painter and sculptor, was also a poet may come as a surprise to some readers. But Michelangelo was, in fact, the author of more than 300 sonnets, madrigals and other verses. To have taken the trouble, in one lifetime, to compose so many works of this kind would seem to indicate a wholehearted dedication to the art of poetry. But how seriously, in practice, did Michelangelo take the writing of verse? Is there evidence anywhere in his work of a talent comparable to that unique genius he possessed as painter and sculptor?

In the field of poetry what most distinguishes Michelangelo's work is its stark confessional power. The poems not only lay bare the human heart behind the life and work of the great artist, but also expose, and with impressive candour, a *nakedness of soul* akin to the great nude figures of saints and sinners which, over a lifetime, Michelangelo created in paint and stone. Readers, not surprisingly, from different disciplines have been drawn to these fascinating verses, mining them for information, both about the man and about the age in which he lived. But the poetry itself – the quality of the verse – how should we regard it? Can we say that the lyrics stand on their own as authoritative works of literature? Or is their importance due simply to their confessional power and to the unique information they provide about Michelangelo the man?

Beauty is the theme which dominates the poetry of Michelangelo – beauty as possessed in particular by certain individuals – the sheer overwhelming power of beauty

---

1. Sonnet G 87, *Michelangelo: Rime e lettere*, ed. Paola Mastrocola (Rome, 2015), p. 149. Hereafter: *Rime*.

to attract and hold in thrall. Along with this susceptibility to beauty, with its all risks and enchantments, Michelangelo was obsessed by the salvific hope of attaining, in both this life and the next, union with divine, immortal beauty. So the question arises: did his enchantment with immediate, palpable beauty serve, in the end, to draw him out of himself towards God, or did it succeed only in distracting him from his divine aim?

In the poetry of Michelangelo, no question is of more fundamental importance, and none more fascinating to observe being answered by the poet. As year follows year, and as his perspective on life and on love changes, the nature of that answer also changes, presenting to us, at one stage, a vision of love that astonishes, and at another, a vision that saddens. But, in the end, what is achieved by Michelangelo, as poet, is a language unlike any other of his time, a discourse able to combine great emotional honesty with a uniquely bold and engaging intellectual passion.

The following five headings represent the different sections of the present chapter: (1) Michelangelo, Poet, (2) Beauty and the Flames of Enchantment, (3) Beauty and the Path to God, (4) The Drama of Enchantment and Disillusion and (5) Michelangelo's Last Testament.

1
Michelangelo, Poet
'The Soul Overflows Its Hidden Springs'

The first response to Michelangelo's achievement in verse was its reception by those friends and literary acquaintances fortunate enough to be sent drafts of the poems. And the response was decidedly favourable. He was celebrated by his immediate contemporaries not only as a great sculptor and painter but also as a poet. 'This excellent artist', declared the Florentine Academy after the artist's death, 'has left to the world the fruits not only of his divine hands, but also of his penetrating intellect, that is, compositions full of gravity and of intelligence ... he no less merits his place among the poets than he has merited the chief place among artists'.[2] *A place among the poets.* Madrigals by Michelangelo were set to music during the artist's lifetime and, in 1546, when Benedetto Varchi delivered lectures on artistic theory in Florence, the exemplary nature of Michelangelo's work as poet was publicly acknowledged.

Such a positive response to the poems, however, was not always maintained in the years following the death of Michelangelo on 18 February 1564. The first printed edition of the poems – the *Rime* – appeared in 1623, edited by the artist's grand-nephew, Michelangelo the Younger. This edition was unfortunate from several points of view. The young Buonarroti, out of a confused wish to protect his grand-uncle from both doctrinal and literary criticism, took the liberty of

---

2. *Esequie del Divino Michelangelo Buonarroti*, Florence, 1564, D2. Facsimile edition by R. and M. Wittkower as *The Divine Michelangelo: The Florentine Academy's Homage on His Death in 1564* (London, 1964), p. 100; cited in A.J. Smith, *The Metaphysics of Love: Studies in Renaissance Love Poetry from Dante to Milton* (Cambridge, 1983), p. 152.

completing lyrics, which were unfinished, and of changing, in other unacceptable ways, several of the sonnets and madrigals. This bowdlerized version of the work was, unhappily, the version which survived in all editions of the *Rime* up to the beginning of the nineteenth century.

Eventually when the poems were restored to their original form, far from making a great and immediate impression, to many readers the work seemed awkward and obscure: awkward, that is, in terms of style and obscure in terms of content. But this very 'awkwardness' in the work – the many rough edges and irregularities – came to be regarded by readers in the twentieth century as an impressive form of stylistic liberation, a poetry of risk and honesty with all the stops and starts of a live, individual voice. Eugenio Montale was so impressed, for example, by the rugged technique – the 'rocky' voice – of Michelangelo that he described it as 'perhaps unparalleled throughout the ages'.[3] In similar vein, centuries earlier, one of Michelangelo's contemporaries, the poet Francesco Berni, comparing Michelangelo's work with that of the more ornate and polished poets of his generation, declared: '*e dice cose, e voi dite parole*' – 'he says things and you speak words!'[4]

What Michelangelo achieved in verse was without question something unique. But his talent as a poet, no matter how striking, cannot be said to rank with his mastery of the other two arts to which he was devoted – his genius, that is, as painter and sculptor. Nevertheless, strong and impressive elements of that genius survive in the poems and even in the way the poems were made. His hammered lines, for example, are unmistakably those of a sculptor. Under the pressure of a great range of emotions and ideas, the lines of the poems – hewn, half-hewn – can sometimes give the impression of being carved not out of words but out of stone. The thoughts and feelings possessing Michelangelo, on these occasions, can be so strong, and so unexpected, they place a huge strain on the forms of verse he has inherited. As a result, like the 'prisoners' we see today in the *Galleria dell'Accademia* in Florence, struggling to free themselves from the rock in which they are encased, the poet in Michelangelo wrestles with both the genius and the limitations of language, striving in every way possible to liberate his own voice.

That 'voice' gives expression again and again to emotions of profound enchantment and obsessive desire. But such emotions are not the feelings expressed in what is probably the most impressive of Michelangelo's early poems. This lyric, sonnet G 5, was composed when the artist was engaged in painting the Sistine Chapel in Rome.[5] Once made aware of that context, one would expect, perhaps,

---

3. Eugenio Montale, *Michelangelo poeta* (Bologna, 1976); cited in James M. Saslow, *The Poetry of Michelangelo: An Annotated Translation* (Yale, 1991), p. 3.

4. Statement made by Francesco Berni in his poem '*Padre a me più che gli altri reverendo*'; cited in Christopher Ryan, *The Poetry of Michelangelo* (London, 1998), p. 4. Among those who translated Michelangelo into English are the following authors: Wordsworth, Longfellow, Emerson and Santayana.

5. Sonnet G 5, *Rime*, pp. 70–1.

to find stanzas expressive of a profound spiritual or artistic concentration. But, here, Michelangelo's dominant emotion is one of sheer exasperation. Painting the ceiling, he finds he has to assume unusually awkward positions. Not only, therefore, is he constrained to suffer paint dripping constantly down on top of his face, he also has to twist his body this way and that in order to achieve his desired aim.

All through his life, Michelangelo regarded himself as a sculptor not as a painter. His choice, therefore, would have been to work with stone not with paint. What, however, the Pope most urgently desired at this time was the adornment of the Sistine vault, and to that papal request Michelangelo felt constrained to yield. In a letter to his friend, Giovanni da Pistoia, the frustrated artist vented his feelings in verse. What's more, on the very page on which he wrote the poem, he drew a comic sketch of himself working on the vault. The poem itself, start to finish, is an explosion of wit and spleen.

> Already I've grown a goitre
>   from this task
> as water swells cats in Lombardy
>   or such-like places,
> forcing my belly to hang
>   under my chin.
> My beard points to the sky,
>   I feel my head
> against my hump, my chest out
>   like a harpy's.
> And, all this while, dripping
>   down on top of me,
> the brush is making of my face
>   a coloured pavement.
> My loins have entered my guts,
>   my arse I've turned into
> a croup as counter-weight,
>   and my feet, both
> out of sight, are hanging aimlessly.
>   In front of me, my hide
> is being stretched, forming a knot
>   as it wrinkles up behind;
> I'm bent now like a Syrian bow.
>   What rises in my brain,
> my own judgment, has become
>   wayward and strange,
> and no wonder: through a twisted
>   blow-gun, a man
> shoots awry. So, right now,
>   Giovanni, defend my
> dead painting and my honour.

> This is no place
> for me, and I'm no painter![6]

Michelangelo's apparent refusal here to take his work as a painter seriously is remarkable, especially when one considers that he is, at this time, engaged in painting one of the greatest masterpieces in the history of art. As to the question of what particular merit, if any, he might himself possess as a poet, Michelangelo is equally harsh in his judgement. His poems, he writes, are 'old things fit for the fire, not for witnesses'.[7] And, in another place, writing to a friend, we find him no less brusque in the way he dismisses his talent, insisting that writing poems is not his profession and that, in fact, work of this kind he finds 'irksome'.[8]

Such declarations, however, should not be taken at face value. The great artist had actually planned, at one point, to publish over a hundred of his poems.[9] Judging by the work which has survived, Michelangelo began writing poetry, it seems, in his late twenties. Many years later, at the age of eighty, we find him still composing verses. His career as poet can be divided, more or less neatly, into four phases:

1. From the period 1503 to 1523, twenty poems have survived. During this time, Michelangelo came to enjoy huge recognition as sculptor and painter. From 1508 to 1512 (aged thirty-three to thirty-seven), he was engaged in painting the Sistine vault in the Vatican.
2. In contrast to the first phase when, on average, he wrote about only one poem a year, during the years 1524 to 1532, his output increased to about four poems a year. 'Most poems from this period are about love and when addressed to an identifiable character, that character is a woman.'[10]
3. The years 1532 to 1548 mark the period of Michelangelo's greatest activity as a poet. More than two hundred verses were composed. In the year 1534, he was invited to return to the Sistine Chapel and begin painting the *Last Judgment*. He was now living permanently in Rome. Two great friendships in these years (friendship, first, with the young Tommaso de' Cavalieri and then with Vittoria Colonna) inspired some of his greatest work.

---

6. Ibid. Although most of Michelangelo's poetry is distinguished by a great seriousness, there is also an unmistakable element of the burlesque in his work. See 'Humour, Transgressions, Ambivalences', Chapter One in Glauco Cambon's *Michelangelo's Poetry* (Princeton, NJ, 1985), pp. 3–40.

7. A disparaging comment by Michelangelo on the draft of one of his own poems (in two parts) sent in 1542 to his friend Luigi del Riccio. See *Il Carteggio di Michelangelo*, no. CMXCIX; cited in Saslow, *The Poetry of Michelangelo*, p. 3.

8. A statement by Michelangelo recorded in a letter by Giorgio Vasari. See Saslow, *The Poetry of Michelangelo*, p. 4.

9. That plan, however, came to nothing owing to the death of Luigi del Riccio, his closest literary adviser.

10. Saslow, *The Poetry of Michelangelo*, p. 14. For much of the information about the different phases of Michelangelo's output as a poet, I am indebted to Saslow, pp. 11–22.

4. 1548–60: A mere twenty-three poems survive from this period. Michelangelo was now in his seventies and no longer able to work with anything like the same energy as before. No poems have survived from the last four years of his life. He died on 18 February 1564.

Already, when halfway through his career as an artist, Michelangelo became a compulsive writer of verses. He was forever engaged, it would seem, in a fury of scribbling: writing poems on the backs of letters, on sheets of half-finished drawings and cartoons, on tails of bills and on any odd scraps of paper that came to hand. All through his life, it's true, he regarded himself as a sculptor – that, first and last – but he was also, astonishingly, and by any standards of creativity, a painter, an architect and a poet of genius.

2
'Fire's My Fate'
Beauty and the Flames of Enchantment

Michelangelo's susceptibility to what he calls 'prodigious beauty'[11] is everywhere evident in the work he created in colour and stone. According to Bernard Berenson,

> Michelangelo joined an ideal of beauty and force, a vision of glorious but possible humanity, which, again, has never had its like in modern times. Manliness, robustness, effectiveness, the fulfilment of our dream of a great soul inhabiting a beautiful body, we shall encounter nowhere else so frequently as among the figures in the Sistine Chapel.[12]

It was not only physical beauty, however, to which Michelangelo was susceptible. Once, in conversation with a friend, he remarked: 'Whenever I see someone who has some virtue, who shows some ingeniousness, who can do or say something more aptly than the others, I am compelled to fall in love with him, and I give myself in thraldom to him so utterly, that I am no longer mine, but his own entirely.'[13] This capacity to be possessed by beauty – now of one kind, now another – helps explain Michelangelo's unique power as an artist. But this gift, this rare vulnerability, came at a price.

It was, by all accounts, as much a cause of anguish as of joy, and it marked him from the beginning to the end of his life. Already, well into his sixties, we find him admitting openly: 'I burn for a lovely face.'[14] And, in one of his earliest poems, stunned by the beauty of a particular individual, and by the sudden and complete loss of control over his own feelings, his own thoughts, he exclaims:

11. Sonnet G 260, *Rime*, p. 266.
12. Bernard Berenson, *The Florentine Painters of the Renaissance* (New York, 1895), p. 89.
13. Words of Michelangelo reported by Donato Giannotti in the *Dialogi*; cited in Cambon, *Michelangelo's Poetry*, p. 42.
14. Madrigal G 144, *Michelangelo: Rime*, p. 190.

> How can it be that I am no longer mine?
> O God, O God, O God!
> Who has taken me from myself
> that she might be closer to me, or have
> more power over me than I myself?[15]

This kind of possession, although it clearly alarms the poet, is also something to which, at one level, he aspires and feels drawn. That's the paradox. Speaking, years later, of his love for his great friend and fellow poet, the Roman aristocrat Vittoria Colonna, he wrote, 'I was taken by her away from myself.'[16] In the same poem, however, a few lines later, addressing Vittoria directly, he makes this brief, urgent appeal: 'See to it that I do not return to myself.'[17] Under the sway of a strong, uplifting love, old patterns of control are lost. And yet, paradoxically, this loss becomes gain. The true self of the poet emerges more completely alive than ever before. 'I am more my own, when yours, than if I were mine',[18] he exclaims in another poem.

By far the most forthright and extravagant declaration Michelangelo made of this kind was in relation to a young man, another Roman aristocrat, called Tommaso de' Cavalieri. Michelangelo addresses Tommaso, in one of his sonnets, with language of such total *identification*, it would seem that, having lost all control, he is now given over utterly and completely in thraldom to his friend:

> Within your will alone is my desire,
> within your heart are my thoughts made,
> within your breath my words are formed.[19]

This tribute in words is reminiscent of the kind of language a creative artist might have used, centuries ago, when addressing in joyous homage a muse or a god.[20] It highlights the extraordinary impact made on Michelangelo by the younger man. Shaken to the core by what he calls the 'infinite beauty'[21] and 'many charms, unique and singular'[22] of Tommaso, Michelangelo declares:

---

15. Madrigal G 8, *Rime*, pp. 73–4. It's not clear in the poem if the individual referred to is man or woman.
16. Madrigal G 235, *Rime*, p. 244.
17. Ibid., p. 245.
18. Poem G 108 (apparently complete), *Rime*, p. 167.
19. Sonnet G 89, *Rime*, p. 151.
20. The astonishing declaration, 'Within your will alone is my desire' (*nel voler vostro è sol la voglia mia*), recalls words spoken by Beatrice to Dante in Canto III of the *Paradiso*: 'In His will is our peace' (*E'n la sua voluntade è nostra pace*).
21. Sonnet G 80, *Rime*, p. 140.
22. Ibid., p. 139.

> What will become of me? With you
> [this close] what guide or escort
> can prove of use or value, if near,
> you burn me and, by leaving, slay me?[23]

The image of 'burning', used to describe the impact of a crazed, possessive love, recurs in many of the poems and madrigals composed by Michelangelo throughout his long career. In an early sonnet, for example, he delivers the following sharp warning: 'Lovers, flee from Love, flee from the fire. / Its burning is fierce and its wound is fatal.'[24] This kind of flame, although it burns and destroys, is the source, he admits elsewhere, of his own ever-renewed creativity. In a poem addressed to Vittoria Colonna, he writes: 'If, in this way, the fire, drawn forth from me, / and playing secretly within me, dissolves me, / then burnt and extinguished, I can have further life.'[25] And elsewhere, in similar vein, he writes: 'My only food is what flares up and burns, / and what others die from I need to live.'[26]

Michelangelo's willing/unwilling surrender to the flames of enchantment and the quite extraordinary flourishing of his own creative genius are acknowledged here as inextricably linked. It comes as no surprise, therefore, at the close of another sonnet, to hear him openly declare that his own inescapable destiny is to *burn*. Or, as one translation puts it: 'fire's my fate'.[27] This particular sonnet – a work addressed to Tommaso de' Cavalieri – begins as follows:

> With a heart of sulphur and flesh of tow,
> dry wood for bones, and having a soul
> with no direction, none, and no control
> over desire, a slave to all excess,
> all loveliness, and blind to reason, weak
> and lame in a world of noose and snare
> ... it's no surprise a man will burst
> into flame at the first fire encountered.[28]

There can be no doubt that, at a certain moment in the life of Michelangelo, Tommaso de' Cavalieri was that 'first fire'. The contemporaries of the two men, learning of the impassioned verses, or actually reading them in manuscript

---

23. Ibid., p. 140.
24. Sonnet G 27 (incomplete), *Rime*, p. 91.
25. Sonnet G 63, p. 122.
26. Poem G 73, *Rime*, p. 134.
27. Sonnet G 97. See Frederick Nims, *The Complete Poems of Michelangelo* (Chicago, 1998), p. 72.
28. Sonnet G 97, *Rime*, pp. 156-7. Two brief phrases in this translation are from a version by Frederick Nims: 'with no direction, none, and no control' and 'noose and snare', the latter a colloquial rendering of Michelangelo's 'birdlime and snares'. See Nims, *Complete Poems of Michelangelo*, p. 72.

form, quickly came to realize this was no ordinary friendship. Giorgio Vasari, Michelangelo's close friend and first biographer, tells us that 'infinitely more than any of the others he loved M. Tommaso de' Cavalieri', adding that the young man was 'a well-born Roman who was intensely interested in the arts'.[29] It was probably in the early summer of 1532 that Michelangelo encountered Tommaso for the first time. By all accounts, the young aristocrat was not only strikingly handsome and endowed with a talent for design he was also, by common consent, notably intelligent and virtuous. Michelangelo, at this time, was fifty-seven years old, Tommaso in his early twenties.

The letters and drafts of letters Michelangelo composed for his friend – not all of which were sent – are candid almost to a fault. And they express a humility so stark at times, they are difficult to interpret and understand. In one letter, describing his new acquaintance as 'the light of our century, unique in the world', he says to Tommaso: 'If I have not the skill to navigate through the waves of the sea of your brilliant mind, you will excuse me and will neither disdain the disparities between me and you, nor desire from me what I do not have.'[30] Unembarrassed by the fire kindled in him by his encounter with the young Roman, Michelangelo speaks of 'the very great, indeed boundless love' he has for him.[31] When, at a later occasion, Tommaso suggested he might have been forgotten by the great artist, not having received a reply to a letter sent earlier, Michelangelo replied at once:

> I know for sure I'll forget your name the day I forget the food on which I live; indeed, I could sooner forget the food I live on, which unhappily nourishes only the body, than forget your name, which nourishes both body and soul, and fills them both with such sweetness that, as long as your name is held in memory, I can feel no annoyance nor fear of death.[32]

A month later, writing to a certain Friar Sebastiano, who had been in contact with Tommaso around that time, Michelangelo asks the friar: 'I beg you, if you see him, to remember me to him a thousand times, and when you write to me, tell me something about him so that I can keep him in memory, for if he slipped from my mind, I am sure I would immediately fall down dead.'[33]

That summer of 1532 found Michelangelo clearly in love, not with a beautiful girl or young woman but with a handsome man. How would he have understood what was happening to him? What name would he have given to the sudden violence of his emotions? And how would contemporary society, his fellow artists, his patrons in the Church, his friends, have viewed this event in his life? These

---

29. Giorgio Vasari, *The Lives of the Most Excellent Painters, Sculptors and Architects*, trans. G. du C. de Vere (New York, 2006), p. 421.
30. Letter G 141. To Tommaso dé Cavalieri, December 1532, *Rime*, p. 468.
31. Letter 143. To Tommaso dé Cavalieri, 28 July, *Rime*, p. 470.
32. Ibid., pp. 470–1.
33. Letter 145. To Sebastiano del Piombo, before August 1533, *Rime*, p. 472.

questions are by no means easy to answer. In the opinion of James M. Saslow, the case of Michelangelo presents almost insuperable challenges when it comes to trying to unravel 'his actions, values, and self-concept regarding sex'.[34]

One problem is that 'the voluminous sources are often frustratingly silent, ambiguous, or misleading'.[35] Added to that, there are the differences 'between the conceptual grid through which Renaissance culture classified and interpreted sexual behaviour and our own modern constructions of sexuality'.[36] Any attempt, therefore, to approach the subject nowadays runs the risk of historical anachronism, of projecting back onto an individual such as Michelangelo our own uniquely modern understanding of same-sex attraction, considering it, in other words, as an 'all-encompassing psychological identity', a view almost totally foreign to the Renaissance mentality.[37] That said, however, what cannot be denied is that, for long periods of his life, Michelangelo found himself overwhelmingly attracted to young men and, most especially, at a certain stage, to Tommaso de' Cavalieri.[38]

The poems Michelangelo dedicated to Cavalieri – those which have survived – number perhaps about twenty or thirty.[39] But that could be a modest estimate. The Italian editor of Michelangelo's poems, E.N. Girardi, has suggested that there might have been as many as forty poems composed for Cavalieri. A number of lyrics were also dedicated by Michelangelo to Vittoria Colonna. The number is smaller than those for Cavalieri, but all are marked by the same language of enchantment. Again and again, in the *Rime*, we hear acknowledged the 'fair eyes' of Vittoria[40] and the 'beautiful eyes' of Tommaso.[41] These declarations apart, however, no other references are made to the *physical* beauty of either Vittoria or Tommaso. These are love poems, it's clear, but love poems of a rather unusual kind.

In one of the poems dedicated to Cavalieri, sonnet G 72, Michelangelo speaks at one point of 'the virtuous fire' he feels burning within him.[42] Then, moments later, as if on impulse, the smitten poet expresses a desire to hold in his arms forever

---

34. James M. Saslow, '"A Veil of Ice between My Heart and the Fire": Michelangelo's Sexual Identity and Early Modern Constructs of Homosexuality', *Genders* 2 (Summer 1988): p. 80.

35. Ibid.

36. Ibid.

37. The word 'almost' is needed here because, as Saslow points out, already during the time of Michelangelo 'elements of the modern conception of homosexuality ... were beginning to emerge'. See 'A Veil of Ice', p. 86.

38. Ibid., p. 79. Worth noting, in this context, is the strength of Michelangelo's affection for two young men in particular: Gherardo Perini and Febo di Poggio. See Martin Gayford, *Michelangelo: His Epic Life* (New York, 2013), pp. 358–9 and pp. 455–6. And see also Saslow, *The Poetry of Michelangelo*, p. 13.

39. Sometimes, based on the manuscript evidence alone, it's difficult to decide the identity of the individual to whom a particular poem is being addressed.

40. Madrigal G 234, p. 243.

41. Sonnet G 89, *Rime*, p. 150.

42. Sonnet G 72, *Rime*, p. 134.

his 'sweet and longed-for lord'. That is, of course, quite remarkable. But even more striking is the formulation of this desire which has survived in one of the poem's early drafts. There, the poet asks that time would stand still for him so that he might be able to embrace 'the breast and neck of my lord'.[43] Ardour to the point of rapture is expressed in a number of the poems Michelangelo addresses to Vittoria, but nowhere, even among those strong lyrics, can be found anything to compare with the bold, physical character of this extraordinary declaration.[44]

Vittoria was, without question, the woman Michelangelo adored more than any other in his life. Attention will be given later to the character of their relationship. But, at this point, it's worth pausing, for a moment, to consider some of the many madrigals and poems composed by Michelangelo on the subject of feminine beauty – the *power* of that beauty. Most of these verses, apart from work dedicated to Vittoria, are regarded by critics as mere literary exercises, artificial constructs inspired by no particular woman, and containing little or no passion.[45] That these lyrics pale (for the most part) by comparison with the work inspired by Cavalieri and Colonna cannot be denied. But it would be a mistaken prejudice, I believe, to imagine it was mere literature and not the actual beauty of a woman, or of several women, which quickened at least a number of these verses into life. I never fail to be struck by the opening of madrigal G 263: 'A woman's fresh beauty / spurs me on, cuts me loose, and lashes me.'[46]

By far the most playful and sensual of all Michelangelo's poems is one of his earliest works, sonnet G 4. Attention in the poem is focused, from beginning to end, on the beauty of a particular girl, the poet playfully imagining how, with enviable closeness, her garment, her *'vesta'*, is pressing all day long against her breast and how the 'small belt', tied around her waist in a knot, is so happily content with its position it seems to be declaring: 'Here I would like to cling forever!'[47] Even this brief, joyous lyric, I'm sorry to say, is viewed as a mere 'exercise in traditional Petrarchan conceit'.[48] But what Michelangelo is attempting here is something different from his predecessor. Petrarch does speak, it's true, of his beloved's 'beautiful eyes', 'golden hair' and 'gentle smile', but he avoids, as if by instinct, language that's explicitly sensual. Nothing in his verse compares with the innocently carnal language used here by Michelangelo to describe a young girl's beauty.

---

43. Eight autograph drafts of sonnet G 72 survive. See Saslow, *The Poetry of Michelangelo*, p. 181.

44. Worth noting, in this context, is the difference between the presentation drawings Michelangelo gave to Cavalieri and those which he gave, some years later, to Colonna. The drawings for Colonna focus exclusively on religious subjects. Those for Cavalieri, in contrast, although some are open to religious interpretation, depict scenes of naked human bodies in playful, heroic or violent action.

45. See, for example, the view expressed by Robert J. Clements in *The Poetry of Michelangelo* (New York, 1966), p. 206.

46. Madrigal G 263, *Rime*, p. 260.

47. Sonnet G 4, *Rime*, p. 69.

48. See Saslow, *The Poetry of Michelangelo*, p. 69, footnote 5.

In another poem, written a few years later, after repeating a traditional lover's lament ('She whom I love so much feels no love. / How can I go on living?'[49]), Michelangelo makes an observation for which there is no precedent in the courtly love tradition. The issue is the young woman's negative attitude towards herself. This detail suggests that here the poet has a particular girl in mind and a very particular dilemma: 'She does not love herself … / How can I hope that she'll take pity on me / if she does not love herself?'[50] The voice behind the question might almost be that of a contemporary author. And that, I would suggest, is no less true of the question posed at the beginning of sonnet G 42. Here, Michelangelo wants to know if the beauty drawing him to the person concerned is real or merely a projection of his own desires:

> Pray tell me, Love, whether my eyes
> really see the beauty I long for,
> or is it just in me when, looking all around,
> that woman's face I see carved
> everywhere.[51]

The impact of beauty, in this case, is so strong the poet loses all inner composure, and yet he declares he is happy to pay the cost and would not ask for 'a less burning fire'.[52] That image of fire returns once again in one of the most explosive stanzas in Michelangelo's work. Here the lines seem almost to burn on the page:

> There's not a single day
>   slips through my fingers
> when I don't see or hear her
>   in my mind. And nowhere
> is there heat so great, in oven
>   or in furnace, that wouldn't
> grow more fiery with my sighs.
>   At times, when I have her
> near me a little, I give off
>   sparks like red-hot iron
> in a blazing fire. And there's so
>   much I want to say
> that even if she waits on me
>   to speak, I say less
> than I would if I were not
>   in such a hurry![53]

49. Madrigal G 11, *Rime*, p. 78.
50. Ibid.
51. Sonnet G 42, *Rime*, p. 102.
52. Ibid.
53. *Capitolo* G 54, stanza 6, *Rime*, p. 114.

The natural excitement experienced by anyone particularly susceptible to beauty – to *physical* beauty – awakened in Michelangelo, the man, an almost continual state of restlessness and longing, an unease of spirit which must have been hard to bear. But in Michelangelo, the artist, it also bred an extraordinary giftedness, a creative flair, a bold imaginative genius second to none. What Michelangelo was able to achieve in the field of the arts – in sculpture and painting – is epic by any standards. But there was, at the core of his being, always another desire, another criterion for human fulfilment, another ambition which possessed him. It was the salvific hope, the dream of attaining communion with God in this life and the next. How, in actual practice, this desire impacted on his life as a man, on his passionate life and on his work as an artist remains now to be considered.

3
Beauty and the Path to God
'My Eyes Eager for Beautiful Things, My Soul No Less for Its Salvation'

Michelangelo's passionate devotion to art has been much more documented than the question of his own private convictions about God and religion. And that, of course, is understandable. Nevertheless, to ignore completely, or almost completely, the question of what he himself actually believed would be a mistake. For even a brief examination of the subject is able to reveal vital aspects of his commitment as a believer and able also to provide us with key information about the man and the artist, affording us access – *closer* access – to the paradoxical origin of his artistic inspiration: the bright, mysterious link, that is, between his heart's urgent desire for earthly beauty and his soul's longing for salvation.

First, then, an exploration of what religion meant in practice to Michelangelo and, second, a reflection on how, as a *religious* individual, he came to understand and accept his most compelling experiences of enchantment, the impact on his life, in other words, of 'prodigious beauty'.

The Practice of Religion

Michelangelo was an observant and devout Catholic all his life. He attended Mass regularly, going to different churches in Rome such as Dodici Apostoli and Santa Maria sopra Minerva. He had a lifelong devotion to the Blessed Virgin Mary, prayed for souls in Purgatory and gave alms to the poor[54] – all typical practices for a Catholic, signs of a strong and simple faith. But there was a complexity as well, an added intensity of religious emotion, a fraught concern regarding the salvation

---

54. On one occasion, entrusting to his nephew the task of handing over alms to some people in need, he wrote: 'As for the donation to charity, it's enough for me to know that it has been done, and enough to have the receipt from the monastery, and you need make no mention of me at all.' See Letter 217. To Leonardo in Florence. 24 September 1547, *Rime*, p. 545.

of his eternal soul, which had its origin, or part of its origin, in sermons he heard preached by a Dominican friar when he was a young man in Florence. The friar in question was the apocalyptic preacher and visionary, Girolamo Savonarola. It's hard to exaggerate the impact which these vivid, fiery sermons made on the young sculptor.

One of Michelangelo's own brothers, Lionardo, was a Dominican friar.[55] He joined the Order in 1491 just at the time Savonarola was making huge waves in Florence. In 1492 Lionardo was professed as a Dominican. Five years later, however, in the summer of 1497, he visited Michelangelo in Rome having found himself thrown out of the Order. 'I should inform you', Michelangelo wrote to his father, 'that Friar Lionardo returned here to Rome and says he had to flee from Viterbo, and had his [Dominican] habit taken from him'.[56] With money supplied by Michelangelo, Lionardo travelled to Florence to see his father. Eight years later, he is once again back in the Dominican Order, living at Cortona. One scholar, citing the opinion of E.N. Girardi, suggests that the reason Lionardo was expelled from the Order was because, at this time, the friars in Italy had become split into two warring factions, divided over the memory of Savonarola, and Lionardo, like his younger sibling, Michelangelo, had always kept a strong and fond memory of the preacher.[57]

Savonarola's name has, over the centuries, been linked with the infamous 'bonfire of the vanities', that event in Renaissance Florence when followers of the friar preacher publicly burned 'objects such as nude statues ... [and] heretical books'.[58] Savonarola was eventually denounced as a heretic, brutally tortured and executed. At the height of his power, the Dominican had publicly campaigned not only against papal corruption but also against what he regarded as the artistic excesses of Renaissance Florence and, in particular, against the Medici and their leader, Lorenzo the Magnificent. But these very 'excesses' – the bright, unembarrassed humanism of the Medici court, the rapt enthusiasm for Graeco-Roman art and literature, the celebration in paint and stone of the beauty of the naked human body – were all enthusiasms and practices which had helped in the shaping and flourishing of Michelangelo's particular genius. How, then, could he of all people be on the side of bonfires and dark admonitions?

Well, it's most unlikely Michelangelo would ever have approved of genuine works of art being destroyed. What is true, however, is that as a young man he was profoundly affected by the austere, apocalyptic preaching of the Dominican, an

---

55. As a young boy, Lionardo had been entrusted by his father to the care of a well-known teacher in Florence. Tragically, the teacher abused the boy, confessing afterwards that he had committed the crime of sodomy 'often, and often from behind with Lionardo'. At the time this took place, Lionardo was ten years old. See Gaylord, *Michelangelo: His Epic Life*, p. 41.

56. Letter G 2. Michelangelo to his Father, 1 July 1497, *Rime*, p. 310.

57. See Paola Matrocola's reflection on this subject in *Rime*, p. 310, footnote 4.

58. From a diary entry of Luca Landucci (27 February 1498), cited in George Bull, *Michelangelo: A Biography* (London, 1996), p. 31.

impression which remained with him all his life. Among the artists and intellectuals of his day, Michelangelo was not alone in being struck by the Dominican. Three other leading figures of the time, Angelo Poliziano, Pico della Mirandola and Sandro Botticelli, became enthusiastic admirers. There was obviously a lot more to the stern preacher than is generally reported by modern historians. A contemporary, the brother of Botticelli, Simone Filipepi, had this to say about Friar Girolamo: 'To observe him when he was not in the pulpit, he seemed like a little lamb, as indeed he was, full of humility and charity.'[59] As for Botticelli himself, Vasari tells us that, for a period, he 'became such a partisan of the [Savonarola] sect he abandoned painting'.[60] It was even rumoured that he had thrown some of his own paintings onto the bonfire!

The impact of Savonarola on Michelangelo is noted by Condivi in his biography. Solid piety is highlighted, but also Michelangelo's clear love of learning:

> Michelangelo ... with great diligence and attention read the holy scriptures, both the Old Testament and the New, as well as the writings of those who have busied themselves with their study, such as Savonarola for whom he has always had a strong affection, and the memory of whose living voice he still carries in his mind.[61]

That voice, and its message, on one side (the proclamation of a demanding path of negation) and, on the other, the voice of an expansive humanism (the proclamation of a rapturous but transient beauty) were the two voices which called to Michelangelo all his life, pulling him now in one direction, now in another: 'Now on the right foot, now on the left, / shifting back and forth, I search for my salvation.'[62]

*

The religious side of Michelangelo's character finds its greatest expression in his work as sculptor and painter. But his strong, natural piety also comes to the surface in many of the letters which have survived. When he discovered, for example, that his father was seriously ill, he immediately wrote to his brother, Buonarroto, wanting to make sure his father would not lack 'what concerns the needs of the

---

59. See 'Cronica', in *Scelta di prediche e scritti di Fra Girolamo Savonarola* (Florence, 1898), eds. P. Villani and E. Casanova. In similar vein, the Dominican Kenelm Foster writes: 'We imagine Savonarola grim; as fierce as his terrible sermons; but his nature, all the evidence shows, was warmly affectionate and even gentle. He won the Florentines, especially the young and the poor, by so evidently loving them.' See Foster, *God's Tree: Essays on Dante and Other Matters* (London, 1957), p. 125.

60. See Vasari, *Le Vite de' più eccellenti architetti, pittori, e scultori Italiani* (Torino, 1986), p. 477.

61. See Ascanio Condivi, 'Life of Michelangelo Buonarroti', in *Michelangelo: Life, Letters and Poetry*, ed. and trans. George Bull (Oxford, 1987), p. 68.

62. Madrigal G 162, *Rime*, p. 207.

soul and the Sacraments of the Church'.[63] Hoping against hope his father would recover, he wrote, 'I would like to see him in any case before he dies', adding, moments later: 'May God take care of him and us.'[64]

After a gap of years, his brother Giovan Simone also died. Michelangelo had been estranged from this particular sibling, but the death affected him all the same: 'I remind you', he wrote to his nephew Leonardo, 'that he was my brother ... and I cannot but grieve for him, and I wish something might be done for the welfare of his soul, as I have done for the soul of your father'.[65] Michelangelo, hearing that Giovan Simone had not received the Last Rites before death, but had nevertheless expressed sorrow for his sins, remarked encouragingly to Leonardo: 'If that's the case, that's enough for salvation.' Then he went on to say: 'Do whatever good you can for his soul.'[66]

In tribute to his own father's memory, Michelangelo composed a long, unfinished elegy which contains lines eloquent not only of his love for his father but also of his faith in eternal life. One particularly moving section in the work reads:

> In your death I am learning how to die,
> O my dear father, and in thought I see you,
> there where the world rarely lets us pass.
> Some think death's the worst, but it's not,
> not for the one whose final day, by grace,
> rises up to the first eternal day, near to the
> divine throne, where I imagine
> and assume you are, there where I hope
> to see you.[67]

Judging by the evidence of his many letters, Michelangelo, as a Christian believer, had no hesitation in asking people to pray for him. And the words and expressions he uses, on these occasions, are always deeply felt. They are not mere fossils of devotion. Once, when quite seriously ill, and in great pain, he wrote to Leonardo, his nephew: 'I have need of the help of God. So tell Francesca to say prayers, and tell her that if she knew how I had been, she would see she is not without company in her misery.'[68] Then, he adds: '*Pazienza!* Perhaps, with God's help, it will turn out better than I imagine.'[69]

---

63. Letter 85. To his brother Buonarroto, 23 November 1516, p. 85.
64. Ibid.
65. Letter 228. To his nephew Leonardo, 28 January 1548, *Rime*, p. 554.
66. Letter 229. To his nephew Leonardo, 4 February 1548, *Rime*, p. 554.
67. *Capitolo* G 86 (unfinished), stanzas 20–1, *Rime*, p. 148.
68. Letter 240. To his nephew Leonardo, 15 March 1549, *Rime*, p. 565.
69. Ibid.

That note of placing trust in God, especially at a time of trial, is struck again and again. To his father in June 1509, he writes: 'I am unhappy here, not in great health, with a great deal of work, no instructions, and no money. Nevertheless, I have good hope God will help me.'[70] And to his brother, Buonarroto: 'If God helps me, as he always has, I hope by this Lent to have done what I have to do here.'[71] And again: 'Because God has shown such kindness to me I am able to bear what I have to bear.'[72] When circumstances happened to turn around in his favour, he was quick to express gratitude and joy. At the end of January 1507, for example, favoured by a visit to his studio by none other than Pope Julius II, and clearly delighted that the pope was pleased with his work, he wrote to Buonarroto: 'He [the pope] indicated he was happy with what I am doing. Accordingly, we have, it seems to me, most especially to thank God, and so I pray you to do, and pray for me.'[73]

That statement and the preceding affirmations might give the impression Michelangelo was, generally speaking, of a benign and accommodating temper. In fact, however, almost the opposite is the case. As a man, as an artist of genius, he didn't suffer fools and, on occasion, could even intimidate popes. One reigning pontiff, Pope Leo X, famously said of him: 'He is terrible ... one cannot deal with him.'[74] One example of how he could hold his ground in the presence of the powerful is the conversation reported by Condivi between him and Pope Julius. Michelangelo had just finished work on the Sistine Chapel vault. The pope, desiring to make it look even more splendid, wanted part of the ceiling retouched with gold. Lacking this addition, the pope declared, 'It will look poor.' To this statement, Michelangelo, thinking of the humble people depicted on the vault, replied at once: 'Those who are painted here were poor themselves!' And that sharp, telling rejoinder carried the day.[75]

At some point, during the bellicose papacy of Pope Julius, the use, the *abuse*, of religion for the sake of profit and military might so scandalized Michelangelo it prompted him to write a number of lines etched with an almost Dantean ferocity and sense of outrage: 'Here they make helmets and swords from chalices / and sell the blood of Christ by handfuls / ... now in Rome his very flesh is being sold, / and all roads to virtue are closed.'[76] Some years later, he remarked: 'Wealth goes about adorned with gold and jewels.'[77] In contrast, 'Poor and naked and alone goes Truth, / esteemed greatly by humble people.'[78] Michelangelo's words of advice to family and friends could quite often be sharp and critical, but they could also be bearers

---

70. Letter 34. To his father Lodovico, 15 June 1509, *Rime*, p. 349.
71. Letter 6. To his brother Buonarroto, 19 December 1506, *Rime*, p. 318.
72. Letter 62. To his brother Buonarroto, 30 July 1513, *Rime*, p. 377.
73. Letter 8. To Buonarroto, 1 February 1507, *Rime*, p. 321.
74. Pope Leo X, cited in George Bull, *Michelangelo: A Biography* (London, 1995), p. 143.
75. See Condivi, 'Life of Michelangelo Buonarroti', pp. 38–9.
76. Sonnet G 10, *Rime*, pp. 75–6.
77. *Capitolo* G 67, stanza 7, *Rime*, p. 125.
78. Ibid., stanza 12, p. 127.

of real insight and wisdom. 'Such pomp', he noted in a letter to his friend Giorgio Vasari, 'does not please me, because no man should laugh when all the world is crying'.[79] Fearing, on one occasion, that his brother, Buonarroto, was about to be seduced by a suspicious offer of a great deal of money, he wrote: 'Again I tell you, I don't like you to get mixed up with baser men than you are out of avarice; avarice is a truly great sin, and wherever there is such a thing, wherever there is sin, nothing can come to a good end.'[80]

Michelangelo was not unaware of his own failings as a man but, when accused of moral dishonesty or blatant corruption, he felt able to declare: 'Among men – I say nothing of God – I consider myself an upright person (*uomo da bene*) who never deceived anyone.'[81] A mixture of pride and humility characterizes many of the observations he makes about himself in his correspondence. When near to completing work on the great bronze statue of Pope Julius in Bologna, he must have felt enormous pride in his achievement. Its completion was, he declared, 'contrary to the opinion of all Bologna that I would ever get it completed'.[82] His pride, on this occasion, was the most natural thing in the world. But, happily, one added phrase, in the same passage, allows humility also to find its voice. He writes: 'I think the prayers of a few people have helped me, and kept me sane.'[83]

For years the contemporaries of Michelangelo had praised his work in the highest possible terms. But, as he got older, the approval he himself most desired was not of earth but of heaven. Responding to a multitude of compliments heaped upon him by a fellow poet, Niccolò Martelli, he replied: 'If I had heaven in my breast less would be enough', adding: 'I am a poor man of little worth, who keeps labouring in the art God gave me, to prolong my life as far as I can.'[84]

Through Finite to Infinite Beauty

If I had heaven in my breast. It's almost impossible to exaggerate the strength of Michelangelo's desire to attain to God and thereby achieve salvation. James M. Saslow writes: 'As a deeply devout man, Michelangelo sought one goal even higher than the love of earthly individuals: the love of God.'[85] This statement, in so far as it touches on the quality and depth of Michelangelo's orientation towards God, finds support in the religious integrity of his work as painter and sculptor and also in his lifelong dedication to the practice of his faith. But one question still remains. How, in light of this manifest dedication, did Michelangelo understand the extraordinary character of his devotion to his friend, Tommaso

---

79. Letter 282. To Giorgio Vasari, 21 or 28 April 1554, *Rime*, p. 600.
80. Letter 46. To his brother Buonarroto, 10 January 1512, *Rime*, p. 362.
81. Letter 168. To an unknown Monsignor, before 24 November 1542, *Rime*, p. 499.
82. Letter 25. To his brother Buonarroto, 10 November 1507, *Rime*, p. 339.
83. Ibid.
84. Letter 160. To Niccolò Martelli, 20 January 1542, *Rime*, p. 486.
85. Saslow, *The Poetry of Michelangelo*, p. 29.

de' Cavalieri? In both letters and poems, do the clearly extravagant – at times almost idolatrous-sounding pronouncements made by Michelangelo – not indicate signs of a civil war in his thinking between the conflicting claims of human passion and religious piety?

To attempt to answer this question, it will be helpful to look back again at sonnet G 89, the poem in which Michelangelo, addressing Tommaso directly, makes bold to confess: 'Within your will alone is my desire.'[86] In this radiant lyric, at no stage do we hear the note of pious complaint. On the contrary, every line, every sentence in the poem, breathes with the confidence of a man happily caught in the throes of a great enchantment. Although effectively reduced to being a slave to this enchantment, he is, at the same time, a man manifestly at ease, a poet unembarrassed by the bright and fierce paradoxes of love. Scarcely able, at one point, to contain the exuberance of his joyous surrender, he exclaims:

> Depending on your whim, I am pale or red,
> cold in the sun, hot in the freezing fog.[87]

The lines immediately preceding this declaration read:

> I fly up, though lacking feathers, with your wings;
> by your brilliance drawn constantly towards heaven.[88]

Here the word 'heaven' might sound like an arbitrary romantic expression, having no particular meaning other than that of bliss in general. But, for Michelangelo, the word contains an idea far more precise and far more remarkable. Contemplating the '*ingegno*', the unique brilliance of his friend, he finds himself being lifted up, quite literally, to the radiance of another world. That journey of the mind from beauty seen on earth to a beginning vision of *heavenly* beauty is something we find recorded many times in the *Rime*. The insistent focus on the role enchantment plays in this drama betrays the strong influence of a particular form of Christian Neo-Platonism, a philosophy he had imbibed as a young man in Florence at the court of Lorenzo the Magnificent.[89]

Marsilio Ficino, one of the most important proponents of this transcendent philosophy, writes in his *Theologia platonica*:

> The splendour of the highest good shines in individual things, and where it shines more fittingly, there it especially allures him who contemplates it, excites him who looks at it, enraptures and takes possession of him who approaches it

---

86. Sonnet G 89, *Rime*, p. 151.
87. Ibid.
88. Ibid.
89. For an illuminating reflection on Florentine Neo-Platonism, see Smith, *The Metaphysics of Love*, pp. 94–102.

... There it is apparent that the soul is inflamed by the divine splendour, glowing in the beautiful person as in a mirror, and secretly lifted up by it.[90]

Michelangelo, addressing Tommaso in sonnet G 105, declares that, gazing into the eyes of his friend, what he sees is something much greater than mere mortal beauty. He catches a glimpse, in fact, of the eternal Source behind all transient appearance. What is, at first, captivating in terms of 'outward beauty', he goes on to explain, is never enough to satisfy human longing. Created in the image and likeness of God, our soul desires always to transcend mere finitude and contemplate what he calls 'the universal form'.[91] With regard to those individuals who find themselves in the flame of love's enchantment – radiant in the glow of a new intimacy – love's demand is not that they deny that fire but, on the strength of the awakening it brings, allow themselves to be lifted up in contemplation of an *eternal* radiance. For that, at core, Michelangelo believed, is what all of us ultimately desire.

In a brief madrigal, though likely to be composed for Cavalieri, he speaks of the 'brilliant light' of heaven whose splendour can be glimpsed here on earth in things of great beauty but, most of all, in the radiant gaze of one's beloved.

> My eyes, eager for things of beauty,
>   and my soul, no less eager
> for its salvation,
>   have no other means by which
> they may ascend to heaven
>   except by contemplating such
> things. For, from the highest stars,
>   descends a brilliant light
> which draws desire to them, and
>   here is called love.
> The noble heart finds nothing else
>   to make it love and burn
> except a face
>   that, in its eyes, resembles them.[92]

This 'resembling', it should be noted, refers not simply to physical attractiveness, evident in the eyes, but also to *moral* beauty, the sheer goodness of the character of the beloved. In sonnet G 78, referring to what he calls, with unguarded rapture, the 'burning bush' of the eyes of Tommaso, Michelangelo exclaims: 'Your beauty is no mortal thing / but something divine among us, made in heaven above.'[93] What holds

---

90. Marsilio Ficino, '*Theologia platonica*', *Opera Omnia* 1 (1576): p. 306; cited in *The Metaphysics of Love*, p. 96.
91. Sonnet G 105, *Rime*, p. 164.
92. Madrigal G 107, *Rime*, p. 166.
93. Sonnet G 78, *Rime*, p. 138.

Michelangelo's attention so powerfully is not an allure of mere passing interest. It is, instead, as he understands it, something of the eternal beauty of God shining through the startling goodness and attractiveness of his young friend. What this means is that, for Michelangelo, there is, at this stage, no war of any kind between the competing claims of human passion and devout piety. He is fully persuaded, in fact, that the enormous regard he has for Tommaso, far from diminishing his piety, actually increases it. Like almost nothing else in his experience, it lifts his heart and mind to the contemplation of things eternal.

Such a metaphysics of love is not something all of Michelangelo's readers are likely to appreciate. Already, during the lifetime of artist, the purity and nobility of his intentions towards Cavalieri were queried by a small number of his contemporaries. These voices of suspicion prompted Michelangelo to compose for Tommaso one of his most impassioned sonnets.

> I see in your handsome face, my Lord,
>   what, in this life, no words can describe.
> For, though my soul is still enclosed in flesh,
>   already, many times, simply
> by looking at you, gazing on your face,
>   I have encountered God.
>
> And should the foolish, malevolent throng
>   point an accusing finger,
> blaming others for what they themselves feel,
>   no less welcome to me will be
> my intense longing in your regard, my love
>   for you, my faith, my honest desire.
>
> To the attentive eye, beauty seen on earth
>   resembles – more than any other thing –
> that Fount of Mercy from which we all derive.
>   We have no other sign on earth of heaven.
> Those able, therefore, to keep faith with beauty
>   rise up to God and render death sweet.[94]

That Michelangelo's relations with Cavalieri were 'platonic' can hardly be doubted. According to James M. Saslow, 'There is no evidence of sexual activity on Michelangelo's part with either men or women.'[95] His relationship, in particular, with Cavalieri, we are reminded in a recent biography, 'was acted out through poems and images that were far from secret'.[96] Accordingly,

---

94. Sonnet G 83, *Rime*, pp. 141–2.
95. Saslow, *The Poetry of Michelangelo*, p. 17
96. Gayford, *Michelangelo: His Epic Life*, p. 457.

even if there were readers inclined not to credit the contemporary reports of Michelangelo's commitment to celibacy, 'Tommaso's high social position and the relatively public nature of their relationship make it improbable that it was not platonic.'[97]

When, after the death of Michelangelo, the artist's grand-nephew, Michelangelo the Younger, planned an edition of the *Rime*, he was clearly worried that some of the more passionate poems might scandalize new readers. Accordingly, he presumed, on several occasions, to change the genders of the addressees from male to female, an intervention clearly reprehensible. What is curious, however, is that Michelangelo himself, when composing drafts of individual poems, was prepared, on occasion, to do something similar, shifting the original gender of a poem's addressee from male to female and female to male. The draft of sonnet G 259, for example, was originally addressed with manifest affection to '*signor mio*', to Tommaso de' Cavalieri. In the poem's final version, however, the invocation of the male addressee is completely gone, and gone also is the gender-identifying phrase '*signor mio*'. It could be that this indicates some instinctive element of self-protection at work. The great artist, rendered vulnerable by the intensity of his emotions, may just possibly have been thinking of 'the malevolent throng' he refers to in sonnet G 83, those of suspicious mind who would seize every chance to 'point an accusing finger'.

In light of all that has been said up to now, it's impossible to doubt the enormous importance of Tommaso de' Cavalieri in the life of Michelangelo. No other relationship, in his long career, brings so starkly into focus the two most dominant aspects of Michelangelo's character, his susceptibility to beauty and his passion for God. For months on end, after his first encounter with Cavalieri, it seemed almost as if the strength of that enchantment was enough by itself to hold in check any real or potential opposition between the demands of human love and religious piety. Events, however, were soon to prove that, in the dramas of heart and soul, nothing stands still. There would be changes ahead, not least among them a fresh enchantment. The flame of religious conviction and Michelangelo's capacity to be held in thrall by beauty would soon find new and powerful expression. A wholly unexpected chapter was about to open for Michelangelo, one in which the two most notable features of his character would, once again, take centre stage.

4
'What Was Once Sweet Tastes Bitter to Me Now'
The Drama of Enchantment and Disillusion

Around the time Michelangelo began painting the *Last Judgement* fresco in the Sistine Chapel, he met Vittoria Colonna. The year was 1536. Vittoria, fifteen years

---

97. Ibid.

his junior, soon became the individual to whom he was most devoted. A poet in her own right, she became his closest friend and the veritable still point of his busy, tumultuous life. She was, he declared, at one point, the woman 'whom I adore, / the soul and the heart of my fragile life'.[98] One lyric, composed in stunned awareness of what he calls her 'immense graciousness'[99] and her 'exalted' beauty,[100] begins: 'You make me rise, my lady, / so far above myself / that I don't know what to say or to think.'[101]

Throughout this period, it's presumed, Michelangelo kept in contact with Tommaso de' Cavalieri. We know that the two remained close friends right up to the time of Michelangelo's death, Cavalieri being one of the few friends permitted to be in the room when the great man was dying.[102] But Michelangelo's meeting with Vittoria was momentous. From this point on, by all accounts, she became the centre of his world. In Condivi's biography we read: 'In particular, Michelangelo greatly loved the Marchioness of Pescara, with whose divine spirits he fell in love, and by whom in return he was himself loved utterly and tenderly.'[103]

Michelangelo, addressing Vittoria in sonnet G 166, exclaims, 'Let there be no part of me that can't enjoy you!'[104] When she died in 1547, Michelangelo was inconsolable. Condivi writes: 'I remember having heard him say that what grieved him above all else was that when he went to see her as she was passing from this life, he did not kiss her brow or her face but simply her hand.'[105] Condivi adds: 'Through her death, he many times felt despair, acting like a man robbed of his senses.'[106]

Two traditions inform the sonnets and madrigals Michelangelo wrote for Vittoria, one literary, the other philosophical. The first was the courtly love tradition as represented most especially by the poetry of Petrarch, the second, the tradition of Christian Neo-Platonism which had so clearly marked his work as an author up to this point. In one of two sestinas for Vittoria, Michelangelo expounds, in brief, his theory of the journey of the soul, noting how, through the contemplation of beauty – the beauty of painting and sculpture in this case – one is led upward from the mortal sphere to the divine, *dal mortale al divin*:

> At birth, as a trustworthy model
> for my vocation, I was given the gift of beauty,
> the lamp and mirror of both my arts.

---

98. Madrigal G 153, *Rime*, p. 200.
99. Sonnet G 159, *Rime*, p. 204.
100. Madrigal G 156, *Rime*, p. 202.
101. Madrigal G 154, *Rime*, pp. 200–1.
102. Cavalieri got married about thirteen years after he first met Michelangelo. He had two sons. After the death of Michelangelo, he helped bring to completion the designs which Michelangelo had made for the square and buildings on the Capitoline Hill.
103. Ascanio Condivi, 'Life of Michelangelo Buonarroti', p. 67.
104. Sonnet G 166, *Rime*, p. 211.
105. Condivi, 'Life of Michelangelo Buonarroti', p. 67.
106. Ibid.

> Should anyone think otherwise, he's wrong.
> For this alone can raise the eye to that height
> which I'm preparing here to paint and sculpt.[107]

This conviction about the power of art – the *beauty* of art – to effect, by its own grace, a profound elevation of spirit corresponds to Michelangelo's abiding conviction about human beauty and the unique spiritual impact it can have on our lives. But this conviction would soon begin to be undermined, not from sceptical voices on the outside but from the voice of a growing *inner* doubt, a first questioning of his own Neo-Platonic philosophy.

A number of the lyrics, it's true, can still sound supremely confident, but behind the confidence, on occasion, one can detect the cadence of a troubled self-questioning. In sonnet G 260, for example, when Michelangelo declares, 'A violent burning for prodigious beauty / is not always a harsh and deadly fault',[108] one has the impression he is trying to persuade himself of something of which he is, at this point, by no means convinced. What eventually he does get around to admitting to himself is that the great dream of being lifted up to God on the impetuous wings of enchantment, and being carried aloft, therefore, by the intensity of burning desire, is a dream that was in large part illusory. Instead of attaining to the radiant beauty of a spiritual realm, he finds himself still very much on earth, his whole attention fixed on the visible, tangible beauty of the woman he loves. In madrigal G 258, which was written for Vittoria, he makes no attempt to hide his spiritual failure in her regard or, for that matter, to disguise his all too human love:

> Lady, although your human face
> makes manifest here below
>   beauty that is divine, enjoyment
> of that high distant pleasure
>   is so fleeting, I can never stop
> gazing at you here, for to my
>   pilgrim soul every other steep
> or narrow path is hard.
>   Thus I allot my time: the day
> for your eyes, the night
>   for your heart, with no interval
> in which to aspire to heaven.
>   And fate, which holds me
> captive to your radiance, does not
>   permit my ardent desires to rise
> unless there's someone else
>   to draw my mind towards

---

107. Sonnet G 164, *Rime*, pp. 208–9.
108. Sonnet G 260, *Rime*, p. 266.

> heaven, whether by grace or mercy.
> The heart is slow to love
> what the eye can't see.[109]

Many years earlier, Michelangelo, in one of his first lyrics, described how love for a particular individual so possessed him that his path to growth in holiness – his ascent of 'the mountain' – was effectively blocked.[110] Now, a much older man, he begins, with a sinking heart, to suspect that even those whom he has loved with the greatest affection throughout his life may have blocked rather than opened his path to God. In one unfinished sonnet, composed when he was nearly eighty years old, he confesses with sadness:

> Love's fire once used to burn even in cold ice,
> but that burning is cold ice to me now …
> That first love which once offered all time and space
> is, to the tired soul, in its final distress,
> a burdensome weight.[111]

In another sonnet, written a short time earlier, he remarked: 'If a burning desire stops short / at mortal beauty, it did not descend / from heaven … and must be earthly.'[112] At this stage of profound disillusion, Michelangelo would seem to have come to the desolating conclusion that even the affection he had felt, many years earlier, for Tommaso de' Cavalieri, had stopped short 'at mortal beauty'. The enchantment had been so strong, at one point, he found himself admitting: 'It's pointless to spur on my flight, / doubling my speed from my enemy, beauty.'[113] Here the word 'enemy' was not, in fact, intended to be taken literally. It was, instead, in its context, intended as a huge compliment, an ironic, roundabout way of affirming the great attractiveness of his friend. In later years, however, Michelangelo's susceptibility to beauty he would come to regard, especially in the context of his spiritual life, as more an enemy than a friend.[114]

Michelangelo, as he grew older, felt compelled to acknowledge that what was at issue was nothing less than the precarious state of his soul. Beauty was no longer the uniquely helpful aid towards contemplation and holiness. It was, instead,

---

109. Sonnet G 258, *Rime*, p. 264. Elsewhere Michelangelo makes the opposite statement, declaring with confidence that the 'human face' of Vittoria was able to lift him joyfully to the contemplation of heaven. See the unfinished sonnet G 279.
110. Poem G 18, *Rime*, p. 83.
111. Sonnet G 281 (incomplete), *Rime*, p. 282.
112. Sonnet G 276, *Rime*, p. 279.
113. Sonnet G 82, *Rime*, p. 141.
114. Addressing the question of Michelangelo's beginning doubts about the nature of his relationship with Cavalieri, Christopher Ryan refers to madrigals 92 and 93 and to sonnet 97 where Michelangelo was 'beginning to acknowledge to himself … that his love for Cavalieri might be morally dubious'. See Ryan, *The Poetry of Michelangelo*, pp. 118–19.

5
'My Soul Desirous of Its Own Salvation'
Michelangelo's Last Testament

Among the late sonnets of Michelangelo, sonnet G 285 ('*Giunto è gia 'l corso della vita mia*') is regarded by many readers as his most accomplished work. Composed between the years 1552 and 1554, it underwent numerous drafts. The final version was eventually sent by Michelangelo to his famous contemporary, Giorgio Vasari, and Vasari included the work (together with a commentary) in his 1568 edition of *Lives of the Most Eminent Painters*. During the years 1552–4, every fragment of verse, every sonnet, composed by Michelangelo, was of an explicitly religious character. And sonnet 285 was no exception. But, in this poem, although the context is religious, we don't hear or overhear Michelangelo addressing God, as he does in the other verses and meditations. Instead, sonnet 285 allows us to hear the elderly poet engaged in honest dialogue with himself.

> Arrived from across
> a stormy sea in a frail boat, the course
> of my life has at length
> brought me to that common port
> where all must render
> account, and give reasons for every
> deed, miserable or good.
>
> Now I see just how
> loaded with errors was that fond
> imagining of mine,
> that fantasy, which made of art
> an idol and a monarch,
> and which, to our common cost,
> we humans still aspire.
>
> What will
> become now of my amorous
> thoughts,
> once vain and giddy,
> now that two deaths
> draw near, one that menaces,
> the other certain?

---

115. A summary paraphrase of the celebrated statement about beauty made by Dmitri Karamazov in *The Brothers Karamazov*, Part One, Book III, Chapter 3.

> For neither
> painting nor sculpture
> can any longer
> bring the peace I crave. And so, to
> Love Divine I turn
> who, from the Cross, extends
> his arms to save.[116]

When the first draft of this poem was completed, Michelangelo was seventy-seven years old. All through his life he had been haunted by the fragility and brevity of human existence. It's no surprise, therefore, to find the theme of transience occurring over and over again in his poetry. And inevitably, perhaps, with the increasing vulnerability of old age, the thought of death – the immanent possibility of his own death – was clearly overwhelming. Michelangelo finds himself confronted not merely by the threat of a single death but by what he regards as 'two deaths'. The first is, of course, the death of the body, that end which is 'certain' for all of us. But there is, for Michelangelo, another possible death, and that is the potential loss or 'death' of his soul – a loss dependent on how divine judgement at the end will assess the life he has lived in this world, his good and bad deeds.

With regard to divine judgement, descriptions of both dread and hope are commonplace in religious literature. But what is not common, indeed wholly unexpected, is the statement Michelangelo goes on to make in the next stanza:

> Now I see how
> loaded with errors was that fond
> imagining of mine,
> that fantasy, which made of art
> an idol and a monarch,
> and which, to our common cost,
> we humans still aspire.

How to understand this extraordinary confession? Is it possible that the man, who is arguably the greatest painter and sculptor in the history of art, is now turning his back on art itself? Is Michelangelo, against all reason, determined somehow to regard as idolatrous his own amazing talent? Whatever is happening here is happening under the shadow of death. That much is clear. The encroaching shadow, which Michelangelo knows will sooner or later extinguish his life, renders even his most treasured artistic ambitions empty and hollow. 'Art and death', he observed, with sharp wit, in an earlier poem, 'do not go well together'.[117]

---

116. Sonnet G 285, *Rime*, p. 284.

117. Poem G 283, stanzas one and two, p. 283. It has been reported that Michelangelo, towards the end of his life, 'wondered whether he should not have been a Dominican friar, as had his brother, the better to serve God.' See Robert J. Clements, *The Poetry of Michelangelo* (London, 1966), p. 53.

This explosive change of attitude on the part of Michelangelo to aesthetic goals and to his own artistic genius – this manifest crisis occurring towards the very end of his life – brings to mind the great crisis, happening centuries later, which affected the life and work of Leo Tolstoy. The obliteration death and time would bring to even the greatest works of art and literature so haunted the imagination of Tolstoy that he came, in mid-career, to the following grim conclusion: 'The truth', he declared, 'is death'. And then he added: 'As for art and poetry – for a long time I managed to convince myself, under the influence of success and praise, that they were a possible form of activity, even though death would destroy all, both my work and the memory of it. Then I realized that this activity was also a lie.'[118]

Though separated by hundreds of years, there is an unmistakable similarity between these two moments of crisis. But, in Michelangelo's case, the apparent rejection of his own genius, though indeed striking, is perhaps less radical than that of Tolstoy. What Michelangelo wants to recoil from is not his own amazing talent but rather what he now perceives as an unhappy lifetime of slavery to something less than God. Not painting, therefore, not sculpture, but the obsessive, slavish nature of his devotion to these two great arts is what he now considers idolatrous.

In the final lines of the lyric we are afforded a glimpse of the artist, the man of faith, turning his attention with relief to what he has come to recognize as the most worthy object of his devotion, namely the redeeming love of Christ Jesus.

> For neither
> painting nor sculpture
> can any longer
> bring the peace I crave. And so, to
> Love Divine I turn
> who, from the Cross, extends
> his arms to save.[119]

Even in modest English translation some measure of the strength of the original work – the lyric, that is, in its entirety – survives. What is immediately striking is the clarity and symmetry of the poem and also the manifest sincerity of the author's emotion. From the insecurity and fear of the 'stormy sea' at the beginning, and from the menacing threat of death and damnation in the middle, we are led, at the end, into a realm of grace, into a beginning sense of blessing and safe harbour.

In a number of different ways, Michelangelo, in his late poems, evokes something of this state or place of grace. But the brightness that comes with the blessing – the manifest relief – is crossed at times, and indeed significantly dulled, by the shadow of guilt. That guilt, however, in its turn, is again and again transformed into brief, powerful lyrics of repentance.

118. Leo Tolstoy, *Confession*. First distributed in Russia in 1882, published in 1884; cited in Henri Troyat, *Tolstoy*, trans. N. Amphoux (London, 2001), p. 521.
119. Sonnet G 285, *Rime*, p. 284. Here is a literal translation of this final stanza: 'Neither painting nor sculpture can ever again satisfy the soul that has turned to that divine love which, on the cross, opens its arms to receive us.'

> There is no earthly thing more lowly or base
> than what I am, and feel myself to be, without you,
> and thus my weak and tired breath
> asks pardon of you, who are the highest desire.[120]

And again:

> O make me see you, Lord, in every place!
> Then, if I feel burnt by mortal beauty,
> compared to yours, it will be but quenched fire,
> and I'll be aflame in yours as I was before.
>
> To no-one, my dear Lord, but you alone I call on
> and invoke against my blind and futile torment.
> You alone can renew, within and without,
> my will, my judgment, my sluggish, meagre strength.[121]

But why should Michelangelo, at this stage in his life, find himself oppressed by such intense feelings of guilt? One probable explanation is the persistence of what Michelangelo had come to regard, with increasing alarm, as 'vain and perilous affections'.[122] He has in mind here, we may presume, the overwhelming passion he experiences when in the presence of great physical beauty, a passion he now judges to be more carnal than spiritual and, for that reason, 'dangerous'. And there may be a further reason for his alarm. According to James M. Saslow, Michelangelo began, at a certain point in his life, to connect love 'with a sense of sin and fear of vengeance ... concepts more suitable to homosexual passion, which was officially and theologically proscribed'.[123]

Whatever the origin, or the cause, these poems of desperation and raw need, together with the insistent appeal they make to divine grace, are, by common consent, Michelangelo's finest achievement in verse.[124] In the opinion of A.J. Smith, 'The impact of these sonnets is extraordinary. They make up as vehemently pungent a set of devotional poems as we shall find anywhere in Christian history.'[125] With

---

120. Sonnet G 289, stanza one, *Rime*, p. 286.
121. Sonnet G 274, stanzas one and two, *Rime*, p. 278.
122. Sonnet 302 (incomplete), *Rime*, p. 294.
123. Saslow, *The Poetry of Michelangelo*, p. 13.
124. For the names of critics who regard Michelangelo's final poems as his best, see Ryan, *The Poetry of Michelangelo*, p. 288, footnote 11.
125. Smith, *The Metaphysics of Love*, p. 161. Smith, in spite of this strong statement of affirmation, avoids speaking of Michelangelo's poetry as 'mystical'. And that's accurate, I believe. For all their devotional integrity, the poems never attain the passion and depth of an author such as St John of the Cross. For a different opinion, see Sarah Rolfe Prodan, *Michelangelo's Christian Mysticism: Spirituality, Poetry and Art in Sixteenth-Century Italy* (Cambridge, 2014).

that judgement I am happy to concur. The work is indeed remarkable. But, with regard to the guilt that weighs so heavily on Michelangelo in his old age, it's hard not to feel enormous sadness. Faults, minor or major, there may well have been, but scrutinized, day after day, by a conscience as unsparing as that of Michelangelo, it's more than likely that at least some part of the enormous guilt he felt on occasion was, at times, exaggerated.

According to contemporary reports, Michelangelo was inclined to judge himself by almost impossibly high standards. All his life he was known not only as an outstanding artist but also as a sculptor and painter of religious subjects. This would have meant, in practice, an unusually heightened focus on the iconography of the sacred. One effect of that intense focus, it would seem, was to quicken in the artist, especially as he got older, something like holy fear. Once, when talking on the subject of religious art with a small group of friends – among them Vittoria Colonna – he remarked: 'It is not sufficient merely to be a great master in painting and very wise, but I think that it is necessary for the painter to be very good in his mode of life, or even, if such were possible, a saint, so that the Holy Spirit may inspire his intellect.'[126] And again: 'One recognizes the knowledge of a great man in the fear with which he does a thing the more he understands it.'[127]

Brief, poignant confessions of guilt can be found in some of the poems dedicated to Vittoria. In madrigal 161, for example (a work composed for her but addressed, in its final lines, to Christ the Saviour), Michelangelo speaks of 'old, habitual ways of behaving' so deep-rooted he despairs of ever being able to escape their stranglehold.[128] At the close of the poem, however, hope overcomes despair. Addressing Christ directly, he exclaims: 'Lord, in my last hours, / stretch out towards me your merciful arms. / Take me away from myself, and make me pleasing to you.'[129]

In one of the very late sonnets, composed 'on the recto of a sheet whose verso bears a sketch for a *Christ in the Garden* [of Gethsemane]',[130] we hear, together with the note of deep humility and sincere repentance, the note of saving hope:

> Relieved of the body's cumbrous and heavy load,
> and freed from the world, I turn to you,
> dear Lord, as a tired and fragile boat
> turns from the frightful tempest to sweet calm.

---

126. Michelangelo in Francis de Holanda, *Dialogues with Michelangelo* (London, 2006), p. 114. Michelangelo noted further: 'even in the Old Testament God the Father wished that those who only had to ornament and paint the *arca foederis* [Ark of the Covenant] should be masters not merely excellent and great, but also touched by His grace and wisdom', p. 115.
127. Ibid., p. 121.
128. Madrigal G 161, *Rime*, p. 206.
129. Ibid., p. 207.
130. See Saslow, *The Poetry of Michelangelo*, p. 484.

> The thorns, the nails, and both your palms,
> and your kind, humble and merciful face,
> promise to my unhappy soul the grace
> of deep repentance and hope of salvation.
>
> May your holy eyes not look upon my past
> with justice alone, nor likewise your pure ear,
> and may your stern arm not stretch out to it.
>
> May your blood suffice to wash and cleanse my sins,
> and the older I grow, the more may it overflow
> with ever-ready aid and full forgiveness.[131]

Nothing, in the late poems of Michelangelo, is more striking than this act of turning, with sheer desperation and hope, to Christ Jesus. In the poems and madrigals composed earlier, things were different. For a start, there was almost no reference to Christ. Instead, in poem after poem, attainment to God was declared to be possible in this life through the rapt contemplation of human beauty. That steep, ascending path from finite to infinite – the way of contemplative ecstasy – Michelangelo fervently believed would save him from himself and bring him to the peace he craved. In the end, however, it is Christ the divine Saviour; Christ lifted up on the Cross, whose presence transfigures the final sonnets. Kenelm Foster writes:

> [Michelangelo] still clamours for the sight of God ... but he now knows that no human means, no beauty of body or mind will avail him to reach it ... Perhaps it was death above all, Vittoria's death and the imminence of his own, that brought this home to him; one by one the images were failing in which he had thought to find God until none was left but Christ; until at last he saw quite clearly that only God's active love, coming to meet his own, could bring his heart to peace.[132]

---

131. Sonnet G 290, *Rime*, p. 287. For the translation of the final two stanzas, I am indebted to Saslow, *The Poetry of Michelangelo*, p. 484.

132. Kenelm Foster, 'Michelangelo's Failure', *Blackfriars* XLIV, no. 519 (September 1963): p. 363.

Chapter 5

APOCALYPTIC VISIONS: THE POETRY OF NATURE AND THE CROSS

The image of nature which emerges from a great number of the verses composed by Christian poets over the centuries is that of an almost un-fallen world, a world which offers with each new season new promise of freedom and freshness, beauty and delight. But in Christian writing from the time of the Gospels, not all descriptions of nature are of this kind. The vision we find, for example, in the Gospel of St Matthew, evoking the impact on nature of the death of Christ, is at once confounding and apocalyptic: 'The veil of the Temple was torn in two from top to bottom; the earth quaked; the rocks split; the tombs opened' (Mt. 27. 51–52).[1]

Countless poems and hymns have been written regarding the death of Christ but only a relatively small number of them have been directly inspired by this account of apocalyptic disturbance in nature.[2] The verses in question are distinctive works of vision – some of them remarkable. They more than match the audacity of the Matthean vision. Their disparate authors represent not only different countries and cultures but also different historical periods. With the exception of one or two of them, however, these poets and their work have been largely overlooked or forgotten. The primary aim of the present chapter, therefore, is presenting a wide selection of texts from the tradition to bring into focus this quite unique poetry of the Cross.

But before turning to that subject (in the second and third sections of the chapter), there is another strain of Christian verse, also connected with the death of Christ, to which attention should first of all be given. Although only on occasion relying on the language of apocalypse, it is also a visionary form of writing, a poetry which delights in finding images and symbols of the Crucified in the world of nature. Thus, 'Nature and the Form of the Cross' will be the title of the first part of the chapter, 'The Poetry of Apocalypse' the title of the second and 'Dreams and Visions: The English Tradition' the title of the third and final part.

---

1. See also Lk. 23.44 and Rom. 8.22–23.
2. 'Apocalyptic' and 'apocalypse' – the words – depending on the context can have different meanings. As used in this chapter, they refer to an event of catastrophic proportion which has been evoked or described in a visionary form of writing.

1
Nature and the Form of the Cross

A not uncommon theme in poetry across the world is the presence of the divine in all creation. But a new and startling understanding of that 'presence' finds expression in both prose and verse in the early Christian centuries. The Cross – the death of Christ – was viewed by some of the Fathers of the Church as a mystery of such cosmic significance that signs and traces of the Cross, they believed, could be found impressed on all the animate and inanimate things in the universe. Accordingly, writing in the second century about the various elements of nature, St Irenaeus does not hesitate to declare, 'In them God's Son is crucified in so far as he stamps upon them the form of the Cross.'[3]

But what exactly did Irenaeus and the other Fathers of the Church understand by this mystical symbolism, this new and decidedly unusual way of reading the universe? By way of explanation, St Justin Martyr (second century) offers us a number of examples. He writes: 'Look upon anything in the world and ask yourself whether it could be used or even go on existing without this figure of the cross … The earth is not ploughed without the cross. Men could not dig or do any other work upon it without tools that bear this shape.'[4] To our modern way of thinking, this vision of the world as a vast but integrated system of symbols and mysteries can appear so strange, at times, as to be almost unreal. What is impressive, however, is the way these early Christians perceived the interconnection of all things in the universe and how they took such clear delight in finding signs of their Creator and Redeemer in the great and small details of nature. 'In every place, if you look', St Ephrem (fourth century) declares, 'His symbol is there.'[5]

Elsewhere Ephrem, in a passage directly connected with this bold declaration, raises a question, and it is one which confronts believers in every age: 'How is it possible to express God in human language?' Ephrem responds, at first, with a simple repeated refrain: 'Blessed is He who has appeared to our human race under so many metaphors.'[6] But Ephrem also offers a more reasoned, more studied reply to the question:

> We should realize that had He not put on names
> of such things
> it would not have been possible for Him
> to speak with us humans.
> By means of what belongs to us did He draw close to us:

---

3. St Irenaeus, *Epideixis: The Demonstration of the Apostolic Preaching*, 1, 34; cited in Hugo Rahner, *Greek Myths and Christian Mysteries*, trans. B. Battershaw (New York, 1963), p. 50.

4. St Justin Martyr, *Apologia*, 1, 55 (Otto, 1, pp. 150 f); cited in *Greek Myths and Christian Mysteries*, p. 56.

5. *Ephrem the Syrian: Hymns*, trans. K.E. McVey (New York, 1989), p. 41.

6. St Ephrem, Hymn 31 of 'The Cycle on Faith', cited in Sebastian Brock, *The Luminous Eye: The Spiritual World Vision of Saint Ephrem* (Kalamazoo, MI, 1992), p. 60.

> He clothed Himself in our language,
> so that He might clothe us in His mode of life.
> He asked for our form and put this on,
> and then, as a father with His children,
> He spoke with our childish state.[7]

Ephrem, in an earlier hymn touching on the same subject, refers to those elements in the natural world which undergo suffering of one kind or another and which, by virtue of that suffering, become useful to the world. The torments they endure the saint regards as illuminating signs or symbols of Christ's Passion. Although this chosen theme of St Ephrem is of serious import, the links he makes between the details of Christ's Passion and the various elements of nature are, at times, so wholly unexpected and so unusual the work betrays, I would suggest, not only a clear determination of will but also a certain playfulness of imagination. Ephrem writes:

> Cut stone becomes
> by its suffering a bulwark for the human being …
> Wood, by means of its harsh treatment,
> resembles the cross:
> it carries in the sea, it bears on dry land …
> Noble gold is beaten without offense.
> To all those who beat it, it gives its sides
> as a symbol of our Lord.
> Its insult is for honour; its suffering is for glory.
> Iron and a sharp stake
> indeed pierce the pearl like that One who was pierced
> by nails and on the cross.
> It becomes by its suffering an adornment for humankind.
> And who will tell the suffering
> of the grain of wheat?
> Indeed, how many scourgings and sufferings it encounters!
> By its torments it gives life to its tormentors …
> So also, when the bird beats the air
> with its wings as with arms, the back [of the air]
> is subjected to it …
> So also the farmer by means of iron
> rends and cleaves the earth, but she [the earth]
> is not angered by her sufferings.
> The sheep in its shame strips off its garment and cloak
> and gives all of it to its shearers,
> like the Lamb who divided His garments for His crucifiers …
> All these things teach by their symbols:

7. Ibid.

they open by their sufferings the treasure of their riches,
and the suffering of the Son of the Gracious One
is the key of His treasures.[8]

Most readers, I imagine, will not expect this symbolic mode of perceiving the Cross in nature to have survived the centuries.[9] One can, however, still find here and there a few indications of its survival. The first which comes to mind is a work by a minor Irish poet of the early twentieth century, Joseph Mary Plunkett (1887–1916).

I See His Blood upon the Rose

I see his blood upon the rose
And in the stars the glory of his eyes,
His body gleams amid eternal snows,
His tears fall from the skies.

I see his face in every flower;
The thunder and the singing of the birds
Are but his voice – and carven by his power
Rocks are his written words.

All pathways by his feet are worn,
His strong heart stirs the ever-beating sea,
His crown of thorns is twined with every thorn,
His cross is every tree.[10]

The quiet mysticism in these lines lifts what would be, by any standards, modest verse to a level of vision, enabling the words and images of the poem to survive in the mind long after one has first read it.

*

---

8. Hymn 11, in *Ephrem the Syrian: Hymns*, pp. 308–9.

9. Already in the Middle Ages, according to Umberto Eco, the world of nature began to be perceived in a new way: 'It was no longer a "forest of symbols." The cosmos of the early Middle Ages gave way to a universe we could call scientific. Earlier, things had possessed a value not because of what they were but because of what they meant; but at a certain point it was realized that God's creative activity was not an organising of signs but a reifying of forms. Even Gothic figurative art, which was the highest point of the allegorical sensibility, reflected the new climate.... Hitherto, no one had really *observed* a bunch of grapes, because grapes had first and foremost a mystical significance. But now one could see stems and shoots, leaves and flowers, decorating the capitals.' See *Art and Beauty in the Middle Ages*, trans. H. Bredin (London, 1986), p. 64.

10. Joseph Mary Plunkett, 'I See His Blood upon the Rose', in *The Oxford Book of Mystical Verse*, eds. D.H.S. Nicholson and A.H.E. Lee (Oxford, 1917), p. 561.

The second work I want to consider is a kind of prose-poem. Its author is the twentieth-century French mystic and philosopher, Simone Weil. The passage I have in mind, although it also possesses an unmistakable mystical quality, is decidedly different from the fragile lyric of Joseph Mary Plunkett. What, however, the two works do have in common is a focus on the presence of the Crucified in nature. Weil begins by reflecting first on the implications of the separation of God from God, of the Son from the Father, which took place at Golgotha. She writes: 'This infinite distance between God and God, this supreme tearing apart, this agony beyond all others, this marvel of love, is the crucifixion. Nothing can be further from God than that which has been accursed.'[11] Weil then goes on to reflect on how all of creation, the entire universe, has itself been affected by this separation of God from God.

> This tearing apart, over which supreme love places the bond of supreme union, echoes perpetually across the universe in the midst of silence, like two notes, separate yet melting into one, like pure and heart-rending harmony. This is the Word of God. The whole creation is nothing but its vibration. When human music in its greatest purity pierces our soul, this is what we hear through it. When we have learnt to hear the silence, this is what we grasp more distinctly through it.[12]

The whole creation is nothing but its vibration. To my knowledge, no writer, no poet since the early Christian centuries, has attempted to write in such a daring, visionary manner on the subject of Christ's Passion and the natural world. But Weil's impassioned statements represent far more than a mere interest in finding symbols of the Crucified in nature. For years I could think of no work of literature, no poem, to set alongside it. But then, by happy chance, I came upon a short work by the Indian Hindu poet, Rabindranath Tagore. Obviously, Tagore, in his lyric, is no way concerned with the poetry of the Passion. Nevertheless, his words concerning the anguish of 'separation' within nature do appear, on one level at least, to echo the extraordinary pathos and beauty of Weil's intuition.

Gitanjali LXXXVI (Song Offerings)

> It is the pang of separation that spreads throughout the world and gives birth to shapes innumerable in the infinite sky.
> It is this sorrow of separation that gazes in silence all night from star to star and becomes lyric among rustling leaves in rainy darkness of July.
> It is this overspreading pain that deepens into loves and desires, into sufferings and joys in human homes;

---

11. Simone Weil, *Waiting on God*, trans. E. Craufurd (London, 1950), pp. 82–3.
12. Ibid., p. 83.

and this it is that ever melts and flows in songs through my poet's heart.[13]

2
The Poetry of Apocalypse

A gifted preacher of the second century, a man who was as much a poet as a preacher – Melito of Sardis – reflecting on the mystery of Christ's Passion and on the violence of nature's response, exclaimed:

> An unheard-of murder has been committed ... And who has been murdered? ... Who is it? It is painful to tell, and yet still more dreadful not to tell. Listen, therefore, and tremble because of him for whom the earth trembled. The One who hung the earth in space is himself hanged. The One who fixed the heavens in place is himself impaled. The One who made all things fast is made fast on a tree. The One who is the Master of all has been affronted ... O frightful murder! O unheard of injustice! The Master is disfigured, and is not deemed worthy of a garment for his naked body ... For this reason, the stars turned and fled, and the day grew dark in order to hide the naked man hanging on the tree ... Although the people did not tremble, the earth trembled; although the people were not afraid, the very heavens grew frightened.[14]

The impressive homily from which this passage has been taken, the '*Peri Pascha – On Easter*', was lost for centuries but was happily rediscovered in 1940.[15] Other works by Melito, or rather fragments of works, have survived. In one of them, the poet imagines the world of nature stunned into speech by the sight of the God-Man dying on the Cross:

> The earth trembled, and its foundations shook,
> the sun fled, the elements turned backwards,
> the day departed. None of the things of nature
> could bear to see their Lord crucified.
> Creation shuddered and exclaimed in fear:
> 'What kind of extraordinary mystery is this?
> The judge is judged and keeps silent.
> The invisible is seen and is not abashed,
> the incomprehensible is grasped and is not irate,

---

13. Tagore, 'Gitanjali, LXXXIV', in *Collected Poems and Plays of Rabindranath Tagore* (London, 1976), p. 39.
14. Melito of Sardis, 'Peri Pascha', 94–8 (A Homily on the Passover), in *Sur la Pâque et fragments*, ed. O. Perler, Sources Chrétiennes, 123 (Paris, 1966), pp. 116–19.
15. 'Introduction', in *Sur la Pâque et fragments*, pp. 14–15.

> the immensity is contained and does not resist,
> the unsuffering suffers and takes no vengeance,
> the immortal dies and says not a word.
> The celestial is buried and does not react.
> What kind of new mystery is this?'
> All creation is seized with astonishment.[16]

*

Around the time the lost manuscript of Melito was discovered – mid-twentieth century – another manuscript of considerable importance, this time for Irish letters, was discovered. It concerns the work of the eighth-century poet Blathmac mac Con Brettan. In Blathmac's work, as in the work of Melito, we find the different elements of nature responding to the event at Golgotha, keening and lamenting together the death of their divine Lord. Blathmac writes:

> The sun hid its own light;
> It mourned its lord; a sudden darkness
> went over the blue heavens,
> the wild and furious sea roared.
> The whole world was dark;
> the land lay under gloomy trembling;
> at the death of noble Jesus
> great rocks burst asunder.
>
> ... ...
>
> It was clearly fitting
> for the elements of God's creation,
> the beautiful sea, the blue heaven,
> the present earth,
> that they should change their aspect
> when keening their hero.[17]
>
> ... ...
>
> Tame beasts, wild beasts, birds
> had compassion on the Son of the living God,
> and every beast that the ocean covers,
> they all keened him.[18]

At one point in the poem, the impact of the death of Christ on the different elements of nature is evoked with an image so powerful it is almost shocking.

---

16. Melito of Sardis, *Fragment* XIII, 'Les Fragments de Méliton', in *Sur la Pâque et fragments*, p. 239.
17. Blathmac mac Con Brettan, '*Tair* cucom, *a Maire boíd*' (A Devoted Offering to Mary), in *The Poems of Blathmac Son of Cú Brettan*, ed. James Carney (Dublin, 1964), p. 23.
18. Ibid., p. 45.

Christ's blood is described not merely as gushing out from his body, and reddening the wood of the Cross, but also as in some remarkable way colouring the whole of creation. Blathmac writes:

> A stream of blood gushed forth
> (severe excess!)
> so that the bark of every tree was red;
> there was blood on the breasts of the world,
> in the tree-tops of every great forest.[19]

Whether or not the poet intends us to take his words literally is not clear. What is clear is the urgency of his desire to communicate to us – in as strong and as visionary a way as possible – that the event at Golgotha is one that concerns the entire universe, all of nature and all of history.

One other Irish medieval text claims our attention here. It is a work of prose rather than poetry and concerns not simply the reaction of nature to Christ's death but also that of a certain hero-warrior called Conchobhar. According to the legend, Conchobhar was 'one of the two men in Ireland who believed in God before the coming of the faith'.[20] Regarding the death of Christ on the Cross, the story of Conchobhar is one of the most truly bizarre to have survived from the Middle Ages. It is, as a literary work, substantially 'pagan' in origin and conception. Custom at that time, in the very early Christian centuries, permitted the '*fili*', the official bard, to take up numerous wild and wonderful tales from the pre-Christian world, colour them and rework them in light of the Christian revelation.

According to this particular legend, it was when Conchobhar witnessed the reaction of nature to the death of the Son of God that he knew, for the first time, that some appalling catastrophe had taken place.

> A great trembling came on the elements at that time, and heaven and earth shook with the monstrous nature of the deed which was done then – Jesus Christ the Son of the Living God crucified though guiltless. 'What is this?' said Conchobhar to his druid, 'what great evil is being done today?' 'It is true,' said the druid, 'it is a great deed that is done there, Christ Son of the Living God crucified by the Jews.'[21]

Hearing this report Conchobhar went wild with grief and anger. 'A thousand armed men shall fall at my hand in rescuing Christ', he shouted.[22] It was, of course, a not unexpected way for a strong warrior-hero to react. But what ensued then

---

19. Ibid., p. 23.
20. 'The Death of Conchobhar', in *A Celtic Miscellany*, trans. J.H. Jackson (Harmondsworth, 1971), p. 56.
21. Ibid., p. 55.
22. Ibid., p. 56.

was almost as comical as it was tragic (a clear foreshadowing, I would suggest, of the valorous Don Quixote): 'He leaped for his two spears then, and brandished them violently so that they broke in his fist; and he took his sword in his hand next and attacked the forest around him, so that he made an open field of the forest.'[23] Conchobhar, in one of his earlier battles, had been severely wounded. This new exertion proved too much for him. His brains, we are told, sprang from his head, and he died on the spot.

*

The last text I would like to quote in this section is from Romanos the Melodist, a saint and poet who is generally regarded as the finest of all the poets and hymnographers of the Syrio-Greek Middle Ages. In one of his hymns on the Passion, he considers the response of nature to the death of the Messiah. But, rather than imagine nature itself speaking, as other poets of the Passion are inclined to do,[24] he chooses instead to address the elements individually and in his own voice:

> Be today struck with astonishment, O sky!
> Do not venture,
> O radiant sun, to gaze at your Master
> on the wood to which, by his own choice,
> he hangs.
> Let the rocks split apart because, at this instant,
> the Rock of life itself is being
> bruised by nails.
> Let the veil of the temple be torn
> because the body of the Lord is being pierced
> by a criminal lance.
> Let all creation shudder and groan before the
> Passion of its Creator.[25]

One theological idea quite often explored in the writings of Romanos is that not merely Christ's death at Golgotha but also his birth at Bethlehem had begun, in some way, to restore to humanity direct access once again to the joys of paradise which had been lost at the Fall. He writes: 'Bethlehem has opened the gates of Eden; come, let us see. In a secret place we have found delight; come, let us partake

---

23. Ibid.
24. Cosmas of Maiuma, for example, reflecting on the death of the Messiah in one of his *Kanons*, writes: 'The universe saw you, who without hindrance hung the whole earth on the waters, hanging upon Golgotha, and it was filled with wonder and cried out: "There is no one holy but you, O Lord!"' See 'Kanon on Easter Sunday', in *The Penguin Book of Greek Verse*, ed. and trans. C.A. Trypanis (Harmondsworth, 1971), p. 432.
25. Romanos the Melodist, 'La Passion', Prooïmion II, 1, Hymne XXXVI, in *Romanos le Mélode, Hymnes*, Vol. IV, ed. J. Grosdidier De Matons (Paris, 1967), p. 205.

of paradise within the cave. In it has appeared a root never watered, blossoming forth forgiveness.'[26]

At one point in the hymn, Mary, the young mother, speaking of herself as a 'mouth-piece' and representative of the human race, says to her divine child: 'Make everything in your creation to stand aright. For this you shone forth to me and to the Wise Men and to the whole earth.'[27] Mary pleads in a particular way for those 'who were cast from the delight of paradise', but she pleads also on behalf of all the things of creation: 'I pray to you on behalf of the winds, and of the fruits of the earth, and of those who live on it; be reconciled to all, for my sake, of whom you were born a little child, God of all time.'[28]

According to Romanos, in the cave at Bethlehem – in the place of birth – something of the wonder and radiance of Eden has been finally restored. But that same radiance is even more powerfully restored, he believes, in the place of death at Golgotha.[29] There, the Good Thief, condemned to death on the cross, has become, in Romanos's understanding, an initiate of the mystery. For, when 'the eye of his heart' was opened, he saw before him the dark tree of the cross shining like the tree of paradise. It was an extraordinary vision: the tree of death transformed into a 'tree of life'. What had once been lost was now found; death had somehow gained access to life and to 'the delights of Eden'.[30]

3

Dreams and Visions: The English Tradition

Although poems describing disturbance in the elements of nature at the death of the Messiah can often be both vivid and memorable, for imaginative daring none compares with the first notable English poem of the early Middle Ages, *The Dream of the Rood*. The work opens with the poet recalling an extraordinary dream. It concerns the Passion of Christ, a subject often depicted in the poetry and hymnody of the period. What is, however, immediately striking about this particular dream-vision is that the voice which speaks to the poet from the Cross is not that of the Crucified but rather that of the Cross itself, the actual wood on which Christ died. This may appear shocking to the uninitiated, but one expert on the period writes: 'That the gallows speaks is in no sense grotesque … the attribution of personality to inanimate objects was an Anglo-Saxon commonplace.'[31]

---

26. Romanos the Melodist, 'Christmas Hymn', in *The Penguin Book of Greek Verse*, p. 392.
27. Ibid., p. 404.
28. Ibid., p. 403.
29. See Romanos le Mélode, *Hymne* XXXIX, 'Adoration de la Croix', 2, in *Hymnes*, pp. 327–8.
30. Ibid., p. 327.
31. Michael Swanton, ed., *The Dream of the Rood* (Exeter, 1992), p. 66.

The Dream of the Rood is thought in its final form to date from the mid-eighth century. Earlier, in that same century, lines practically identical with those of the poem survive in the form of runic verses on a freestanding stone monument in Scotland called the Ruthwell Cross. Statements such as the following, as bold as they are moving, are etched into the stone:

> I raised up a powerful King,
> the Lord of Heaven. I dared not topple.
> They reviled us both together.
> I was drenched with blood from the man's side.[32]

The author of *The Dream* is unknown, so the question of authorship has effectively been left to conjecture. Two Anglo-Saxon poets, however, are often mentioned by scholars as likely or possible authors: Caedmon and Cynewulf.[33] Caedmon came to prominence in the middle of the seventh century. According to the account of St Bede in his *Ecclesiastical History of the English Nation*, Caedmon was an illiterate who received his gift of songcraft in a dream. Asleep on one particular night in a stable of the monastery (he had been allotted that day the task of looking after the animals), he dreamt that a figure stood close by him and commanded: 'Caedmon, sing some song to me.'[34] Caedmon knew he had no ability of any kind to sing, so he was naturally puzzled. Nevertheless, he asked, 'What shall I sing?' The figure replied: 'Sing the beginning of created things.' At this juncture, according to the report, Caedmon began there and then 'to sing verses to the praise of God', a combination of words and music he had never heard in his life.[35] The one work of Caedmon which has survived, *Caedmon's Hymn*, is regarded as one of the earliest surviving examples of Old English.

As for Cynewulf, the other possible author of *The Dream*, almost nothing is known of his life. Fortunately, however, a number of Cynewulf's poems came to light in a tenth-century codex known as *The Vercelli Book*.[36] In that same codex there was also discovered the single surviving manuscript of *The Dream of the Rood*, a fact which has prompted speculation that Cynewulf and not Caedmon was the work's likely author.

The poem is in three separate sections: first, a report by the poet concerning a vision he had of the glorious Rood which appeared to him one night in an

---

32. See *Stone, Skin and Silver: A Translation of the Dream of the Rood*, eds. R.J. Kelly and C.L. Quinn (Middleton, Cork, 1999), p. 39.

33. For a helpful reflection on the question of authorship, see Swanton, *The Dream of the Rood*, pp. 58–62.

34. The Venerable Bede, *The Ecclesiastical History of the English Nation*, Chapter XXIV, ed. V.D. Scudder (London, 1910), p. 206.

35. Ibid.

36. *The Vercelli Book*, an anthology of Old English prose and verse, was found in the Cathedral Library at Vercelli, northern Italy. It was most probably brought from England by one of the many English pilgrims on the way to Rome.

astonishing dream; second, the Rood's account of its own history, the journey from the forest to Calvary and beyond; third, a new and determined resolution on the part of the visionary poet to seek, for both himself and others, salvation in and through the Cross. Such a manifest seriousness of purpose might well have produced in the end a poem or hymn of merely dogmatic verse. But instead, what has been achieved is a work of great imaginative power, a visionary text formed out of disparate elements and diverse styles of writing, most notably heroic action described in vivid prose but also hortatory preaching, elegy and riddle.

At first, a considerable mystery surrounds 'the wondrous tree' raised aloft in the sky and shining with gemstones. No explicit mention is made of Christ or Calvary. On one level at least, therefore, the work we can say opens as a riddle.[37] So sacred in appearance is the vision, the poet, the dreamer, conscious of his past 'sins' and 'evil deeds', is at first pierced through by a feeling of unworthiness.[38] But, gazing further at the tree bedecked with gold and precious gems, he becomes aware of something else – blood pouring out from under the gold on the right side. This phenomenon awakens in the poet feelings of the deepest awe and fear. What's more, even as he looks, the vision begins to change:

> I observed the urgent portent
> shift its coverings and its hues;
> at times it was soaked with wetness,
> drenched by the coursing of blood,
> at times adorned with treasure.[39]

At a later stage, still rapt in contemplation, the poet becomes aware, against all expectation, that the tree has begun to speak to him, describing first of all how it was cut down in the forest and then carried by strong enemies to 'the hill'. Calvary is still not mentioned by name, but it now becomes clear that 'the hill' is indeed Calvary and the tree none other than the Cross to which Christ is now to be nailed. That wood, even as an instrument of torture, knows that it must yield to the will of its 'brave King' and not fail in its task. The tree becomes the most intimate, privileged witness of the Passion, able to describe, as we discover, how Christ strides towards his death more like a hero than a victim, more in glorious triumph than defeat:

> Then I saw, marching toward me,
> mankind's brave King;
> He came to climb upon me.

---

37. The title 'The Dream of the Rood' did not accompany the poem when it was first written.

38. 'The Dream of the Rood', in *Anglo-Saxon Poetry*, trans. S.A.J. Bradley (London, 1982), p. 160.

39. Ibid.

> I dared not break or bend aside
> against God's will, though the ground itself
> shook at my feet. Fast I stood,
> who falling could have felled them all.
>
> Almighty God ungirded Himself,
>   eager to mount the gallows,
> unafraid in the sight of many:
>   He would set free mankind.[40]

Commentators, reflecting on these lines, often remark on the image of Christ as a young, athletic warrior, an image so unexpected at first reading that it might seem to suggest a vision of the Cross altogether different from that of the Christian Gospels. In one commentary, for example, we read:

> The scene of Christ resolutely running to the Cross differs from the biblical accounts of the Passion, which depict Christ as a tortured and exhausted figure personally carrying his Cross to the place of execution. This shift of emphasis displays the astuteness of the Anglo-Saxon poet to culturally tailor his subject-matter for his audience. Anglo-Saxon society valued strong and brave heroes who were assisted by loyal and worthy thanes.[41]

That in terms of both imagery and atmosphere a resolution of some kind has been achieved between the competing cultures of the period cannot be doubted. But it would be a mistake to suggest that the scene of the Passion, as we find it presented in the poem, differs *radically* from the biblical accounts. Rosemary Woolf has tellingly observed: 'The medieval picture of Christ exhausted and struggling beneath the weight of the Cross is so well known and so moving that it is easy to forget nowadays that it is not a literal illustration of the gospel narrative but a medieval interpretation.'[42] Also, the Christ who appears in the Gospel of St John is not, by any standards, a passive victim. In Jn 10.17–18, for example, we hear Christ declare to his disciples: 'No one takes my life from me. I lay it down of my own accord.'

One vivid image in *The Dream* is of Christ, at the foot of the Cross, stripping himself of his own garments. This action is thought by some scholars to differ from the account in the Gospels where they presume the soldiers stripped Christ of his garments before he was nailed to the wood. But, as it happens, the stripping of Christ at this point in the story of the Passion is not mentioned in any of the

---

40. 'The Dream of the Rood', in *The Earliest English Poems*, trans. Michael Alexander (Harmondsworth, 1966), p. 107.
41. *Stone, Skin and Silver*, pp. 17–18.
42. Rosemary Woolf, *Art and Doctrine: Essays on Medieval Literature*, ed. H. O'Donoghue (London, 1986), p. 38.

four Gospels.[43] The notion of a young hero ungirding himself rather than being forcibly stripped is one which would naturally have appealed to the Anglo-Saxon mentality of the time, and this may well be the reason for its inclusion here. But the ungirding image in fact closely follows a particular Patristic tradition. In St Ambrose of Milan's commentary on Luke's Gospel, we find a description of 'Christ as kingly victor removing His clothes: *Pulchre ascensurus crucem regalia vestimenta deposuit* (Very fitting when about to ascend the Cross, He laid down His royal vestments)'.[44] That said, however, the local Anglo-Saxon element remains strong throughout. In the staunch character of the Rood whose great height the King now eagerly ascends, there is unquestionably something of the loyal and worthy thane:

> I shook when his arms embraced me
> but I durst not bow to ground,
> Stoop to Earth's surface.
> Stand fast I must.
>
> I was reared up, a rood.
> I raised the great King,
> Liege lord of the heavens.[45]

The Dream of the Rood is at last approaching its climax, and the name of Christ is about to be revealed for the first time. The extraordinary device in the poem of allowing inanimate wood to speak matches the extraordinary nature of the event itself. There are no words one can find to describe the brilliance and pathos of the effect achieved.

> Wry weirds a-many I underwent
> up on that hill-top; saw the Lord of Hosts
> stretched out stark. Darkness shrouded
> the King's corpse. Clouds wrapped
> its clear shining. A shade went out
> wan under cloud-pall. All creation wept,
> keened the King's death. Christ was on the Cross.[46]

---

43. There was an earlier stripping by the soldiers recorded in the Gospel of Matthew after which Christ was given a purple robe (Mt. 27.28).

44. St Ambrose of Milan, *Commentary on St Luke's Gospel*, cited by Woolf in *Art and Doctrine*, p. 40. Woolf speaks of the probable influence on the *Dream of the Rood* of liturgical hymns such as *Vexilla regis prodeunt* and *Pange lingua* by Venantius Fortunatus (sixth century). On this question of influence, see also J.A.W. Bennett, *The Poetry of the Passion: Studies in Twelve Centuries of English Verse* (Oxford, 1982), pp. 11–14.

45. 'The Dream of the Rood', p. 107.

46. Ibid., p. 108.

All creation wept. But the Rood is itself part of that creation. It is a witness, and yet it is something more, a passive yet active participant in the agony of the King.

> They drove me through with dark nails:
>   on me are the deep wounds manifest,
> Wide-mouthed hate-dents.
>   I durst not harm any of them.
> How they mocked at us both!
>   I was all moist with blood
> Sprung from the Man's side
>   after He sent forth His soul.[47]

The Rood, the talking tree, 'speaks not only for the cosmos but as part of it',[48] writes J.A.W. Bennett. He also adds, 'This is not simply a literary device but the very *raison d'être* of the poem.'[49] That said, what is achieved with regard to the event of the crucifixion – simply in terms of writing, of *literature* – is incomparable. It marks, one can say, a uniquely Anglo-Saxon, Anglo-Celtic achievement. David Jones, writing as a representative of that dual tradition, and speaking first of all of the fragment of 'this great poem' originally carved 'on the Anglo-Celtic Ruthwell Cross in Scotland', says of *The Dream*:

> The northern poem could not have been written except Mediterranean man had brought the story, but no Mediterranean man could have told the dream that the Rood dreamed. He would not have known how to make that particular shape. We know still, even after 1300 years, that it is our shape, that it is how we would sing of the Passion had we the genius.[50]

---

47. Ibid., pp. 107–8.
48. Bennett, *The Poetry of the Passion*, p. 3.
49. Ibid.
50. David Jones, *Epoch and Artist: Selected Writings* (London, 1959), pp. 269–70.

Chapter 6

GOD'S SPY: SHAKESPEARE AND RELIGIOUS VISION

If there is one characteristic which can be said to distinguish the truly great artist or poet, it is comprehensiveness of vision or what T.S. Eliot calls 'width of emotional range', the ability, that is, to express 'everything in the way of emotion between depravity's despair and the beatific vision'.[1] But does Shakespeare, in fact, possess such a comprehensive vision? Does he follow Dante, for example, in an exploration of the higher states and stages of religious feeling? Can we locate anywhere in his writing that form of expression described once by Eliot as 'man in search of God, and trying to explain to himself his intenser human feelings in terms of the divine goal'?[2] Is it possible that Shakespeare, arguably the greatest poet and artist of all time, failed to explore that one fundamental dimension of human life we call religion or the religious experience?

In the opinion of the philosopher George Santayana, 'the choice', for Shakespeare, 'lay between Christianity and nothing'. And, according to Santayana, 'He chose nothing', – chose that is, 'to leave his heroes and himself in the presence of life and of death with no other philosophy than that which the profane world can suggest and understand.'[3] Santayana's judgement here raises questions not only about Shakespeare the author but also about Shakespeare the man.

Over the centuries, as opinion's wheel has turned, the Stratford dramatist has been made to assume by critics many different forms and identities. At one end of the spectrum, for example, he appears as a Renaissance sceptic or pessimist and at the other, as a benign establishment figure, a sort of Anglican icon. His most recent appearance as a devout Papist has sent more than a few shock waves across the literary establishment. The poet Ted Hughes, after looking into the question, came to believe that Shakespeare, from a young age, had instinctively identified

---

1. T.S. Eliot, 'What Dante Means to Me' (1950), in *To Criticize the Critic and Other Writings* (London, 1965), p. 134.
2. A comment made by Eliot to William Force Stead. See Helen Gardner, *The Composition of Four Quartets* (London, 1965), p. 134.
3. George Santayana, *Interpretations of Poetry and Religion* (New York, 1967), p. 152.

with the Roman Catholic tribe.[4] For Hughes, Shakespeare was 'the shaman of old Catholicism', a man deeply disturbed by the savage persecution and even near extermination of the faith in which his own father and mother had most probably lived and died.

The question of Shakespeare's personal religion has been for years the subject of a lively ongoing debate.[5] It's a topic which holds considerable fascination for many readers. It is not, however, the focus of interest in these pages. Even a tentative judgement on the question would require far more research and far more careful sifting of the information available than is possible within the limits of the present chapter. What can be said at once, however, is that in coming to a decision about Shakespeare's personal religion, one must be wary not only of possible conditioning by the secular and literary establishment but also of one's own dominant bias and religious enthusiasm. And this advice holds true, of course, as much for the sceptic as for the believer.

One notable sceptic, George Bernard Shaw, being convinced that he could find in Shakespeare's work evidence of an all-pervading pessimism, produced, as a kind of proof, the 'out brief candle' soliloquy from *Macbeth*:

> And all our yesterdays have lighted fools
> The way to dusty death. Out, out, brief candle!
> Life's but a walking shadow, a poor player
> That struts and frets his hour upon the stage
> And then is heard no more: it is a tale
> Told by an idiot, full of sound and fury,
> Signifying nothing. (Act V, Scene 3)

G.K. Chesterton objected to Shaw's 'pessimistic' reading and took him to task with characteristic wit and wisdom. 'The speech', Chesterton observed, 'is not a metaphysical statement at all; it is an emotional exclamation. Mr Shaw has no right to call Shakespeare a pessimist for having written the words "out, out, brief

---

4. Ted Hughes, *Shakespeare and the Goddess of Complete Being* (London, 1993), pp. 77 and 90. That Shakespeare enjoyed an impressively wide range of Catholic contacts is by now well established. See Peter Ackroyd, *Shakespeare: The Biography* (London, 2005), pp. 422, 446, 468–9.

5. See, for example, Richard Wilson, *Secret Shakespeare: Studies in Theatre, Religion and Resistance* (Manchester, 2004); Peter Milward, *Shakespeare the Papist* (Ann Arbor, MI, 2005); Eamon Duffy, *Saints, Sacrilege and Sedition: Religion and Conflict in the Tudor Reformation* (London, 2012); David N. Beauregard, *Catholic Theology in Shakespeare's Plays* (Newark, 2007), and David Scott Kastan, *A Will to Believe: Shakespeare and Religion* (Oxford, 2014). John Finnis and Patrick Martin argue that the 'phoenix' in Shakespeare's 'The Phoenix and the Turtle' is none other than the Catholic martyr St Ann Line. See 'Shakespeare's Intercession for Love's Martyr', *Times Literary Supplement*, no. 5220, 18 April 2003, pp. 12–14.

candle"; he might as well call Shakespeare a champion of the ideal of celibacy for having written the words, "Get thee to a nunnery"!'[6]

Chesterton's writings on Shakespeare are nowadays all but forgotten, and that's a pity. For, like his writings on Aquinas, they are, at times, quite extraordinarily intuitive. When Chesterton discusses the question of Shakespeare and religion, he doesn't insist, unlike some more recent commentators, that the Bard was all his life a secret, committed Catholic. Instead, he is inclined to the view, and I think here he is correct, that 'Shakespeare was not ... a man with a very definite doctrinal point of view.'[7] He writes: 'To live in the thick of the Renaissance and the Reformation was to live in the thick of a scepticism and philosophical confusion as great, if not greater than our own.' But then adds at once: '[Shakespeare] had a great deal of traditional and inherent religious emotion, and what there was of it was mainly Catholic.'[8]

In the present chapter, attention will be focused on three themes or patterns in Shakespeare's work: first, and in relation principally to *Sonnet 27*, the theme of love and vision; second, and in relation to some of the late visionary plays and also to *Sonnet 146*, the theme of death and immortality; and third, in the final section, the theme or the pattern of contemplative vision with respect to this world. These three different sections represent three rather different methods of approach to Shakespeare's work or three different ways in which Shakespeare's work can be said to stand in relation to the literature of religious vision and to theology. The first section explores the contrast, in terms of theme and imagery, between a representative love poem by Shakespeare and a poem chosen from the spiritual tradition. The interest here, I should point out at once, is not in Shakespeare's religious vision as such but simply in the richness of exchange – particularly in terms of language – between two very different worlds of experience. In the second section, however, where the theme is death and immortality, attention will be centred on the evidence to be found of Shakespeare himself – as poet and as author – entering into the field of religion and into the realm of interiority. Finally, in the last section, taking my cue from a single line out of one of the plays, I will reflect on the meaning of Shakespeare's contemplation of things and ask whether, in any sense, that contemplation can be thought of as a form of religious vision.

1

Passion and Prayer
Shakespeare's 'Black Night'

In the winter of 1582, Shakespeare, at the age of eighteen, married Anne Hathaway whom he had got pregnant three months earlier. And in that same winter, towards the end of January, a contemporary of Shakespeare, a poet in his fortieth year,

---

6. 'The Great Shawkspear Mystery', in *Chesterton on Shakespeare* (London, 1971), p. 149.
7. Ibid., p. 148.
8. Ibid., p. 149.

arrived at Granada in Spain and there began to write a commentary on what is his most outstanding achievement in verse, *La Noche Oscura*. The poet in question is the saint and mystic, John of the Cross. What I propose now is to offer a comparison between St John's poem and Shakespeare's *Sonnet 27*. Inevitably, since I will not be quoting *The Dark Night* in the original Spanish, much will be lost in translation, in terms of both meaning and music. However, there is, I am glad to say, an English version of *La Noche Oscura* available, translated by Roy Campbell, which not only is faithful to the spirit of the original but is also a remarkable poem in its own right.[9]

Both St John's poem and Shakespeare's sonnet are poems of passionate love, and both describe a journey by night. For John the journey takes place within the night of faith. The awakened soul of the contemplative, 'attracted by God and enkindled with love for Him alone,'[10] happily takes the risk of going out alone into the night, in great secrecy, in order to meet with the Beloved.

> Upon a gloomy night,
> With all my cares to loving ardours flushed,
> (O venture of delight!)
> With nobody in sight
> I went abroad when all my house was hushed.
>
> In safety, in disguise,
> In darkness up the secret stair I crept,
> (O happy enterprise!)
> Concealed from other eyes
> When all my house at length in silence slept.
>
> Upon that lucky night
> In secrecy, inscrutable to sight,
> I went without discerning
> And with no other light
> Except for that which in my heart was burning.
>
> It lit and led me through
> More certain than the light of noonday clear
> To where One waited near
> Whose presence well I knew,
> There where no other presence might appear.[11]

---

9. See *The Poems of St John of the Cross*, trans. R. Campbell (London, 1986), pp. 10–13.

10. John of the Cross, *The Ascent of Mount Carmel*, Book I, 1, 4, in *The Collected Works of St John of the Cross*, trans. K. Kavanaugh and O. Rodriquez (Washington, 1973), p. 74.

11. St John of the Cross, 'Song of the Soul in rapture at having arrived at the height of perfection, which is union with God by the road of spiritual negation', in *Poems of St John of the Cross*, trans. Roy Campbell (London, 1983), p. 11.

St John's lyric continues for three more stanzas. The final one reads:

> Lost to myself I stayed,
> My face upon my lover having laid
> From all endeavour ceasing:
> And all my cares releasing
> Threw them amongst the lilies there to fade.[12]

This remarkable poem, *La Noche Oscura*, although it reads on the surface as a simple drama of encounter between a young woman and her lover, is intended by John to represent, first of all, the journey into the night of faith and then the extraordinary rapture that occurs when the bride soul – the *anima* – finds herself utterly and completely absorbed in the love of her divine Lord. In Shakespeare's *Sonnet 27*, what we find described is a love obsession, a thraldom of a different kind altogether. The journey the poet finds himself making by night is a journey which takes place entirely inside his own mind, and the vision which he attains in the end, and which hovers before him like a dark 'jewel', is the imagined presence of the one he loves obsessively. But that presence, though it is real only in his imagination, and therefore in a sense illusory, is to the fevered brain of the poet-lover, something wondrous and vivid. Thus, in spite of great tiredness, his 'drooping eyelids' are kept 'open wide'. Even the 'black night' itself, which surrounds him, is made 'beauteous'.

> Sonnet 27
> Weary with toil, I haste me to my bed,
> The dear repose for limbs with travel tired;
> But then begins a journey in my head,
> To work my mind when body's work's expired:
> For then my thoughts, from far where I abide,
> Intend a zealous pilgrimage to thee,
> And keep my drooping eyelids open wide,
> Looking on darkness which the blind do see:
> Save that my soul's imaginary sight
> Presents thy shadow to my sightless view,
> Which, like a jewel hung in ghastly night,
> Makes black night beauteous and her old face new.
>   Lo, thus, by day my limbs, by night my mind:
>   For thee, and for myself, no quiet find.

The 'black night' in Shakespeare and the 'dark night' in St John of the Cross describe two very different states of mind and soul. But common to both 'nights'

---

12. Ibid., p. 13.

is the paradox of a total darkness somehow mysteriously lit from within, a 'night' transformed, in one case, by a depth of human passion and, in the other, by an intensity of mystical love. It is this paradox, the wonder of an illuminating darkness, which St John praises and celebrates in stanza five:

> Oh night that was my guide!
> Oh darkness dearer than the morning's pride,
> Oh night that joined the lover
> To the beloved bride
> Transfiguring them each into the other.[13]

In or around the time Shakespeare wrote *Sonnet 27*, he also composed a long poem on the subject of the two lovers Venus and Adonis. At one point in the poem, Venus refers to what she calls 'this dark night'. And, by way of reply to Adonis's statement, 'And now 'tis dark, and going I shall fall', Venus, in full and calm possession of a lover's knowledge and intuition, declares, 'In night ... desire sees best of all.' And, then, a few lines later: 'Now of this dark night I perceive the reason.' Clearly, the 'dark night' of St John of the Cross is not to be confused with the 'dark night' of Venus! St John, in *La Noche Oscura*, dares, it is true, to use the imagery of human passion and, at times, even of erotic love in order to describe the soul's communion with God. But the overwhelming, divine love of which he is speaking is, at root, something utterly different from the force and mystery of an absorbing sensual and romantic passion. All the same, so daring is St John as poet that the voice we hear in stanzas six and seven might almost be that of Venus herself or, more likely perhaps, that of young Juliet:

> Within my flowering breast
> Which only for himself entire I save
> He sank into his rest
> And all my gifts I gave
> Lulled by the airs with which the cedars wave.
>
> Over the ramparts fanned
> While the fresh wind was fluttering his tresses,
> With his serenest hand
> My neck he wounded, and
> Suspended every sense with its caresses.[14]

What, in John's poem, are simply vivid metaphors – the obsessive need to meet with the beloved and the complete surrender to a sensual, absorbing love – are

---

13. Ibid., pp. 11 and 13.
14. Ibid., p. 13.

for Shakespeare (I think it can be assumed) the form of an experience he knew very well as a young Stratford male. And when, in his work, he writes about the adventure of human love, Shakespeare – almost as if to match the imaginative daring of the Carmelite mystic – is not shy to steal, as it were, metaphors from the world of religion and religious experience. Thus, Romeo, for example, is described by Juliet as 'the god of my idolatry'. And Romeo himself, with a lover's playfulness and passion, refers to Juliet as a 'holy shrine' and speaks of his own lips as 'two blushing pilgrims':

> Then move not, while my prayer's effect I take.
> Thus from my lips, by thine, my sin is purged.

Likewise, in *Sonnet 27*, in order to evoke the intensity of human passion, Shakespeare does not hesitate to employ explicit religious imagery. He speaks of his 'soul's imaginary sight' and of how, in the 'black night', his 'thoughts' are so focused on his beloved, they 'intend' what he calls 'a zealous pilgrimage'. An equally obsessed lover, the protagonist in Graham Greene's novel *The End of the Affair*, speaks of this kind of imaginative criss-crossing from one world of experience to another, from sacred to profane and from profane to sacred. I can think of no better way of ending this brief reflection on the two nights – the '*noche oscura*' of St John of the Cross and the 'black night' of Shakespeare – than by quoting a few lines from Greene's remarkable novel:

> The words of human love have been used by the saints
> to describe their vision of God, and so, I suppose, we
> might use the terms of prayer, meditation, contemplation
> to explain the intensity we feel for a woman. We too
> surrender memory, intellect, intelligence, and we too
> experience the deprivation, the *noche oscura*, and
> sometimes, as a reward, a kind of peace.[15]

Just after that reflection, the tone changes. Greene's protagonist speaks in a more urgent, more personal vein: 'It is odd to find myself writing these phrases … Sometimes I don't recognize my own thoughts. What do I know of phrases like "the dark night" or of prayer, who have only one prayer?'[16] The note of exasperated passion there is pure Shakespeare. And the statement or question of Greene's obsessed lover might almost serve as a gloss, hurriedly dashed off, in the margin alongside Shakespeare's *Sonnet 27*.

---

15. Graham Greene, *The End of the Affair* (London, 1975), p. 47.
16. Ibid.

2
'Be Absolute for Death'
The Theme of Immortality

Of the 154 sonnets of Shakespeare, *Sonnet 146* is the most straightforwardly spiritual and religious. One of its central themes echoes the dominant preoccupation of many of the other sonnets, an obsessive concern with death and immortality. Regarding the question of how to overcome the ravages of Time, the answer Shakespeare's sonnets offer is not religion but art, and not art in general but the art of the poet, William Shakespeare.

> Yet do thy worst, old Time: despite thy wrong,
> My love shall in my verse ever live long. (*Sonnet 19*)

But *Sonnet 146* breathes a decidedly different atmosphere. It opens with the poet upbraiding himself for spending so much time and energy on mere outward show.

> Why so large cost, having so short a lease,
> Dost thou upon thy fading mansion spend?

A sense of guilt and a stark awareness of the inevitable decay and death of the body's 'outward walls' encourage the poet 'to buy terms divine' and recover within himself an inner world of meaning, a realm of the spirit that will not pass away.

> Poor soul, the centre of my sinful earth,
> [Press'd by] these rebel powers that thee array,
> Why dost thou pine within and suffer dearth,
> Painting thy outward walls so costly gay?
> Why so large cost, having so short a lease,
> Dost thou upon thy fading mansion spend?
> Shall worms, inheritors of this excess,
> Eat up thy charge? Is this thy body's end?
> Then, soul, live thou upon thy servant's loss,
> And let that pine to aggravate thy store;
> Buy terms divine in selling hours of dross;
> Within be fed, without be rich no more:
>   So shalt thou feed on Death, that feeds on men,
>   And Death once dead, there's no more dying then.

The bold confidence of these lines, the declaration concerning the paradox of life-in-death and the claim that while being poor 'without', one can be rich 'within' are all commonplaces in the literature of Christian spirituality and mysticism. St John of the Cross, for example, speaks on one occasion of the person who is genuinely detached as 'one who though having nothing yet possesses all things'.[17] Shakespeare, in his play *Timon of Athens*, allows Timon himself, at the end of his life, to repeat this idea but to repeat it with at least as much desperation and bravado as mystic rapture. Thus: 'My long sickness of health and living now begins to mend / And nothing brings me all things' (Act V, Scene 1). Likewise, in *Measure for Measure*, Claudio, encouraged by the Duke to resign himself to what seems an inevitable death, turns to the Duke and says:

> I humbly thank you.
> To sue to live, I find I seek to die,
> And, seeking death, find life: let it come on.

In his heart, of course, Claudio simply wants to live. He is no more convinced by his own brave rhetoric than the Duke (who has disguised himself as a friar) is convinced by the pseudo-spiritual homily which he delivers to Claudio and in which he paints such a grim and negative picture of our earthly life:

> Be absolute for death; either death or life
> Shall thereby be the sweeter. Reason thus with life:
> If I do lose thee, I do lose a thing
> That none but fools would keep

Some lines further on, still addressing life itself, the Duke declares:

> If thou art rich, thou'rt poor;
> For, like an ass whose back with ingots bows,
> Thou bearest thy heavy riches but a journey,
> And death unloads thee. (Act III, Scene 1)

At first hearing, the 'friar's' words might seem to echo the traditional, ascetical counsel of that *real* friar, the austere poet and contemplative, St John of the Cross. But John's ascetical path, his own version of being 'absolute for death', is not based on any kind of recoil from life but springs rather from a deep, personal desire for communion with God.

That desire, that urgent thirst for contact with the author of life itself, is nowhere expressed in the Duke's words to Claudio, and indeed it is questionable if it finds expression anywhere in Shakespeare's work. Are we to conclude, then, that there was nothing whatever of the mystic in Shakespeare's character? Was it enough for him to contemplate the great spectacle of human existence without ever registering, as man and artist, a thirst like that of Dante, an urge to range beyond the limits of this mortal life? Whatever conclusion we reach with regard to this question,

---

17. 'The Ascent of Mount Carmel', Book II, 4, 5, in *The Collected Works of St John of the Cross*, p. 114.

one thing is clear: no poet or dramatist ever succeeded better than Shakespeare in presenting what Anthony Burgess has described as 'man', or the human being, 'lost, bewildered, baffled, looking for meaning, hungering and thirsting after justice'. And might it not, therefore, be the case, as Burgess contends, that 'what Shakespeare's work implies is less the existence of God than the need for God to exist'?[18]

Many more references to religion can be found in Shakespeare than the few noted by George Santayana. And a number of these are by no means fossils of piety. In relation, for example, to the great themes of dedicated, faithful love and compassion, many texts could be quoted from the plays, and a poem such as *Sonnet 116* could also be cited ('Let me not to the marriage of true minds / Admit impediments') and compared with St Paul's hymn to love or charity. That said, it would not be helpful to characterize Shakespeare as a religious dramatist. Shakespeare chose, by and large, to leave religion alone. Unlike Dante, he was writing *plays* most of the time, not poems. And it's hard to see how the interior life of faith, or the world of the afterlife, could be depicted convincingly on a public stage. With respect to religion in general, Shakespeare may well have felt constrained, in any case, owing to the manifest danger of the times and the strength of the religious ferment in Elizabethan England, to remain silent on the subject of his own personal faith and/or his tribal loyalty. 'But break, my heart; for I must hold my tongue!'

Sonnet 146, the poem we have been considering, is of course nothing if not an open, personal meditation of a religious kind. But the man we are overhearing in meditation is not actually talking to God but to himself: 'Poor soul, the centre of my sinful earth'. God – apart from the one reference to 'terms divine' – is never mentioned. Instead, the poem's spiritual interest finds expression in the themes of loss and gain, death and immortality. Needless to say, the poet is well able to ring the changes on these two great themes. But, from beginning to end, the tone of *Sonnet 146* is rather strictly homiletic and exhortatory. It is not a work of vision. Only towards the end of Shakespeare's career as a dramatist did these two themes come together with visionary force, allowing him to invent what has been called a 'myth of immortality'.

The form which this myth takes is that of a young girl or a woman thought dead or lost being miraculously restored. Wherever this image is found, and it occurs in a number of the late romances, the aim of Shakespeare is not to assert a temporal survival after death. His mysterious task, rather, is to reveal that a love which was real once but now seems lost or dead cannot in fact be dead. Somehow, even in the face of death and failure, love survives. But that is not all. In these late plays, the world of vision being enacted or being created before our eyes draws our attention to what was once referred to by T.S. Eliot as Shakespeare's 'deeper religious sensibility'.[19] Eliot, in an unpublished lecture on Shakespeare, goes so far as to say:

---

18. Anthony Burgess, 'Foreword', in *Playing with Fire: A Natural Selection of Religious Poetry*, ed. Susan Dwyer (Dublin, 1980), p. 21.

19. T.S. Eliot, 'What Is a Classic?' (1945), in *On Poetry and Poets* (London, 1957), pp. 60–1.

The personages in *Cymbeline, The Winter's Tale, The Tempest* and *Pericles* are the work of a writer who has finally seen through the dramatic action of men into a spiritual action which transcends it ... They [e.g. Perdita, Miranda and Marina] belong to a world from which some emotions have been purified away, so that others, ordinarily invisible, may be made apparent.[20]

Eliot's poem *Marina* was directly inspired by the 'recognition scene' in *Pericles*, and this scene he regarded, in fact, as 'the finest of all the recognition scenes'. In it, he says, 'Shakespeare's consummate dramatic skill is as bright as ever; his verse is as much *speech* as ever: only, it is the speech of creatures who are more than human, or rather, seen in a light more than that of day.'[21] The restoration of Marina, the lost daughter, is mysteriously accompanied by music. Pericles, her father, exclaims: 'Now, blessing on thee! rise, thou art my child./Give me fresh garments' (Act V, Scene 1). And again:

> Give me my robes. I am wild in my beholding.
> O heavens! bless my girl. But hark! what music?
> Tell Helicanus, my Marina, tell him
> O'er, point by point, for yet he seems to doubt,
> How sure you are my daughter. But, what music?

Commenting on this remarkable passage, Eliot writes: 'The "Give me fresh garments" emphasized presently by "Give me my robes" has great significance. The scene becomes a ritual; the poetic drama developed to its highest point turns back towards liturgy: and the scene could end in no other way than by the vision of Diana.'[22] Just moments earlier, when Pericles first began to realize that his 'dead' child was alive, and was there standing in front of him, he was overcome by an almost unbearable flood of joy. Turning around in his bewilderment to Helicanus, he exclaimed:

> O Helicanus! strike me, honoured sir;
> Give me a gash, put me to present pain,
> Lest this great sea of joys rushing upon me
> O'erbear the shores of my mortality.

---

20. Extracts from Eliot's unpublished essay, 'Shakespeare as Poet and Dramatist', are quoted in the Appendix to G. Wilson Knight's *Neglected Powers* (London, 1971), p. 490, and in Appendix I in John E. Freeh's unpublished doctorate thesis, *Eliot, Shakespeare and the 'Ultra-dramatic'*, Oxford, 1999, pp. 255–61. See also Paul Murray, *T.S. Eliot and Mysticism* (London, 1991), p. 209.
21. Ibid., p. 490.
22. Ibid.

Here the ecstasy is so great, and the expression of it so powerful, one is reminded at once of certain passages from the mystical tradition. There is, for example, one particular passage in St John of the Cross in which the saint notes how, on occasion, God's 'visit' to his bride, the soul, is so overwhelming that the soul is unable in her weakness to endure such excess. John writes: 'The torment experienced in these rapturous visits' is such that were God not to intervene to help the soul, 'she would die'. In fact, to the soul, 'it seems that she is being set free from the flesh and is abandoning the body'.[23] This contemplative rapture, although it bears a striking resemblance to the ecstasy of Pericles, is not, of course, the same thing. John himself remarks: 'This rapture is not like other natural transports and swoons in which one returns to self when pain is inflicted.'[24] Nevertheless, when the recognition scene in *Pericles* is read in context, or watched live on the stage, it makes, I believe, an impression on the reader or on the listener that one can only call 'spiritual'.

If, at this point, someone were to ask 'What, then, is the philosophy or the theology that lies behind "the recognition scene" in *Pericles*?' I am not sure what I would reply. Of course, on one level, considering the apparition of the goddess Diana to Pericles, and the placing, in the scene which follows, of a Greek temple, the theology is Hellenistic. But, given Shakespeare's 'intuition of immortality' in the later plays and the recurrent death and rebirth symbolism which appears to 'corroborate', in G. Wilson Knight's phrase, 'the death-conquest announced by Christianity',[25] there are, it would seem, at least some grounds for considering the underlying theology or philosophy of the plays to be Christian.

Earlier I remarked that Shakespeare was not a religious dramatist. In the light of all that has been said, however, I cannot bring myself to agree with George Santayana when he says that, in the writing of his poems and plays, Shakespeare relied on 'no other philosophy than that which the profane world can suggest and understand'. Shakespeare, it is true, can be neither named with any confidence a secret, committed Catholic nor held up as a great religious dramatist. But neither, I think, can he be dubbed, like poor drunk Barnardine in *Measure for Measure*,

> a stubborn soul
> That apprehends no farther than this world,
> And squar'st [his] life according. (Act V, Scene 1)

However hard we try, we cannot, in the end, successfully 'square' Shakespeare's life or his work. Shakespeare, whether we think of him as an artist or as a man, will always, I suspect, be able somehow to 'disappear' at the last and elude both our sacred and our profane categories. That doesn't mean, however, we should

---

23. 'The Spiritual Canticle', stanza 13, 4, in *The Collected Works of St John of the Cross*, p. 459.
24. Ibid., stanza 13, 6, p. 460.
25. G. Wilson Knight, 'Myth and Miracle', in *The Crown of Life* (London, 1965), p. 31.

abandon all effort at understanding. 'About anyone so great as Shakespeare', Eliot once remarked, 'it is probable that we can never be right; and if we can never be right, it is better that we should from time to time change our way of being wrong'.[26]

3
Shakespeare and 'the Mystery of Things'

I began the present chapter by asking if Shakespeare, in spite of his manifest genius as author, somehow failed to explore the dimension of life we call religion or the religious experience. The answer to this question will obviously depend on the meaning we give to the term 'religion'. If we take, for example, 'religious experience' to mean the exploration of states of feeling beyond the ordinary spectrum of human emotion, then Shakespeare's late romances certainly qualify as being in some sense 'religious'. But if 'religion' means for us, instead, a personal devotion to God, a hunger to see God and even a mystical thirst for intimate communion with God, then Shakespeare's work, though comprehensive to a degree probably unsurpassed in world literature, cannot be described or circumscribed by the word 'religious'.

Eliot says somewhere that whereas the mystic looks at God, the poet looks at things. God is approached by the mystic, that is to say, as an object – the supreme 'object' of his or her attention. This way of thinking about religious experience is, of course, entirely valid and acceptable. But there is a passage in Simone Weil, the modern French mystic and philosopher, in which, with characteristic daring, she suggests that this matter can be viewed, as it were, back to front. Instead, therefore, of thinking in terms of the individual looking at God, and perhaps thus looking away from things, and away from the world, we can think of ourselves as somehow coming out from God *towards* things and of being called, in some sense, to share in God's gaze – that is, with God as 'Subject', looking at the world and at things with us and through us. Weil writes: 'The real aim is not to see God in all things; it is that God through us should see the things that we see. God has got to be on the side of the subject.' And again: 'We imitate the descending movement of God … [when we] turn ourselves toward the world.'[27]

I quote this passage from Weil because I believe that there is a hint of something like it in Shakespeare. The passage in question occurs towards the end of *King Lear*. It is spoken by Lear to his daughter, Cordelia. Already immense suffering has broken the king's heart. He is barely sane. And yet, paradoxically, though stripped of all his former glory, and half-crazed with sorrow, the words he speaks are instinct with strange wisdom and compassion. 'Come,' he says to Cordelia, 'let's away to prison':

---

26. T.S. Eliot, 'Shakespeare and the Stoicism of Seneca' (1927) in *T.S. Eliot: Selected Essays* (London, 1951), p. 126.
27. Simone Weil, *The Notebooks*, Vol. 2, trans. A. Wills (New York, 1956), p. 358.

> We two alone will sing like birds i' the cage:
> When thou dost ask me blessing, I'll kneel down
> And ask of thee forgiveness: so we'll live,
> And pray, and sing, and tell old tales, and laugh
> At gilded butterflies, and hear poor rogues
> Talk of court news; and we'll talk with them too,
> Who loses and who wins; who's in, who's out;
> And take upon's the mystery of things,
> As if we were God's spies. (Act V, Scene 1)

Things. The poet, every poet, every sculptor, every painter, looks at things. But the truly astonishing depth and range of Shakespearian vision – the poet's wide and wise perceptiveness – might it not be explained, in part, by the proposal voiced here, 'to take upon's the mystery of things, / As if we were God's spies'?

The contemplation of the world has come to be regarded as a task belonging not so much to the ecclesiastical tradition but rather to that tradition referred to once by the Dominican Cornelius Ernst as 'the tradition of the human heart: novels, art, music, tragedy'.[28] But genuine religious contemplation does not, of course, necessarily exclude the contemplation of things. In prayer, it is true, what matters first and last is the contemplation of God. But as Josef Pieper reminds us, there is 'a contemplative way of seeing the things of creation'. Pieper continues: 'I am speaking now of actual things, and of seeing with the eyes; I mean also hearing, smelling, tasting, every type of sense-perception, but primarily seeing.' And he adds: 'Out of this kind of contemplation of the created world arise in never ending wealth all true poetry and all real art.'[29]

It is noteworthy that, in all the great religious traditions, there can be found innumerable examples, both in story and in art, of the contemplation of the world. There is, for example, a wonderful story told by Evagrius Ponticus about St Anthony in the desert. One day Anthony was asked by a philosopher: 'How do you ever manage to carry on, Father, deprived as you are of the consolation of books?' He replied: 'My book, sir philosopher, is the nature of created things, and it is always at hand when I wish to read the words of God.'[30] Evagrius himself, in the very first lines of his *Praktikos*, lists as part of our essential task two things, 'the contemplation of God' and 'the contemplation of the physical world'.[31] In this context, there is one other Christian contemplative who comes immediately to mind, Gerard Manley Hopkins, the great Jesuit poet. As man and as poet, Hopkins

---

28. See Cornelius Ernst, *Multiple Echo: Explorations in Theology*, eds. F. Kerr and T. Radcliffe (London, 1979), p. 1.

29. Josef Pieper, *Happiness and Contemplation* (London, 1958), pp. 88–9.

30. See Evagrius Ponticus, 'Sayings of the Holy Monks', no. 92 in *The Praktikos: Chapters on Prayer*, trans. J.E. Bambinger (Spencer, 1970), p. 39.

31. 'The Hundred Chapters', 1, in *The Praktikos*, p. 15.

is aware of God, both as the transcendent object of his devotion in prayer and as the immanent 'Subject' in his life, utterly hidden in some sense and yet completely revealed:

> For Christ plays in ten thousand places,
> Lovely in limbs, and lovely in eyes not his
> To the Father through the features of men's faces.[32]

There are many other examples in religious literature, one could cite here, which give attention to 'the mystery of things'. But I will restrict myself to two short texts, one from the world of the Hasidim, the Jewish tradition, and one from the Hindu tradition. The Jewish text first:

> Rabbi-Shalom said: 'The Talmud tells of a wise
> man versed in the lore of the stars, and relates that
> the paths of the firmament were as bright and clear
> to him as the streets in the town of Nehardea
> where he lived. Now if only we could say about
> ourselves that the streets of our city are as clear
> and bright to us as the paths of the firmament! For
> to let the hidden life of God shine out in this lowest
> world, the world of bodiliness, that is the greater
> feat of the two!'[33]

The text from the Hindu tradition is a short poem composed by Rabindranath Tagore. The poet, in his meditation, is beginning to sense with awe that God – God who is also a 'poet' – desires somehow to contemplate his own creation in and through him. And so he exclaims:

> What! Is it possible, God, that you desire
> to drink from the cup of my life?
>   Is it your joy, my Poet,
> to contemplate your own creation through
> my eyes, and stand at the portal
>   of my ears silently listening
> to your own eternal harmony? Your world
> weaves words in my mind.
>   Your joy adds music to them.

---

32. 'As Kingfishers Catch Fire …' See *Gerard Manley Hopkins: A Selection of His Poems and Prose*, ed. W.H. Gardner (Harmondsworth, 1963), p. 51.
33. See Martin Buber, ed., *Tales of the Hasidim: The Later Masters*, trans. O. Marx (New York, 1948), pp. 50–1.

> You give yourself to me in love,
> and then experience your own entire
> sweetness within me.[34]

That image of God contemplating his own creation through the eyes of the poet immediately brings to mind the short passage in *Lear* we've been considering. But in the king's words, in marked contrast to the language of Tagore or Hopkins, there is no suggestion whatever of actual religious devotion. In fact, it is worth noting that Shakespeare, in the composition of *King Lear,* seems purposely to have removed a number of the religious and Christian references from the source on which his play is based. This detail, incidentally, infuriated Tolstoy. In a blistering essay, the great Russian author complained that the original *King Lear*, an anonymous work entitled *True Chronicle History of King Leir*, had been stripped by Shakespeare of much of its spiritual depth and Christian meaning.[35] Tolstoy is, of course, an important witness here for the prosecution. But, in spite of his brilliance, he failed utterly to grasp the strange and terrible beauty of Shakespeare's play. In particular, Tolstoy failed to see how Shakespeare, by composing a play that was in no way obviously religious, could at the same time explore certain basic aspects of our human and spiritual condition. In this context, I am reminded of a comment made in a letter by Flannery O'Connor about the modern Catholic novelists, Bernanos, Mauriac and Greene. O'Connor writes: 'At some point reading them reaches the place of diminishing returns.' One gets 'more benefit' by reading authors not thought to be religious but in whom 'there is apparently a hunger for a Catholic completeness in life'. O'Connor then adds, and the idea is wonderful: 'It may be a matter of recognizing the Holy Ghost in fiction by the way He chooses to conceal himself.'[36]

But does this idea apply to Shakespeare? No artist in history, it is still generally agreed, contemplated the reality of things with greater breadth and depth of vision than William Shakespeare. So when King Lear, towards the end of the play, speaks of taking upon himself 'the mystery of things', is it possible that his words indicate something of Shakespeare's own sense of his task, as artist and playwright, looking at the things of this world from such a broad perspective that it's *as if he were God's spy*? The question is, of course, impossible to answer. The reason it has seemed worth asking here is because the springs of Shakespeare's genius remain such a mystery and puzzle to this day. The wisest thing, no doubt, would have

---

34. An adaptation by the present author of the translation of no. LXV of 'Gitanjali', in *Collected Poems and Plays of Rabindranath Tagore* (London, 1977), p. 31.

35. In what he calls 'the older drama', Tolstoy notes that Lear's abdication had a profound spiritual basis: '[L]ear thinks only of saving his soul.' See L.N. Tolstoy, 'Shakespeare and the Drama', trans. V. Tcherkoff, in *Shakespeare in Europe*, ed. Oswald LeWinter (London, 1963), p. 242.

36. Letter of 16 January 1936, in *The Habit of Being: Letters of Flannery O'Connor*, ed. S. Fitzgerald (New York, 1979), p. 130.

been simply to avoid the question and say nothing: 'Whereof one cannot speak, thereof one must be silent.'[37] Not once but a number of times in the writing of this particular chapter on Shakespeare I have felt the shadow of Ludwig Wittgenstein fall across my pages, recalling to mind in particular one gnomic remark he made about the English playwright: 'I could only stare in wonder at Shakespeare; never do anything with him.'[38]

So a presence at the margins of my work has been that of Wittgenstein. But there has been another presence, one as innocent and sweet of temper as Wittgenstein's is huge and formidable, a child's philosopher of fun, a seer of laughter conjured by Shakespeare out of words in *A Midsummer Night's Dream*, a simple, earthy character, and the last, perhaps, we would ever think of as being religious – Bottom! Bottom, as is well known, can probably count almost everyone familiar with the *Midsummer* play among his admirers. But no one can have praised him with more generous wit and insight than G.K. Chesterton. Here he is, in rare form, talking about *A Midsummer Night's Dream*:

> It is difficult to approach critically so great a figure as that of Bottom the Weaver. He is greater and more mysterious than Hamlet ... We are the victims of a curious confusion whereby being great is supposed to have something to do with being clever ... Greatness is a certain indescribable but perfectly familiar and palpable quality of size in the personality, of steadfastness, of strong flavour, of easy and natural self-expression. Such a man is as firm as a tree and as unique as a rhinoceros.[39]

And earlier in the piece, Chesterton writes:

> *A Midsummer Night's Dream*. The sentiment of such a play, so far as it can be summed up at all, can be summed up in one sentence. It is the mysticism of happiness ... The soul might be rapt out of the body in an agony of sorrow, or a trance of ecstasy; but it might also be rapt out of the body in a paroxysm of laughter ... We cannot have *A Midsummer Night's Dream* if our one object in life is to keep ourselves awake with the black coffee of criticism.[40]

Criticism! I have been trying in this chapter to reflect with some seriousness on the question of Shakespeare and religious vision. But, at times, I have felt intimidated not only by the shadow of Wittgenstein looming across my pages but also by the glad, exuberant presence of Bottom the Weaver – intimidated, most

---

37. Ludwig Wittgenstein, *Tractitus Logico-Philosophicus*, trans. C.K. Ogden (Sweden, 2016; first published 1922), p. 65.
38. Wittgenstein, *Culture and Value: A Selection from the Posthumous Remains*, ed. G.H. Von Wright (Oxford, 1998), p. 95e.
39. G.K. Chesterton, 'A Midsummer Night's Dream', in *Chesterton on Shakespeare*, p. 107.
40. Ibid., p. 104.

of all, I would have to say, by the memory of the words he speaks in the play about vision and about those who presume to talk or to 'expound' at length on the subject. Clearly, words of criticism are mere straw to a man like Bottom who has had the experience! Here is what he says, talking to himself, when, finally, he wakes up from his dream vision (Act IV, Scene 1):

> God's my life! ... I have had a most rare vision. I have had a dream, past the wit of man to say what dream it was: man is but an ass, if he go about to expound this dream. Methought I was, – there is no man can tell what. Methought I was and methought I had, but man is but a patched fool if he will offer to say what methought I had. The eye of man hath not heard, the ear of man hath not seen, man's hand is not able to taste, his tongue to conceive, nor his heart to report, what my dream was. I will get Peter Quince to write a ballad of this dream: it shall be called Bottom's dream, because it hath no bottom; and I will sing it in the latter end of a play.

Chapter 7

AT THE THRESHOLD OF WONDER:
POETRY AND RELIGION: FRIENDS OR FOES?

'Threshold of wonder' – that phrase immediately brings to mind images and incidents from the lost, everyday world of my own childhood, that illiterate world of innocence and adventure prior to education. But it also brings to mind many fine statements from the *literate* world of philosophy, theology and poetry, lines and texts of startling insight and beauty to which over time, as a young adult, I was happy to be introduced. One of the great wisdom texts I remember is a passage from St Thomas Aquinas's Commentary on Aristotle's *Metaphysics*. I cite it here because it brings together, in easeful concord, all three disciplines, philosophy, theology and poetry. Thomas writes:

> Because philosophy arises from wonder it is evident that the philosopher is, in a sense, a lover of myths and fables, something characteristic of poets. The first to deal with the principles of things in a mythical way such as Perseus and certain others (who were the Seven Sages) were called theologizing poets. Now the reason why the philosopher is compared to the poet is that both are concerned with wonders. For the fables, with which poets are concerned, are composed of wonders, and likewise philosophers find themselves moved to philosophize because of wonder.[1]

A passage worth setting beside this text from Aquinas is the following brief entry in a journal, written two centuries later, by the artist Leonardo da Vinci. Da Vinci is, of course, an artist in the strict sense of the word but he is also, if judged merely by the evidence of this passage alone, a fine artist of words, indeed something of a poet. The *admiratio* – the wonder evoked by the beauty and terror of the unknown – has seldom been described with such simplicity and such power.

> Drawn by my eager wish, desirous of seeing the great confusion of the various strange forms created by ingenious nature, I wandered for some time among the shadowed cliffs, and came to the entrance of a great cavern. I remained before

---

1. St Thomas Aquinas, *In libros Metaphysicorum Aristotelis expositio*, Book 1, lect. 3, no. 55, Marietti edition (Rome, 1950), p. 18.

it for a while, stupefied, and ignorant of the existence of such a thing, with my back bent and my left hand resting on my knee, and shading my eyes with my right, with lids lowered and closed, and often bending this way and that to see whether I could discern anything within; but this was denied me by the great darkness inside. And after I had stayed a while, suddenly there arose in me two things, fear and desire – fear because of the menacing dark cave, and desire to see whether there were any miraculous thing within.[2]

It is precisely this experience of *passive awe* and wonder, which awakens in the poet, according to W.H. Auden, 'the desire to express that awe in a rite of worship or homage'. In the case of poetry, he tells us, 'the rite is verbal; it pays homage by naming'.[3] In the case of philosophy, the rite, it seems natural to add, is intellectual; it pays homage by thinking, by profound reflection.

But what are we to say of theology? The vision of the theologian, man or woman, is inspired first and last by divine revelation, the task demanding adherence to certain revealed truths about God. So, unlike poetry and unlike philosophy, theology, it would seem, begins not so much in wonder but rather in a kind of humble, obedient surrender. This idea, this statement, contains a truth that is undeniable. Nevertheless, it fails to take into account the fact that what faith attains to – the faith, in this case, of the theologian – is not something merely second-hand truths *about* God but rather the reality and wonder of the divine presence itself.

1
Theology at the Threshold

St Gregory of Nazianzen, in one of his most memorable poems and prayers, describes something of the intimate, profound shock provoked by that divine presence. Gregory is clearly stunned by the unspeakable mystery confronting him. One has the impression, reading the work, that within the prayer – in terms of both form and content – philosophy, theology and poetry all come together. The saint, the author of the work, is clearly someone who has entered already into the dark cave of the divine mystery. And there, in a rapture of knowing and not-knowing – in a state of graced bewilderment – he exclaims:

> O you who are beyond anything ... What hymn could tell about you, what language? No words can express you. What could our mind cling to? You are beyond any intelligence. Only you are unutterable, for all that is uttered comes

---

2. Leonardo da Vinci, Codex Arundel 263, folio 115 r, cited in Martin Kemp, *Leonardo da Vinci: The Marvellous Works of Nature and Man* (London, 1981), pp. 98–9.
3. W.H. Auden, 'Making, Knowing and Judging', in *The Dyer's Hand and Other Essays* (New York, 1962), p. 57.

from you ... All beings, those who speak and those who are silent, proclaim you. Universal desire, universal groaning calls you ... For all beings you are the end; you are all thoughts and you are none of them. You are not one sole being, you are not the totality of beings. Yours are all the names, and how will I call you, you, the only one who cannot be named? ... Have mercy, O you who are beyond everything. Isn't this all that can be sung about you?[4]

In all the texts quoted so far, there is not the least hint to suggest anything other than an easeful relationship, a manifestly relaxed and potentially fruitful dialogue between the three disciplines under consideration, theology, philosophy and poetry. All three of them standing, as it were, at the threshold of wonder, appear to be in happy concord, the best of friends. But is this, in fact, a true picture of their relationship? Can we say that the conversation between them, over the centuries, has always proved fruitful, the dialogue always benign?

2
Christianity and Poetry: A Troubled Dialogue?

Pope John Paul II, at the beginning of his 1999 *Letter to Artists*, showed not the least hesitation in speaking about what he called 'the fruitful dialogue between the Church and artists which has gone on unbroken through 2,000 years of history'.[5] But was John Paul perhaps exaggerating? How fruitful in reality, we need to ask, has the centuries-long dialogue between faith-tradition and the world of the arts proved to be in practice and, in particular, the conversation between theology and poetry?

On this topic, the contemporary poet Robert Bly makes bold to declare that, far from being fruitful, the impact of the Christian religion on poetry and poets has been decidedly negative. At the core of all creativity, he believes, there is 'a leap from the conscious to the unconscious and back again, a leap from the known part of the mind to the unknown part and back to the known'.[6] That graced freedom, however, that 'long floating leap', is inevitably and unhappily interrupted, according to our poet, by the ethical and dogmatic demands of Christianity. Christian belief, Bly declares, is both dualist and oppressive. He writes: 'As Christian civilization took hold, and the power of the spiritual patriarchies deepened, this leap occurred less and less often in Western literature. Obviously, the ethical ideas of Christianity inhibit it. From the start Christianity has been against the leap.'[7]

A no less negative assessment has been made by Amos N. Wilder. Poets, he writes, find themselves instinctively opposed to the asceticism proposed by Christ.

---

4. St Gregory Nazianzen, *Dogmatic Hymn* 1; 1, 29, PG 37, 507–8; cited in Samuel A. Nigro, *The Soul of the Earth* (St Louis, 2012), p. 43.
5. Pope John Paul II, *Letter to Artists*, 1 (Chicago, 1999), p. 1.
6. Robert Bly, *Leaping Poetry: An Idea with Poems and Translations* (Boston, MA, 1975), p. 1.
7. Ibid., pp. 1–2.

The things which most matter to them – 'the gamut of human living, emotions, drama' etc. – are renounced in Christianity for 'some wan empyrean of spiritual revery'.[8] The Cross, he declares, far from being a blessing for humanity, 'draws away all the blood from the glowing body of existence and leaves it mutilated and charred'. In effect, Wilder concludes, 'The wine of life', under the oppression of Christian dogma, 'is changed to water'.[9]

These bold, astonishing claims, needless to say, do not represent the opinions of all modern and contemporary poets. But neither are they the opinions of a small minority. The views of Robert Bly and Amos Wilder, if read as part of the ongoing dialogue between poets and the Christian faith-tradition, would seem to indicate that the dialogue, at least in its modern expressions, is a lot more troubled than fruitful.

But what of poets whose lives and works clearly affirm the Christian vision? What of authors such as Gerard Manley Hopkins, St Francis of Assisi, John Donne, Charles Péguy, St Hildegard of Bingen, R.S. Thomas, Dante Alighieri, George Herbert, Anna Akhmatova, St Simeon the New Theologian, Boris Pasternak, David Jones, Patrick Kavanagh, Denise Levertov, Elizabeth Jennings, Czeslaw Miloz, Richard Crashaw and T.S. Eliot? The writings of each of these authors – almost all of them well known – are clearly marked by the Christian vision. And yet not one of them allowed faith conviction to limit or diminish in any way their talent as poets. On the contrary, their achievement in verse, although often inspired by religious conviction, was never reduced to mere religious propaganda. Formed and quickened by the vision of life proclaimed in the Christian gospel, their genius flourished.

One aspect of that flourishing involved, now in one form, now in another, an impressive joining of artistic expression with whatever theological vision, implicit or explicit, had shaped their understanding. No matter how distinctive in practice the nature and source of their inspiration as authors, between the different demands of poetry and religion, there appeared to be no hint of enmity or suspicion. If, however, we turn our attention back to the very early centuries after Christ, and to some of the first observations regarding poetry and poets made by Christian authors and theologians, we find significant elements of unease and even of antagonism.

3
Christian Truth vs Pagan Myth

Not untypical of the theological attitude adopted by the Fathers at a certain stage is the view expressed in *Exhortation to the Heathen* by St Clement of Alexandria. Clement contrasts the 'vain fables' of paganism with the radiant truth of the

---

8. Amos N. Wilder, *The Spiritual Aspects of the New Poetry* (Eugene, OR, 2014), p. 196.
9. Ibid.

Gospel.[10] The 'song' he wants to sing, he declares, follows faithfully 'the immortal measure of the new harmony which bears God's name – the new, the Levitical song'.[11] It has nothing whatever to do, therefore, with the old poetry of paganism. 'Stop, O Homer, the song!' he exclaims, 'It is not beautiful; it teaches adultery.'[12] And, speaking of the authors of verse as 'raving poets' and 'deceivers', he tells us that 'under the pretence of poetry' they have corrupted human life and were, in fact, the first 'to entice men and women to idols'.[13] In his lengthy diatribe against the old gods, Clement is most especially determined to expose the myth of the god Zeus, dismissing as unreal the many colourful disguises which the poets, over the centuries, had attributed to the god. He writes:

> Zeus is snake no longer, nor swan, nor eagle
> Nor erotic man.
> He does not fly as god, nor chase boys
> Nor make love …
> Where then is that eagle? Where that swan?
> Where Zeus?
> He and his wings have mouldered …
> Zeus, like Leda, is dead
> Dead as a swan, dead as an eagle, as erotic man
> And dead as a serpent![14]

So stark at times, in terms of content, is the contrast between the invented fables of the pre-Christian world and the living truth of the Gospel, such a negative reaction to poetry and poets on the part of a theologian such as Clement of Alexandria is not difficult to understand. The early Christian believers, and especially the theologians among them, were aware of bearing an enormous responsibility. All around them were not only the signs of great political power but also the evidence of an astonishing civilization, innumerable living monuments of Graeco-Roman culture. And yet it was to the humble Christians, the least of all people, that God had revealed his final, saving truth. Not poetry, therefore, not the genius of human creativity, but the witness and defence of truth was the most immediate obsession of these first believers. It never seemed to occur to them, at least not for a few generations, that the truth in which they so strongly believed might find in the arts, as almost nowhere else, an invaluable friend. That knowledge, however, was slow to

---

10. St Clement of Alexandria, *Exhortation to the Heathen*, Chapter 1, in *The Anti-Nicene Fathers: The Writings of the Fathers down to A.D. 325*, Vol. II: *Fathers of the Second Century*, eds. A. Roberts and J. Donaldson (Edinburgh, 1986), p. 171.
11. Ibid.
12. Ibid., Chapter 4, p. 189.
13. Ibid., Chapter 1, p. 172.
14. 'Zeus Is Dead', *Exhortation to the Heathen*, Book 2, trans. T. Merton in *The Collected Poems of Thomas Merton* (New York, 1980), p. 934.

awaken and was hampered in no small part by one aspect of their Judaeo-Christian inheritance – the Mosaic condemnation of graven images.

4
St Jerome: The Divided Self

It cannot be doubted that more than a few of the early Church Fathers were natural lovers of words, scholars who were clearly capable of that imaginative play of words and meanings which makes for great writing and great preaching. And they were also what we might call born *readers*, men gifted with a capacity to enjoy great literature. One among them, who clearly possessed an unusual capacity in this regard, was the austere, biblical scholar St Jerome. Jerome, all through his life, seemed unable to contain his enthusiasm for literature, his passion, that is, for both the prose and poetry of certain pre-Christian authors such as Horace and Cicero, Virgil and Plautus. In Rome, and just around the time when he was becoming famous for the radical nature of his ascetical practice, Jerome managed to amass a huge library of 'pagan' literature. Obviously, the brilliance and power of that literature held him in thrall. He was, one could say, a man seduced. In spite of all his best efforts, St Jerome simply could neither detach himself from his books nor stop reading the poets. To a friend, with arresting candour, he wrote:

> I was going to Jerusalem to fight for Christ. But I had not been able to dispense with the library I had collected at Rome with so much labour and care. Unhappy man that I was! I fasted, and it was to prepare me to read Cicero. I spent entire nights in vigil, I shed the bitter tears that the memory of my past sins wrenched from my very entrails, and it was only to pick up Plautus.[15]

Worn down at length by the unrelenting drama and pressure of this inner conflict, St Jerome fell seriously ill. He seemed, in fact, to be on the point of death. It was just then, when the fever was at its height, that he had an extraordinary dream. The vision he witnessed on this occasion has been described by one commentator as the effect of 'repression', in other words 'the unconscious creation of Jerome's remorse'.[16] That may well be the case but, for Jerome, this night vision, at least at first, was nothing less than a revelation. Here is Jerome's own compelling account of what happened:

> They were getting ready to bury me, for my body was so icy cold that the only place where the breath and the heat of life could be felt was my still warm breast. It was then that, all of a sudden, I was caught up in an ecstasy. I was haled before

---

15. St Jerome, Letter XXII to Eustochium, 30; cited in Jean Steinmann, *St Jerome and His Times*, trans. R. Matthews (Notre Dame, IN, 1959), p. 40. For an alternative translation of Jerome's Letter XXII, see *Select Letters of St Jerome*, ed. F.A. Wright (New York, 1933), p. 125.
16. Steinmann, *St Jerome and His Times*, p. 42.

the court of the judge, and I saw a light so dazzling that I did not dare to lift my eyes from the ground where I was lying. They asked me my religion. 'I am a Christian,' I answered. 'You lie,' replied he who was on the bench. 'You are a Ciceronian, not a Christian' ... I held my tongue at once. He had ordered that I should be flogged. But my conscience hurt me more than the blows ... I started to cry out and to beseech him, saying: 'Have mercy on me, Lord! Mercy!' My appeal rang out between the lashes of the whip. Then those who were present fell prostrate before the knees of the judge and begged him to pardon my youth, to grant me time to do penance for my errors, even though he resumed the well-deserved punishment later, if I ever went back to reading the literary works of the pagans. As for me, in such a perilous pass, I was ready to promise far more. I took an oath by the name of the Judge. 'Lord, if ever I own profane books again, or if I read them, it will mean that I have denied you!' Upon this oath, they dismissed me. I came back to earth. To everyone's surprise, I opened my eyes. They were bathed in tears.[17]

At this point, as if anticipating our scepticism, St Jerome makes bold to declare: 'This was not one of those empty nightmares of which we are sometimes victims.' On the contrary, on coming back to consciousness, his shoulders, he tells us, were 'black and blue'.[18] He had no doubt whatever about the objectivity of his dream vision. He wrote: 'I could still feel the bruises when I woke up', adding: 'Since that day, I have studied the divine works with the same assiduity with which I used to read those of men.'[19]

Well, that would seem to be that, a new and complete conversion of life. Out with Virgil, out with all the literary works of the pagans, out with the poets! And, yes, out with the dazzling texts of Cicero and Horace! An inner eruption of some kind had clearly taken place, a veritable shaking of the foundations. There was now a new, radical focus on the study of Sacred Scripture, a disciplined turning in that direction. So strong, however, was the pull of literature, with the passing of a number of years, we find Jerome back reading Vergil as before, this time at Bethlehem, and happily also reading and teaching Cicero. Needless to say, in the intervening period, he had remained a devoted student of *divine* works – a student like no other of his generation – but he was also now, once again, a student of the so-called *profane* works of the pagans. Our great ascetic was back with the poets.

This complete volte-face, this conversion within a conversion, did not go unnoticed in the wider world. A certain Rufinus Tyrannius, once a close friend of Jerome but now a mortal enemy, openly taunted the saint for the scandalous way in which he had perjured himself. To this accusation, Jerome replied with a counter charge, dismissing Rufinus, in the first place, as a hypocrite who was himself secretly reading the works of pagan authors. Then Jerome declared and without, it seems, the least blush:

17. St Jerome, Letter XXII, 30, pp. 40–1.
18. Ibid., p. 41.
19. Ibid.

> If Rufinus is attacking me on account of a dream, let him note the teaching of the prophets: we should not believe in dreams. Adultery committed in a dream no more condemns a man to hell than martyrdom in a dream assures him of heaven. How many times have I not dreamed that I was dead and buried? How many times have I not felt myself flying through the air, crossing land and sea, over hill and dale? ... People [when fast asleep] drink oceans of water in their thirst, and they awake with burning and parched throats. And you expect me to keep a promise made in a dream?[20]

However we understand the sentiments expressed in this remarkable passage, one thing is clear: St Jerome is now experiencing, as a committed Christian, a new sense of freedom, a new confidence with regard to secular literature. From this point on, in fact, we find him quoting texts from pagan authors – poets among them – with increasing frequency.

Harsh critics of St Jerome, such as Rufinus, would no doubt judge this new spirit of acceptance, this new ease, as a form of betrayal, a final succumbing to the glamour of the pagan world. But such critics would be mistaken. What the change represents is, in fact, a dawning realization on the part of Jerome that what was strong and beautiful in the literature of the pre-Christian world is not in any way negated by the truth of the Gospel. Other Christian authors and theologians, in that same period, arrived independently at much the same conclusion. St Basil of Caesarea, for example, in his *Address to Young Men on the Right Use of Greek Literature*, encouraged his students to become, among other things, 'conversant with poets'.[21] As a devout Christian, Basil held to the view that whereas the writings of the pre-Christian authors possessed truth, it was not truth in its fullness. Truth perceived in some measure, yes, but as if 'in shadows and in a mirror'.[22]

In time, as the logic of Incarnation impressed itself more and more on the minds of Christian thinkers, that acknowledgement – that recognition of the elements of truth and beauty present in the work of non-Christian artists and poets – became almost the accepted norm among believers. A point had been reached, at last, when what Pope John Paul called 'the fruitful dialogue between the arts and Christianity' had begun in earnest, a dialogue that, in time, would blossom and flourish beyond all expectation. That said, however, as one generation succeeded another, it soon became clear that by no means all participants in the ongoing 'conversation' between theology and poetry were equally enthusiastic.

---

20. St Jerome, *Apology against Rufinus*, Book 1, 30; cited in Steinmann, *St Jerome and His Times*, p. 43. See also *St Jerome: Dogmatic and Polemical Works*, trans. J.N. Hritzu (Washington, 1965), pp. 102–3.

21. St Basil of Caesarea, *Address to Young Men on the Right Use of Greek Literature (Oratio ad adolescentes, 2)*; cited in P.G. Padelford, *Essays on the Study and Use of Poetry by Plutarch and Basil the Great* (New York, 1902), p. 2.

22. Ibid.

5
Theology and Poetry in the Middle Ages

On one occasion, when St Thomas Aquinas was speaking about theological poets such as Orpheus, Museus and Linus, he remarked: 'These poets deal to some extent with the nature of things by means of figurative representations and myths.'[23] That tiny phrase, 'to some extent', is worth noting. The 'fabulous stories' told by the poets do indeed, Thomas admits, reveal *something* about 'the nature of things'. But that something, when compared with the insights and illuminations offered by the work of a speculative theologian, for example, is of decidedly minor importance. For Aquinas, poetry, in the end, in spite of its undoubted charm, remains an *infirma doctrina*.[24]

A much more positive assessment of the value and attractiveness of the poet's use of myths and metaphors can be found in the work of Meister Eckhart, the Dominican preacher and mystic of the fourteenth century. He writes:

> All the ancient theologians and poets generally used to teach about God, nature and ethics by means of parables. The poets did not speak in an empty and fabulous way, but they intentionally and very attractively and properly taught about the natures of things divine, natural and ethical by metaphors and allegories. This is quite clear to anyone who takes a good look at the poet's stories.[25]

The fact that poetry, and indeed all the creative arts, by the imaginative use of 'metaphors and allegories', can reveal critically important truths about human life is something happily taken for granted in the modern period. The Irish poet Seamus Heaney writes: 'It is precisely this masquerade of fictions and ironies and fantastic scenarios that can draw us out and bring us close to ourselves. The paradox of the arts is that they are all made up and yet allow us to get at truths about who and what we are or might be.'[26] That is, of course, a fundamental insight, well expressed. But the world of literature did not have to wait for the modern or contemporary period for this truth to be acknowledged and given flesh. Already, in the High Middle Ages, a number of Christian writers and poets had discovered different ways in which a 'masquerade of fictions' and 'fantastic scenarios' could be made to serve the communication not only of ordinary truths about ourselves but also of *visionary* and *theological* truths. And, by far, the most notable of these poets was, not surprisingly, the author of the *Divina Commedia*, Dante Alighieri.

23. St Thomas Aquinas, *In Libros metaphysicorum Aristotelis expositio*, Book 1, lect. 4, no. 83, Marietti edition (Rome, 1950), p. 25.

24. Although, in Aquinas's scholastic thinking, poetry occupied a relatively low position, he himself was a very considerable poet. See Paul Murray, *Aquinas at Prayer: The Bible, Mysticism and Poetry* (London, 2013).

25. Meister Eckhart, 'The Book of the Parables of Genesis', 2, in *Essential Sermons*, trans. E. Colledge and B. McGinn (London, 1981), p. 93.

26. Seamus Heaney, *Finders-Keepers: Selected Prose 1971–2001* (London, 2003), pp. 68–9.

I know of no poem in any tradition which contains such a wealth of theology, ranging from expressions of devotion, both personal and practical, to the highest forms of speculation. And yet it remains, first and last, a work of imaginative genius. Here poetry and theology, we can say, come together and create not only a rare masterpiece of literature but also a work acknowledged universally as probably the greatest poem that has ever been written.

6
Dante and Pagan Mythology

Much of the poetry in the *Divina Commedia* depends on pagan myth and on the legends and stories of pagan gods and monsters. Thus, the three-headed dog Cerberus makes an appearance, as do also many other figures out of Graeco-Roman mythology such as Icarus, Phaeton and Medusa. How to explain this reliance, on the part of Dante, on such unusual material? Why, as a poet, does he deliberately include pagan mythology in a poem concerned with the journey – the Christian journey – of the soul to God?

As it happens, there is one statement made by Dante in the *Inferno* which can be taken as a beginning answer to this question. In context, his words refer most immediately to the myth of Medusa and to the terrifying lesson which that myth represents. But his words can also be taken as referring in general to the many unexpected truths waiting to be discovered *under the veils* of pagan mythology. In Canto number IX, choosing at one point to address the reader of his poem directly, Dante exclaims: 'O you who are of sound intellect, / Take note of the teaching that is hidden under the veils / Of these strange verses.'[27]

Not all Dante's contemporaries – theologians among them – were convinced that the myths and legends of the ancient world contained a 'teaching' which could prove useful to the Christian poet. But Dante was well aware that certain truths could only be expressed through allegory, and many of these truths had already, over the centuries, been brilliantly expressed in the '*versi strani*', in the strange and wondrous verses of the pre-Christian poets. One memorable echo of Dante's way of thinking can be found in a work by Boccaccio entitled *Genealogy of the Gentile Gods*. Boccaccio, with reference to what he calls the 'old theology' of the pagan poets, declares that such literature 'can sometimes be employed in the service of Christian truth, if the fashioner of the myths should so choose'.[28] And he notes further: 'I have observed this in the case of more than one orthodox poet in whose investiture of fiction the sacred teachings were clothed.'[29]

---

27. Dante Alighieri, *Inferno* IX, 61–3.
28. Giovanni Boccaccio, 'The Pagan Poets of Mythology Are Theologians', Book XV, 8, *The Genealogy of the Gentile Gods (Genealogiae deorum Gentilium)*, in *Boccaccio on Poetry*, ed. Charles G. Osgood (Princeton, NJ, 1930), p. 123.
29. Ibid.

7
Dante as Visionary Poet and Theologian

When, in the *Paradiso*, Dante the pilgrim finally arrives at the highest, most sacred place of all, and stands face-to-face with the Holy Trinity, the wonder is so great, the mystery so immense, he knows that he will never, afterwards, be able to find adequate words to communicate the experience.

> What then I saw is more than tongue can say.
> Our human speech is dark before the vision.
> The ravished memory swoons and falls away.[30]

In the same canto, several stanzas later, Dante does attempt to express something of the astonished awe he felt when beholding the divine vision. Here, one might expect, at this most exalted moment in the *Commedia*, he will make reference to some image or event from the Christian tradition, some telling religious story that evokes wonder. Instead, however, the image employed is that of the journey of the Argo, the mythical ship which carried Jason and his companions in their quest for the Golden Fleece. This journey, according to the myth, was the first attempt ever made to sail the ocean. Dante imagines the god Neptune looking up in absolute wonder from the bed of the ocean as the shadow of the Argo passes over his head. It is, by any standards, an astonishing conceit and one of the most remarkable moments in the entire poem.

Here, translated by John Ciardi, is the relevant passage, preceded first by a number of fine, memorable stanzas:

> Oh grace abounding that had made me fit
>   to fix my eyes on the eternal light
>   until my vision was consumed in it!
>
> I saw within its depth how It conceives
>   all things in a single volume bound by Love,
>   of which the universe is the scattered leaves;
>
> substance, accident, and their relation
>   so fused that all I say could do no more
>   than yield a glimpse of that bright revelation.
>
> I think I saw the universal form
>   that binds these things, for as I speak these words
>   I feel my joy swell and my spirits warm.
>
> Twenty-five centuries since Neptune saw
>   the Argo's keel have not moved all mankind,
>   recalling that adventure, to such awe

---

30. Dante, *Paradiso* XXXIII, 55–7, trans. John Ciardi, *The Paradiso* (New York, 1970), p. 362.

> as I felt in an instant. My tranced being
>   stared fixed and motionless upon that vision,
>   ever more fervent to see in the act of seeing.
>
> But oh how much my words miss my conception,
>   which is itself so far from what I saw
>   that to call it feeble would be rank deception![31]

Dante is here contemplating the Holy Trinity and, although in the stanza which follows he begins by addressing God the Father, his attention turns almost at once to the Second Person of the Trinity. What most holds him in thrall is the realization that, at the heart of the Godhead, at the very centre of the unspeakable mystery itself, the image of Christ as *man* survives. The wondrous aureole – the circling light he sees before him – possesses not only a divine but also a truly human radiance.

> O Light Eternal fixed in Itself alone,
>   by Itself alone understood, which from Itself
>   loves and glows, self-knowing and self-known;
>
> that second aureole which shone forth in Thee,
>   conceived as a reflection of the first –
>   or which appeared so to my scrutiny –
>
> seemed of Itself of Its own coloration
>   to be painted with man's image. I fixed my eyes
>   on that alone in rapturous contemplation.[32]

In these astonishing lines, as throughout all the stanzas of this final canto, the poet in Dante and the theologian, far from being at odds with one another, are clearly one and the same visionary genius. Reading through Canto XXXIII of the *Paradiso*, it is impossible to separate the theological intelligence at work and the sheer mastery of poetic form. Here the theologian and the poet are unmistakably friends, not foes.

8
The Poetry of Faith in an Age of Unbelief

The achievement of the *Divina Commedia* was made possible by the individual genius of one man, Dante Alighieri. That goes without saying. However, genius alone is not, in this case, the only determining factor. The masterpiece that is the *Commedia* would never have been produced if Dante's own vision of life, including

---

31. *The Paradiso* XXXIII, 82–99 and 121–3, pp. 363–4.
32. Ibid. *The Paradiso* XXXIII, 124–32.

his religious and theological convictions, had not been shared by the society in which he lived. Dante's most fundamental beliefs were the beliefs of an entire culture. There was, we can say, a pre-existing poem, a Christian 'myth' to which people gave instinctive and unquestioned assent. It was, for Dante's contemporary readers, therefore, the most natural thing in the world to enter imaginatively into his religious and theological vision. Nowadays, however, the situation has changed. The Christian vision, the Christian 'myth', no longer enjoys the support of the dominant culture. The once revered images and symbols of Christian faith are no longer the shared inheritance of the majority of readers, a fact which presents an enormous challenge for the poet who happens to be a Christian believer. In an age dominated by secularism, how can the religious artist, or poet, find imaginative expression for core Christian beliefs?

Already by the sixteenth and seventeenth centuries, poets and artists of profound faith conviction found themselves facing an enormous challenge. John Donne, for example, writing in a letter to one of his friends about his attempt to write religious verse, remarked: 'You know my uttermost when it was best, and even then I did best when I had least truth for my subjects. In this present case there is so much truth as it defeats all poetry.'[33] In the twentieth century, T.S. Eliot betrayed a similar unease at one point when working on the composition of what is arguably the greatest Christian poem of the century, *Four Quartets*. In the draft of his third *Quartet*, Eliot chose to alter a particular passage, considering it 'rather too heavily loaded theologically'.[34]

This hesitation had nothing to do with a lack of conviction. It represented rather a desire on the part of Eliot to write a poem and not 'a piece of artless religious testimony'.[35] Eliot knew well that, in the modern age, theological conviction, being no longer supported by a structure or scaffolding of belief *accepted by most readers*, could very easily come across as a kind of dogma with palpable designs on the reader, mere propagandist verse. This cultural reality presented a tough challenge. And the situation was further complicated by the fact that religious conviction, which had once been regarded with instinctive respect, had increasingly come to be viewed in the West as a kind of fundamentalism. Christianity, instead of being identified with the exuberant humanism it had supported for centuries, was now unhappily identified, in the minds of many, with the grim, life-denying traditions of Puritanism and Jansenism.

This horribly distorted picture of the Christian tradition helps explain how a contemporary poet such as Robert Bly was capable of regarding Christianity's influence on poetry and the arts in a wholly negative light. That, in America,

---

33. John Donne, Letter to Sir Robert Ker, March 1625, *John Donne*, The Oxford Authors, ed. John Carey (Oxford, 1990), p. 358.

34. T.S. Eliot, cited in Helen Gardner, *The Composition of Four Quartets* (London, 1978), p. 147.

35. A phrase of Robert Lowell in conversation with Frederick Seidel. See 'An Interview', in *Modern Poets on Modern Poetry*, ed. J. Scully (London, 1971), p. 253.

he and an author such as Amos N. Wilder should find it necessary to reject the life-denying strictures of *extreme* Puritanism is wholly understandable, indeed commendable. But the further leap Bly takes, the projection of that negative view onto almost the entire Christian tradition, is simply inaccurate and uninformed. Here, what should not be forgotten is that corresponding to the extreme, *negative* side of the Puritan tradition, there exists in the Catholic tradition a near twin, a heresy known as Jansenism. Even though Jansenism was roundly condemned by the Church, certain theological ideas, truly poisonous notions tinged with Jansenism, remained in circulation in different parts of Europe for many years after the condemnation.

Was Ireland one of the countries directly or indirectly affected by the heresy? This question has been hotly debated by Irish historians. Whatever the truth of the matter, one thing is clear: already, prior to the emergence of Jansenism, there was present in the Irish Church a rigorist mentality, a phenomenon which would certainly have had a negative impact on the way people came to regard some of the most basic joys and pleasures of life. Rigorism, therefore, as much any other factor, was the likely cause of the unhappy relationship which developed in twentieth-century Ireland between creative writers, on one side, and the Catholic religion, on the other. It's possible that, of late, this relationship may have begun to improve. But there are no grounds for complacency. The history of distrust and repression – rooted in the distorted thinking of the past – has left its mark. Today the majority of Irish writers and poets still tend to be wary of the official Church and of its dogma. Although not foes exactly, neither can they be described as the best of friends.

*

Protest – enlightened protest – against unhappy and repressive forms of religion has, over the centuries, found expression in many different kinds of eloquence and bravery and in many different voices. Some of these voices are linked forever with straightforward, condemnatory speech in the form of either prose or verse. But there are other voices, other forms of protest, no less effective, and not least among them are the bright, subtle voices of humour and satire, of hard-hitting caricature and of irrepressible playfulness.

One text, which stands out in this regard, is a passage from a fourteenth-century Welsh poet, Dafydd ap Gwilym. It records an encounter between the poet and a religious friar in which the friar not only expresses suspicion of the craft of verse but also actually dismisses it out of hand.[36] The poet had gone to the priest (a Grey Friar) to confess his sins, and he explained to the priest that he was 'a sort of poet'. His 'confession' came to this: he was hopelessly in love with a beautiful girl, but his

---

36. Dafydd ap Gwilym, 'The Poet and the Grey Friar', in *A Celtic Miscellany: Translations from the Celtic Literatures*, no. 178, ed. K.H. Jackson (Harmondsworth, 1971), pp. 213–14. For a complete edition of the poet's work, see *Dafydd ap Gwilym*, ed. T. Parry (Cardiff, 1952).

love had found no response. 'I had', he said, 'neither profit nor reward from my lady; only that I loved her long and lastingly and languished greatly for her love, and that I spread her fame throughout Wales, and failed to win her for all that; and that I longed to have her in my bed between me and the wall'.[37]

The friar, clearly scandalized, immediately announced that the poet must immediately abandon the writing of verse. If not, he would face a harsh judgement:

> Make less the punishment on the Day that will come; it would profit your soul to desist, and to be silent from your poems and busy yourself with your beads. Not for poems and verses did God redeem Man's soul. You minstrels, your art is nothing but jabber and vain noises, and incitement of men and women to sin and wickedness.[38]

The onslaught was harsh and unrelenting, but the poet, holding his ground, answered the 'mouse-coloured Friar' with a few sentences of wit and wisdom, declaring:

> God is not so cruel as the old folk say, God will not damn a soul of a gallant gentleman for loving woman or maid. Three things are loved throughout the world – woman, fair weather, and good health; a woman is the fairest flower in heaven beside God Himself ... Therefore, it is not strange that one loves girls and women. From heaven comes good cheer and from Hell every grief; song gladdens the old and young, sick and whole. I must needs compose poems just as you must preach, and it is as proper for me to go wandering as a minstrel as it is for you to beg alms. Are not hymns and church sequences only verses and odes? And the psalms of the prophet David are but poems to blessed God. God does not nourish Man on food and seasoning alone; a time has been ordained for food and a time for prayer, a time for preaching – and a time to make merry. Song is sung at every feast to entertain the girls, and paternosters in the church to win the land of Paradise.[39]

So, yes, religion has the task of alerting everyone to the seriousness of life, but it should not, the poet insists, negate the immediate joys and pleasures of life. 'A glad house', he declares, 'means a full house, a sad face comes to no good'. And again: 'Though some love piety, others love good cheer; few know the art of sweet poetry, but everyone knows his paternoster. Therefore, scrupulous Friar, it is not song that is the greatest sin.'[40]

*

37. Ibid., p. 213.
38. Ibid.
39. Ibid., pp. 213–14.
40. Ibid.

Three centuries later, this time in Ireland, a no less impressive protest was made against clerical opposition to the making of verses. This time, however, the mood of the protest, far from being one of playful exuberance, was of an almost Dantean ferocity. The protest, in the form of a poem, was composed by the Dominican friar and poet Pádraigín Haicéad, one of the four leading Irish poets of the seventeenth century. Haicéad (*c.*1600–54) was abroad when news reached him that the clerical establishment in Ireland had banned the friars from writing songs and poems. The response of the friar was immediate. Seldom, I would say, has unspeakable rage been more successfully transmuted into verse.

> I will not spring at the flank of their argument
> now that the time is past when I could utter
> each thought erupting from the scope of my mind,
> when the edge of my intellect was a thing to fear
>
> showering with no loss of pliant force
> into the general flank of those arrogant priests
> or down on top of their bald malignant skulls
> a hard sharp fistful of accomplished darts.
>
> I will stitch my mouth up with a twisted string
> and say no word about their mean complaining,
> merely condemn the herd of narrow censors
> and the hate they bear my people, O my God.[41]

*

Taking into account the witness of all the voices we have heard so far, it's clear that the relationship between Christianity and the arts has been, at times, decidedly complex and uneasy, a pattern which has also characterized the relationship between theology and poetry. That said, however, it's important not to lose sight of the quite unique and indeed overwhelmingly positive impact made by the Christian faith on all the creative arts, on poetry, music, sculpture, painting etc., an influence, a force for creativity, unparalleled in the history of Western civilization.

Few people have written with more conviction and insight on this matter than the twentieth-century Russian poet, Osip Mandelstam. In one of his essays, Mandelstam makes bold to declare:

---

41. Extract from Haicéad's poem 'On Hearing it has been Ordered in the Chapterhouses of Ireland that the Friars make no more Songs or Verses.' Translation by Thomas Kinsella. See *The New Oxford Book of Irish Verse*, ed. T. Kinsella (Oxford, 1986), p. 170. For a translation of the complete poems of the Dominican poet, see Michael Hartnett, *Haicéad: Translations from the Irish* (Dublin, 1983).

Our entire two-thousand-year-old culture, thanks to the marvellous charity of Christianity, is *the world's release into freedom* for the sake of play, for spiritual joy, for the free imitation of Christ. Christianity adopted a completely free relationship to art which no human religion either before or since has been able to do ... There is no way to sufficiently emphasize the fact that European culture owes its eternal, unfading freshness to the mercy of Christianity with respect to art.[42]

Part of the freedom enjoyed, after the Incarnation, by the Christian artist is the freedom to absorb influences from sources foreign to the Christian religion, while at the same time holding fast to 'the truth heard from the beginning'. For the poet, it is a task of transformation, an invitation to salt with Christ's salt the partial but manifestly radiant truths encountered in non-Christian literature and mythology. In this regard, no one showed greater freedom, as a creative artist, than Dante Alighieri. But Dante is not unique. The daring openness and the surprising grace of welcome to what is clearly foreign and unfamiliar – both manifest qualities of his work – are not only Dantean gifts but qualities which have characterized Catholic Christianity in general and the innumerable works of art which it has inspired.

9

Welcoming the Poet's Vision

My principal concern up to this point has been to explore under the rubric of wonder the nature of the relationship between Christianity and the arts and between theology and poetry. This has necessitated making reference to a number of different texts from different worlds. Now, by way of conclusion, I would like to draw attention to a work which relates directly to our topic and which happens to be one of the finest literary achievements of medieval Ireland. It is entitled *The Frenzy of Sweeney*.[43] Earlier I quoted Aquinas saying that 'the fables, with which poets are concerned, are composed of wonders', and *Frenzy* is nothing if not a story of wonders.

Sweeney's tragic story begins when, cursed by an angry cleric called Ronan, he is condemned to fly around Ireland as an outcast in the shape of a bird, exposed to snow and rain and to every cold gust of wind. He becomes the Bird Man:

---

42. Osip Mandelstam, 'Pushkin and Scriabin (Fragments)', in *Osip Mandelstam: The Collected Prose and Letters*, ed. and trans. J.G. Harris (London, 1991), p. 92.

43. The work has been translated by Seamus Heaney and given a new title: *Sweeney Astray: A Version from the Irish* (Derry, 1983).

> A shape that flutters from the ivy
> to shiver under a winter sky,
> to go drenched in teems of rain
> and crouch under thunderstorms.[44]

A haunted and hunted outsider, an excommunicate, Sweeney is at the same time a visionary poet, a representative 'figure of the artist' (according to the Irish poet Seamus Heaney) 'displaced, guilty, assuaging himself by his utterance'.[45]

> My life is steady lamentation
> that the roof over my head has gone,
> that I go in rags, starved and mad,
> brought to this by the power of God.[46]

At one point, with terrible poignancy, he declares, 'I have endured purgatories since the feathers grew on me.'[47]

> My cut feet, my drained face
> winnowed by a sheer wind
> and miserable in my mind …
>
> Unsettled, panicky, astray,
> I course over the whole country …
>
> Still without bed or board,
> Crouching to graze on cress,
> drinking cold water from rivers …
>
> Never to hear a human voice!
> To sleep naked every night
> up there in the highest thickets,
>
> to have lost my proper shape and looks,
> a mad scuttler on mountain peaks,
> a derelict doomed to loneliness.[48]

Poets are often accused of speaking about nature in a sentimental way, but there is nothing whatever sentimental about Sweeney's bright and sharp lyrics. The voice we hear in *The Frenzy* has almost no parallels in Western literature. It is the voice

---

44. *Sweeney Astray*, 27, p. 28.
45. Heaney, 'Introduction', in *Sweeney Astray*, p. viii.
46. *Sweeney Astray*, 27, p. 28.
47. Ibid., 60, p. 62.
48. Ibid., 62, pp. 62–4.

of a man condemned and yet also somehow blessed to live out in the open, a poet, a singer, compelled to explore states of thought and feeling beyond the ordinary spectrum. Mad Sweeney's is a language, a music, with no protective cover, a poetry, in Heaney's phrase, 'piercingly exposed to the beauties and severities of the natural world'.[49]

> The Mournes are cold to-night,
> my station is desolate:
> no milk or honey in this land
> of snowfields, gusting wind.
>
> In a sharp-branched holly tree,
> exhausted, nothing on me,
> chilled to the bone, every night
> I camp on the mountain summit.[50]

Eventually Sweeney is welcomed and finds himself befriended by a compassionate monk called Moling. Sweeney's story, Moling realizes, is so unique and so remarkable it deserves to be recorded. Accordingly, Moling encourages Sweeney to return often to the monastery, and he takes care, as abbot, to see that Sweeney is properly fed. At one point, speaking to the outcast, hungry Bird Man, Moling says: 'Come here and share / whatever morsels you would like.' To this Sweeney replies: 'There are worse things, priest, than hunger. / Imagine living without a cloak.' Stunned by these words, Moling exclaims: 'Then you are welcome to my smock, / and welcome to take my cowl.'[51]

Official religion, at the beginning of Sweeney's story, had been poorly represented by Ronan the priest. But here, at the end, Sweeney finds in Moling a man, a priest, wonderfully kind. But, in the eyes of Moling, Sweeney is no mere object of charity. From the beginning he recognizes in the crazed visionary something which commands respect. Sweeney, for his part, is aware that, in meeting Moling, he is encountering a man who has knowledge of the Gospel – living knowledge – and he is happy to acknowledge that authority. 'If you are Moling', he declares, 'you are gifted with the Word.'[52]

At the same time, Sweeney is no less aware that, as a poet, he is in possession of another kind of knowledge and one which has its own importance. Without the least hesitation, therefore, with a poet's natural pride, he declares, 'The Lord makes me his oracle / from sunrise till sun's going down.'[53] To these words,

---

49. Heaney, 'Introduction', in *Sweeney Astray*, p. viii.
50. *Sweeney Astray*, 58, pp. 60–1.
51. Ibid., 75, p. 71.
52. Ibid., 75, p. 70.
53. Ibid.

Moling replies with an affirming statement, happy and willing to acknowledge the poet's special authority: 'Then speak to us of hidden things, / give us tidings of the Lord.'[54]

So far in this chapter our attention has been focused almost exclusively on the anguish experienced by the mad, naked Bird Man. But that very nakedness of his, that unprotected exposure to the natural world, resulted at times in moments of contemplative stillness and sheer joy. What we find, therefore, in *The Frenzy of Sweeney* are not only lyrics of bitter and unhappy lament but also, on occasion, poems of bright observation, lyrics of manifest delight.

> The alder is my darling,
> all thornless in the gap,
> some milk of human kindness
> coursing in its sap.
>
> The blackthorn is a jaggy creel
> stippled with dark sloes;
> green watercress in thatch on wells
> where the drinking blackbird goes.
>
> Sweetest of the leafy stalks,
> the vetches strew the pathway;
> the oyster-grass is my delight
> and the wild strawberry.[55]

These lines, and others like them, contain a beginning sense of gratitude and wonder, a revelation of piercing beauty, a manifest joy in the natural world – all of which come together to form the poet's gift to Moling. It's no surprise, therefore, to hear the following words of acknowledgement spoken by Moling after the sudden death of the Bird Man. Standing beside his grave, Moling exclaims:

> The man who is buried here is cherished indeed. How happy we were when we walked and talked along this path. And how I loved to watch him yonder at the well. It is called the Madman's Well because he would often eat its watercress and drink its water, and so it is named after him. And every other place he used to haunt will be cherished, too.[56]

Here there is no enmity but rather a revelation of deep and lasting friendship, something which, in the final lyric voiced for Moling, becomes even more manifest.

---

54. Ibid.
55. Ibid., 40, pp. 39–40.
56. Ibid., 84, p. 75.

I am standing beside Sweeney's tomb
remembering him. Wherever he
migrated in flight from home
will always be dear to me.

Because Sweeney loved Glen Bolcain
I learned to love it, too. He'll miss
the fresh streams tumbling down,
the green beds of watercress.

He would drink his sup of water from
the well yonder we have called
the Madman's Well; now his name
keeps brimming in its sandy cold.

I waited long but knew he'd come.
I welcomed, sped him as a guest.
With holy viaticum
I limed him for the Holy Ghost.

Because Sweeney was a pilgrim
to the stoup of every well
and every green-filled, cress-topped stream,
their water's his memorial.
… … … … … … … … … … … … … …

I ask a blessing, by Sweeney's grave.
His memory flutters in my breast.
His soul roosts in the tree of love.
His body sinks in its clay nest.[57]

---

57. Ibid., 85, p. 76.

FINALLY COMES THE POET: AN AFTERWORD

> After the noble inventors, after the scientists, the
> chemist, the geologist, ethnologist,
> Finally shall come the Poet, worthy that name,
> The true son of God shall come singing his songs.
>
> <div align="right">Walt Whitman: <i>Leaves of Grass</i></div>

What is poetry for? How best explain its magic, its meaning? How necessary for our lives is the witness of poets and artists, whether major or minor? Does their work, their vision, have an impact that is unique in the way we understand the world around us and our place in the world? According to Ottavio Paz, 'The relationship between poetry and humanity is as old as our history: it began when human beings began to be human. The first hunters and gatherers looked at themselves in astonishment one day, for an interminable instant, in the still waters of a poem. Since that moment, people have not ceased looking at themselves in this mirror.'[1]

But is there a way to describe the nature of that 'looking', the strange magic of that enthrallment? Is there a way to explain the impact of great literature? What Ottavio Paz has called the 'mirror' contains, I think we can say, not only poems in the strict sense of the word but also verses and songs, images and stories, prose-poems and plays from the many different places and occasions in recorded history where authentic vision has found a voice.

But should it happen, for one reason or another, that the gaze of the average individual in society today be deflected away from that 'mirror', should we begin to live deprived of the artist's freshness of vision, and never allow ourselves to be affected by the power of a painting or a poem, or ever permit ourselves to be stirred by the impact of music or drama, in time our own innate sense of things will start to atrophy. We will begin living, in effect, at one or two removes from reality. For, without the voices and visions of the artists, without the living witness they bear to the naked human heart, even 'religion', according to

---

1. Ottavio Paz, *The Other Voice: Essays on Modern Poetry*, trans. H. Lane (New York, 1990), p. 159.

T.S. Eliot, 'tends to become either a sentimental tune, or an emotional debauch; or in theology, a skeleton dance of fleshless dogmas, or in ecclesiasticism a soulless political club'.[2]

Religion needs the arts; it needs the vision offered by painters, sculptors, poets and musicians. But the arts themselves? Do they not, in their turn, draw inspiration of some kind from religion? Doesn't the creativity we associate, for example, with the making of great poetry require at least some form of orientation towards the transcendent? Addressing, in this context, the question of Catholicism's impact on the arts, the Irish poet Seamus Heaney made a number of striking observations in an interview conducted in 1995.[3] He noted, first of all, that since the time of Joyce, the Catholic Church in Ireland had come to be viewed by creative writers as 'an oppressive, guilt-inducing, repressive organization'.[4] But then he added: 'I do think that that has been stated and overstated. We know it's true and it has also been blown away, in fact, recently, to some extent.'[5]

What, then, at the level of vision in Heaney's opinion, is the contribution to the arts in general, and to poetry in particular, of Catholicism? The answer which Heaney gives to this question is in no way hesitant or ambiguous. His words are as direct as they are illuminating:

> What should be said in terms of poetry ... is that Catholicism gives from the very beginning a wonderful sense of radiance, of boundlessness and also of a significant placing within the boundless ... the sense of the imperial behind the usual and the sense of an economy of merit and an economy of deserving and of virtue, the sense of a chord that would transcend the impositions or the imperfections, the sense that there was somewhere else to appeal to that was watching but not speaking – all that I think is deeply, deeply important for poetry.[6]

Heaney is not alone in his conviction that 'somehow there is an appeal to the God or the gods at the basis of the poetic imagination'.[7] George Steiner, in *Real Presences*, notes that although a notion of God still 'clings to our culture' and 'to our routines of discourse', this 'God', surviving in our everyday vocabulary, is dismissed by thinkers since Nietzsche as a mere 'phantom of grammar, a fossil embedded in the childhood of rational speech'.[8] But Steiner argues the reverse. He is persuaded that creativity in literature and the arts 'infers the necessary possibility of this "real presence"'.[9]

---

2. T.S. Eliot, 'Religion without Humanism', in *Humanism and America: Essays on the Outlook of Modern Civilization*, ed. N. Foerster (New York, 1930), p. 111.
3. Heaney was interviewed by Hans-Christian Oeser and Gabriel Rosenstock in his Dublin home, October 1995.
4. 'Interview with Seamus Heaney', *Cyphers*, Spring/Summer 2014, p. 12.
5. Ibid.
6. Ibid., pp. 12–13.
7. Ibid., p. 13.
8. George Steiner, *Real Presences* (Chicago, 1989), p. 3.
9. Ibid.

Steiner writes: 'What I affirm is the intuition that where God's presence is no longer a tenable supposition and where His absence is no longer a felt, indeed overwhelming weight, certain dimensions of thought and creativity are no longer attainable.'[10] In support of this conviction, Steiner cites, first of all, a passage from D.H. Lawrence: 'I always feel as if I stood naked for the fire of Almighty God to go through me – and it's rather an awful feeling. One has to be so terribly religious, to be an artist.'[11] And also this passage from W.B. Yeats: 'No man can create as did Shakespeare, Homer, Sophocles, who does not believe, with all his blood and nerve, that man's soul is immortal.'[12]

These are strong statements, and eloquent, but one wonders how many of the present generation in the West, and elsewhere in the world, are likely to find them meaningful. Perhaps only a small minority of readers today permit themselves to be inspired by the visions and intuitions of poets. We are living in an age of astonishing technological progress, and for that reason, no doubt, people are inclined to turn, first and last, to the world of science for an understanding of the world around them and within them. The quotation from Walt Whitman, cited at the head of these reflections, announces the arrival in our midst of 'the scientists, the chemist, the geologist' etc., an arrival saluted by the poet for they are, given the nature of their work and mission, among the bright, necessary practitioners of modern technology. Nevertheless, Whitman, with quite conscious deliberation, reserves his last salute for a voice and vision of a very different kind, declaring, 'Finally shall come the Poet.'

The emphasis on *finally* suggests at once that poets bring to our world something which even the genius of science cannot bring, something of unique importance. That 'something', far from being a dreamy remoteness, a kind of escapist reverie, is 'fresh as snow, cold as water, hard as stone.'[13] A single line from a great poem can bring us to our senses and can awaken our minds like almost nothing else. But poetry, when it is genuine, will always resist definition. It is knowledge certainly but not knowledge obtained and tested by scientific method. Poetry enjoys an audacious freedom in the pursuit of truth. It is as much a disciple of fiction as of fact, its meaning, its music, able, on occasion, to be as simple as a song of sixpence or as deep and moving as a Bach sonata.

The beauty of art, the beauty of poetry, possesses an authority all its own. Great works of art and literature not only charm us but also *disarm* us, their beauty, their vision, able, by sheer force of integrity, to challenge some of our old ways of looking at things. Uniquely, they compel the attention not only of our imagination but also

---

10. Ibid., p. 229.
11. Ibid., p. 228. Lawrence to Ernest Collins, 25 February 1913. See *The Letters of D.H. Lawrence*, Vol. 1, ed. J.T. Boulton (Cambridge, 2002), p. 519.
12. Ibid. The Yeats passage (August 1924) is from an editorial composed anonymously by Yeats for the first edition of a short-lived review, *To-Morrow*. See Roy Foster, *W.B. Yeats: A Life*, Vol. II: *The Arch-Poet 1915–1939* (Oxford, 2003), pp. 268-9.
13. A phrase descriptive of poetry in Peter Levi's *The Art of Poetry: The Oxford Lectures 1984–1989* (London, 1991), p. 303.

of our passions and our reason. The fact that beauty, in its many different forms, has enormous power goes without saying. But, conscious of the phenomenon of evil in our world, and of the sad fact of human helplessness in the face of the horrors of history, what was it that prompted Dostoevsky, or rather Prince Myshkin, the central character in Dostoevsky's *The Idiot*, to declare, in the teeth (it seems) of all the evidence, 'Beauty will save the world'?[14]

Alexander Solzhenitsyn, happening to come upon this statement in the days of his 'self-confident, materialistic youth', dismissed it out of hand: 'When in bloodthirsty history did beauty ever save anyone from anything?'[15] Years later, however, reflecting on 'the essence of beauty', its 'convincingness' and the way 'works of art have scooped up the truth and presented it to us as a living force', he began to suspect that 'the trinity of Truth, Goodness and Beauty' was not after all 'an empty, faded formula', as he had once believed, and that, at a time such as ours, when in some measure 'the stems of Truth and Goodness are crushed, cut down, not allowed through – then, perhaps, the fantastic, unpredictable, unexpected stems of Beauty will push through, and soar to that very same place, and in so doing will fulfil the work of all three'.[16] A statement on the same theme no less memorable, no less passionate, can be found in the poetry of Czeslaw Milosz:

> When people cease to believe that there is
>   good and evil
> Only beauty will call to them and save them
> So that they still know how to say: this is true
>   and this is false.[17]

*

The poets of vision included in the present study represent many different worlds and many different kinds of writing. Other works of vision, other 'stems of beauty', needless to say, might have been included, inspired writing from poets of the twentieth century – such as Boris Pasternak, Elizabeth Bishop, David Jones, Anna Akhmatova, Dylan Thomas, T.S. Eliot, Hart Crane and Rainer Maria Rilke, to list the first names which come to mind – and, of course, from the nineteenth century, that poet of unique vision, Gerard Manley Hopkins. The first time Hart Crane heard Hopkins's poetry being read, it was 'a revelation'. He wrote: 'I hadn't realized that words could come so near a transfiguration into pure musical notation – at

---

14. Fyodor Dostoevsky, *The Idiot* (1868), trans. R. Pevear and L. Volkhonsky (New York, 2003), p. 382.

15. Alexander Solzhenitsyn, 'Nobel Lecture in Literature 1970', in *Nobel Lectures: 1968–1980*, ed. A. Sture (Singapore, 1994), p. 35.

16. Ibid., pp. 35–6.

17. Czeslaw Milosz, 'One More Day', in *The Collected Poems: 1931–1987* (London, 1988), p. 408.

the same [time] retaining every minute literal signification! What a man and what daring!'[18]

To most readers it will come as no surprise to discover that there are as many different kinds of vision as there are poets represented in *God's Spies*. Some of these poets are minor figures relative to the great visionary authors such as Dante and Shakespeare. But, whether major or minor, the works of vision included here have one distinctive quality in common: audacity. All, without exception, offer a bold and wholly unforeseen perspective on reality. All are among 'the fantastic, unpredictable, unexpected stems of beauty'.

18. Hart Crane to Yvor Winters, 27 January 1928, in Thomas Francis Parkinson, *Hart Crane and Yvor Winters: Their Literary Correspondence* (London, 1978), p. 114.

INDEX

Aelred of Rievaulx, St 30
Akhmatova, Anna 150, 172
Ambrose of Milan, St 126
Ann Line, St 130 n.5
Anthony, St 142
Armstrong, Edward A. 10 n.10, 23 n.49
asceticism 12, 20, 22, 34, 41–2, 137, 149–50, 152, 153
audacity 1, 3, 113, 173
Auden, W.H. 148
Augustine of Hippo, St 14, 18
 and Francis of Assisi 22–3
austerity 2, 21, 22, 94, 137, 152

Balthasar, Hans Urs von 68
Basil of Caesarea, St
 Address to Young Men on the Right Use of Greek Literature 154
Baudelaire, Charles 60, 61
Beatitudes 37–8
Bede the Venerable, St 123
Bennett, J.A.W. 127
Berenson, Bernard 86
Bergson, Henri 79
Bernanos, Georges 144
Bernard of Clairvaux, St 30
Berni, Francesco 83
Bishop, Elizabeth 172
Bloy, Léon 64 n.5
Bly, Robert 149, 150, 159–60
Boccaccio
 Genealogy of the Gentile Gods 156
Bodo, Murray 44
Bonaventure, St 34, 39 n.124, 42–3
Botticelli, Sandro 95
Bremond, Henri 3
Bridges, Robert 65
Browning, Robert 61
Buonarroto (Michelangelo's brother) 95–6, 97, 98
Burgess, Anthony 138

Caedmon 123
 Caedmon's Hymn 123
Campbell, Roy 132
Canticle of the Three Young Men, The 28, 29, 31
Carney, James 12 n.15
casualty 55–6, 58, 60, 61
Celano, Thomas 18, 20–1, 28–30, 32–3, 37–9, 43–4
 Life of St Francis 30
Chesterton, G.K. 40, 130–1, 145–6
Ciarán of Saigir, St 9–10
Ciardi, John 157
Cicero 152, 153
Clement of Alexandria, St
 Exhortation to the Heathen 150–1
Coleridge, Samuel Taylor 49 n.8, 53, 61
Colonna, Vittoria 4, 85, 86–7, 88, 90, 91–2, 102–5, 110, 111
Columba Marmion, Blessed 71
Conchobhar 120–1
Condivi, Ascanio 95, 97, 103
contemplation 4, 18–19, 23, 49, 70, 99–101, 103, 105, 111, 124, 131, 132, 135, 137, 140, 142–4, 158, 166
Cosmas of Maiuma 121 n.24
Crane, Hart 172–3
Crashaw, Richard 2, 150
creation 7–44, 114, 117, 118, 119, 120, 121–2, 126–7, 142–4, 152
Cynewulf 123

Dante Alighieri 97, 129, 137–8, 150, 162, 163, 173
 Divina Commedia 1, 155–6, 157, 158–9
 fundamental beliefs 158–9
 Inferno 156
 Paradiso 1–2, 87 n.20, 157–8
 as poet and theologian 157–8
 Vita Nuova 1
da Pistoia, Giovanni 84

da Vinci, Leonardo 147
de' Cavalieri, Tommaso 4, 85, 87–91, 98–102, 103, 105
de Chardin, Pierre Teilhard
    'Mass on the World, The' 76
della Mirandola, Giovanni Pico 95
Desert Fathers 7, 150–4
di Poggio, Febo 90 n.38
doctrine of transcendence. *See* poetry of transcendence
Donne, John 150, 159
Dostoevsky, Fyodor 106
    Idiot, The 172
Dover Wilson, John 47
Dream of the Rood, The (anon) 122–7
Dreyfus Affair 3, 79

Eckhart, Meister 155
Eco, Umberto 22, 116 n.9
Eden 7, 8, 14, 15, 16, 30, 42, 121, 122. *See also* paradise
Eliot, George 53–5
Eliot, T.S. 2, 4–5, 129, 138–9, 141, 150, 159, 170, 172
    Four Quartets 64, 159
    Marina 139
    on Péguy 63–5
Emerson, Ralph Waldo 83 n.4
Ephrem, St 114–16
Ernst, Cornelius 142
Evagrius Ponticus
    Praktikos 142

Ficino, Marsilio
    Theologia platonica 99–100
Filipepi, Simone 95
Finnis, John 130 n.5
Flower, Robin 10
Foster, Kenelm 95 n.59, 111
Francis of Assisi, St 1, 150
    Admonitions 21, 32–3, 34
    and Augustine of Hippo 22–3
    Canticle of the Creatures, The 10, 17–44
    composition of melody 26–7
    Earlier Rule 38
    and early Irish monks, similarities between 9, 10
    elements of nature 18, 23, 28, 29, 31, 32, 39, 40–3
    illnesses and troubles of 25–6, 34, 36–8
    immanence and affirmation in 18–20
    La Verna vision and experience 33–4
    Letter to the Entire Order 32–3
    path towards freedom 20–2
    pilgrimage places associated with 41
    Pope Francis' quotation of 40–1
    Salutation to the Virtues 39
    spirituality of 21–2
    sympathy and regard for creatures 38–41
    Testament 21
Freeh, John E. 139 n.20
Frenzy of Sweeney (Buile Shuibhne), The (anon) 1, 4, 163–7
Freud, Sigmund 2
    'Some Character-types Met with in Psychoanalysis Work' 51–3

Gide, André 68
Giovan Simone (Michelangelo's brother) 96
Girardi, E.N. 90, 94
Greene, Graham 135, 144
    End of the Affair, The 135
Gregory Nazianzen, St 3, 148–9
Guaire of Connaught 12
Gwilym, Dafyddap 160–1

Haecker, Theodor 58 n.28, 60 n.36
Haicéad, Pádraigín 162
Halévy, Daniel 65
Hall, Edward
    Union of the Two Noble and Illustre Famelies of Lancastre and Yorke, The 55
Hasidim 143
Heaney, Seamus 7, 155, 163 n.43, 164–7, 170
Herbert, George 150
hermit songs 11–16
    Manchán of Liath's 12–14
    Marbán's 11–12
    Monk and the Cat, The 14–16
Hildegard of Bingen, St 150
Hill, Geoffrey
    'Mystery of the Charity of Charles Péguy, The' 64–5
Homer 171
homosexuality 90–1, 109
Hopkins, Gerard Manley 18, 29–30, 65, 142–3, 150, 172–3

Horace 152, 153
Hughes, Ted 129–30
humanism 94, 95, 159

Idiot, The (Dostoevsky) 172
incarnation 33, 35, 69, 70, 71–2, 154, 163
intimacy with God 2, 7
Irenaeus, St 114
Irish monk-poets 7–10
Irish (nature) poetry 11–16, 160–7
  *Frenzy of Sweeney (Buile Shuibhne),
    The* 1, 4, 163–7
  Hermit Song, A 11–12
  Another Hermit Song 12–14
  Monk and the Cat, The 14–16

Jansenism 159, 160
Jennings, Elizabeth 150
Jerome, St 152–4
John of the Cross, St 1, 2, 18, 109 n.125
  La Noche Oscura 2, 132–7, 140
Johnson, Samuel 53
Johnson, Timothy J. 23 n.49, 43 n.139
Jones, David 127, 150, 172
Joyce, James 170
Justin Martyr, St 114

Kavanagh, Patrick 150
Kierkegaard, Søren
  'Of the Difference between a Genius
    and an Apostle' 27
  on *Richard III* 58–61
Kinsella, Thomas 162
Knight, G. Wilson 139 n.20, 140
Knowles, Dom David 30

Laforgue, Jules 64
Landucci, Luca 94 n.58
Laudato Si' (Pope Francis) 40–1
La Verna 26, 33–4, 41
Lawrence, D.H. 171
Leaves of Grass (Whitman) 169
Leclerc, Eloi 23 n.49
Leonardo (Michelangelo's nephew) 96
Letter to Artists (Pope John Paul II) 149
Levertov, Denise 150
Lionardo (Michelangelo's brother) 94
Logan, William 64
Longfellow, Henry Wadsworth 83 n.4

Lorenzo the Magnificent 94, 99
Lotte, Joseph 65, 74, 76, 77
Lowell, Robert 159 n.35

mac Con Brettan, Blathmac 119–20
Mallarmé, Stephane 64, 78
Manchán of Liath 12–14
Mandelstam, Osip 162–3
Manichaeism 22
Manselli, Raoul 17
Mansfield, Katherine 67, 68
Marbán 11–12
Mauriac, François 144
Melito of Sardis 118–19
  Fragment XIII 118–19
  'Peri Pascha – On Easter' 118
Mendl, R.W.S. 46
Meyer, Kuno 13–14
Michelangelo
  affection for Tommaso de' Cavalieri 4,
    85, 87–91, 98–102, 103, 105
  affection for Vittoria Colonna 4, 85,
    86–7, 88, 90, 91–2, 102–5, 110, 111
  Christ in the Garden 110
  death of 82, 102, 103
  enchantment and disillusion 102–6
  Last Judgment 85, 102
  last sonnets/days 106–11
  Pietà 4
  as poet *vs.* painter and sculptor 82–6
  religion and piety 93–102
  Rime 82–3, 90, 99, 102
  sexual identity 86–91
  susceptibility to 'prodigious beauty'
    86–93
Michelangelo the Younger 82–3, 102
Miloz, Czeslaw 150, 172
Moloney, Brian 23 n.49
Montale, Eugenio 83
mysticism 17, 22 n.45, 70, 116, 136, 145

Neo-Platonism 99, 103, 104
Newman, John Henry 3
Nietzsche, Friedrich Wilhelm 170
Nims, Frederick 88 nn.27–8.

Ó Clabaigh, Colmán 10 n.13
O'Connor, Flannery 61, 144
O'Connor, Frank 33 n.91

Ó hÚigínn, Tadg Óg 8
Orage, A.R. 67

paganism 14, 20, 120
   Christian truth *vs.* 150–4, 156
Pange lingua (Venantius Fortunatus) 126 n.44
paradise 4, 7–8, 15, 30, 41–4, 121, 122, 161. *See also* Eden
Passion of Christ 33–4, 113–27. *See also* poetry, of the Cross
Pasternak, Boris 150, 172
Paz, Ottavio 169
Péguy, Charles 1, 150
   hope and despair 73–5
   Le Mystère de la Charité de Jean d'Arc 68, 71–2, 73
   life and liturgy 75–7
   literary style 65–6
   literature and truth 67–8
   military service and death of 77–8
   Mystery of the Holy Innocents, The 3
   Portal of the Mystery of Hope, The 3, 73–4
   and theologians 68–9
   views and reviews on 63–5
Petrarch 91
Pieper, Josef 142
Plato 29–30, 99, 102
Plautus 152
Plunkett, Joseph Mary 116, 117
poetry
   of the Cross 8, 36–8, 111, 113–27, 150
   poetry of faith 158–63
   and religion 147–67
   poetry of transcendence 18
Poliziano, Angelo 95
Pope Francis 40–1
Pope John Paul II
   Letter to Artists 149, 154
Pope Julius II 97, 98
Pope Leo X 84, 97
prayer
   passion and 131–41
   and penance 21
   and poetry 63–79
   practice of 69
   and praise 27
Pseudo-Dionysius 18

Purgatory 93, 164
Puritanism 2, 159, 160

Rabelais, François 68
Renaissance 90, 94, 129, 131
Richard III, Duke of Gloucester
   Freud on 51–2
   in *Henry VI, Part 3* 45–51, 56–8
   Johnson on 53
   Kierkegaard on 58–61
   in *Richard III* 55–6
   unearthing of bones of 45
Richard of St Victor 18
rigorism 21, 22, 160
Rilke, Rainer Maria 172
Robinson, Henry Crabb 41
Robson, Michael 17, 43 n.139
Rolland, Romain 67
Romanos the Melodist, St 121–2
Rufinus Tyrannius 153–4
Ruthwell Cross, The 123, 127

Santayana, George 83 n.4, 129, 138, 140
Saslow, James M. 90, 98, 101–2, 109
Savonarola, Girolamo 94–5
Shakespeare, William 1, 171, 173
   Cymbeline 139
   Henry VI 5, 45–51
   King Lear 5, 141–2, 144
   Macbeth 130
   Measure for Measure 137, 140–1
   Midsummer Night's Dream, A 145–6
   Pericles 139–40
   'Phoenix and the Turtle, The' 130 n.5
   religious vision 129–46
   Sonnet 116 138
   Sonnet 146 131, 136–41
   Tempest, The 139
   Timon of Athens 137
   Winter's Tale, The 139
Shaw, George Bernard 130
Simeon the New Theologian, St 150
Sistine Chapel 83–4, 85, 86, 97, 102–3
Smith, A.J. 109
Solzhenitsyn, Alexander 172
Sophocles 171
Sorrell, Roger D. 22, 23 n.49
Steiner, George
   Real Presences 170–1

stigmata 26, 34
symbolism 113–17, 140, 159

Tagore, Rabindranath 117
   'Gitanjali, LXV' 143–4
   'Gitanjali, LXXXIV' 117–18
Teresa of Avila, St 2 n.3
Thérèse of Lisieux, St 71
Thomas, Dylan 172
Thomas, R.S. 150
Thomas Aquinas, St 43 n.139, 76, 131, 155, 163
   Commentary on Aristotle's *Metaphysics* 147
Thompson, Augustine 17, 32
Tolstoy, Leo 108, 144
Tommasini, Anselmo M. 10

Valéry, Paul 64
Varchi, Benedetto 82
Vasari, Giorgio 85 n.8, 89, 95, 98, 106

Vauchez, André 17
Vaughan, Henry 2
Vercelli Book, The 123
Vexilla regis prodeunt (Venantius Fortunatus) 126 n.44
Virgil 152, 153
virtue 21, 35, 39, 40, 57, 73–4, 86, 97, 115, 170
Vitae Sanctorum Hiberniae 9

Weil, Simone 117, 141
Whately, Thomas 46–7
Whitman, Walt 65, 171
   Leaves of Grass 169
Wilder, Amos N. 149–50, 160
Winters, Yvor 173 n.18
Woolf, Rosemary 125, 126 n.44
Wordsworth, William 29, 30, 66, 83 n.4
   'Cuckoo at Laverna, The' 41–2

Yeats, W.B. 74, 171